Praise for other writings on public policy and the law by Peter Eric Hendrickson

"...a judicious and thoughtful work written by an American patriot deeply dedicated to the rule of law." "Skepticism and doubt will slowly be replaced with certainty and conviction as Hendrickson systematically walks his readers through the law and the tax code's maze of confusion."
Steve Thomas, The Mackinac Center for Public Policy, Midland, Michigan

"Thank you so much for your exquisitely documented and beautifully written "Cracking the Code"- "This book is a masterpiece of analysis, clarity and revelation." "This is brain candy for patriots!"
Christiane Sauter, Syracuse, New York

"Wow!!!! I've been studying this for 10 years and haven't gotten anything as clearly as you have put it in your book." "I cannot thank you enough..."
Joyce Cox, Afton, Wyoming

"All American Citizens who truly love their freedom and have a healthy skepticism of the federal government will add this book to their evidentiary foundation..." "...it's a beautiful thing you've done."
John Carpenter, Ann Arbor, Michigan

"Read the book in about 2 days. Very well done. I have been looking at the issue for about 5 years and you distill the info down in a way even the newbies can absorb. Well worth the asking price. I hope this really sells."
Ed Wahler, Fletcher, North Carolina

"EXCELLENT" "...very well written and accurate." "... I would highly recommend."
Dave Wissel, Lebanon, Ohio

"...a valuable tool, and a wealth of knowledge." "Thank you for all your research..."
Arleen Miller, Page, Arizona

"I found the book to be extremely beneficial even though I was fairly knowledgeable on the subject prior to reading the book." "It is definitely on my list of 'recommended reads. Thanks for a great book."
Phil Patana, St. Louis, Missouri

"...haven't been able to put it down. Great information and fabulously put together!"
Bart Goss, Stockbridge, Georgia

"This is a fabulous book I would highly recommend..."
Larry Golson, Montgomery, Alabama

After reading your book, I knew that you had found the answer that everyone has been looking for."
Arthur Pollock, Perryville, Mai

To get a copy of 'Cracking the Code- The Fascinating Truth About Taxation In America' (ISBN 0974393606) or 'Upholding the Law And Other Observations' (ISBN 0974393614), visit www.losthorizons.com or your favorite bookstore.

Was Grandpa Really a Moron?

Critical Inquires for a New American Century

by

Peter Eric Hendrickson

Printed in the United States of America
First printing December 2009
ISBN 0-9743936-2-2

The cover art is a detail from 'The Ring' by the author;
oil on board, 32" x 40"

To order additional copies of this book, or other titles by Peter E. Hendrickson,
visit www.losthorizons.com or your favorite bookstore

This book is dedicated to all those who hold these truths to be self-evident: that all Men are created equal, that they are endowed by their Creator with certain unalienable Rights, that among these are Life, Liberty and the Pursuit of Happiness.

That to secure these Rights, Governments are instituted among Men, deriving their just Powers from the Consent of the Governed,

That whenever any Form of Government becomes destructive of these Ends it is the Right of the People to alter or to abolish it, and to institute new Government, laying its Foundation on such Principles, and organizing its Powers in such Form as to them shall seem most likely to effect their Safety and Happiness.

"In a time of universal deceit, telling the truth is a revolutionary act."

-George Orwell

Foreword

Most intellectual exercises require a bit of equipment if one is going to profit from the effort. If, for instance, the goal is to bulk up one's understanding of what is going on in the marketplace and why, it is important to keep on hand and in constant view the basic laws of supply, demand, and the function of prices; and a comprehension of what constitutes real money as distinct from fiat currency and other types of "securities".

Where economic behavior and processes are concerned, equipment of this sort is not a matter of "perspective" or "position". It is not a matter of one's ideology or politics or preferences, with its utility in economic analysis being therefore a matter of choice. In economics, the principles of supply, demand, price and money are principles in the hard sense of the word-- inescapable realities which WILL have their effect, regardless of our ideology, politics or preferences.

A failure to acknowledge these principles and their inevitable effects won't make their effects vanish. On the other hand, a failure to acknowledge these principles when attempting to exercise one's understanding of economics will ensure that gains from the effort will never appear.

Economic analysis unanchored in the core principles of the dismal science is like exercising with styrofoam barbells. One may work vigorously all day long, but will have nothing to show for it but the same flab with which one began, a circular rut worn into one's synapses, and a disinclination to soon return to a study that has proven to be a greater source of confusion than of illumination.

Useful and productive consideration of government and law, particularly Constitutional law, also requires the firm possession and crisp deployment of certain basic pieces of intellectual equipment. Some of these are very simple to state and understand.

For example, there is the core principle that when a government is established by an explicit charter, that is, by a constitution, any act or behavior which is outside the scope permitted by that charter, or which is prohibited by it, is inherently and inescapably an act or behavior devoid of general governmental authority. Such behavior simply is not, and cannot be, that of the established government acting in its capacity as such, since the establishing instrument does not provide for it, or specifically provides against it.

The implications of this simple principle are similarly straightforward. For example, if the United States Constitution is the instrument by which a general government is established, and that Constitution specifies that, "Congress shall make no law abridging the freedom of speech," then any act of Congress abridging any freedom of speech is self-evidently not an act of that government acting in its capacity as a government, and is devoid of general authority. Such an act can impose no obligation or restraint on any undistinguished person-- at least, not as an expression or invocation of any legitimate general legal jurisdiction possessed by the Constitutionally-established government.

Another of these basic pieces of intellectual equipment is an understanding of the fact that no governmental enactment is legitimate unless it is an expression of the deliberate purpose and intent of those to whom it statically applies. That is, unless the members of a polity have deliberately delegated an authority upon which a government enactment can be based, that enactment possesses no general authority over those members.

Yet another of these basic pieces of intellectual equipment necessary to the productive consideration of government and law, and perhaps the most important, is an understanding that members of a polity are incapable of delegating any power to any government or other agent which they themselves do not individually possess to begin with. If you can't do it, you can't give someone else permission to do it.

Like economic laws, these "natural laws" are not a matter of ideology or perspective, but are immutable and inescapable elements of reality. It does not matter how much one might think it a good idea if one's agents were "authorized" to do this or that. If one has no right to do this or that oneself, one simply has no means to equip an agent to do these things.

It does not matter how much one might think that others ought to share one's own views of what should or should not be delegated. No one has the right to impose such choices on others, nor make them unwillingly subject to the exercise or implementation of choices made by others.

It does not matter how expedient the exercise of a power not granted might seem to some at some time or in some circumstance. If the power has not been granted, it cannot be exercised as a legitimate governmental act of general authority.

There is no evading these laws. No mechanism for selecting one's agents, or supervising or adjudicating the legislation or administration of this or that by those agents; nor any other principle, practice or procedure can equip an agent to do what these laws do not permit.

This is not a matter of wisdom or prudence or position or policy. It is a matter of cold fact. If one possesses no apples, one cannot give an apple to someone else. It simply can't be done. It can't be done by electing a committee or congress of "apple givers", or establishing courts to supervise and adjudicate the giving of apples, or even by voting to rename oranges "apples".

Applying these simple, inflexible laws to the subject of taxation, for instance, it is clear that since I have no right to take any of my neighbor's property just because I want to, or because I think I would use it for a more beneficial purpose that he would, or for any reason whatever, I cannot authorize my agent to do so. Nor can I authorize my agent to do so simply by acting in concert with a majority of my other neighbors, none of whom themselves possess the right to take property in this manner any more than I do.

Further, it cannot be argued that the neighbor whose property is the object of my desire has somehow irrevocably *agreed* to allow another (or others) to decide the disposition of that property. No one could credibly be held to have ever delegated the disposition of his own property against his own will-- whether that coerced disposition is to happen in the immediate moment or at some point after the making of the alleged agreement. To purport to make such a delegation would be a self-evident act of madness, and thus of no legal effect.

Indeed, it is not even credible to suggest that such a delegation has ever been made. Try securing such an agreement sometime, and see what happens.

Approach any group you care to, even your closest friends or members of your own family, and propose that they select from among themselves one person who will be given superseding authority over everyone's bank accounts. This authority is only to be deployed when that delegatee deems it to be in the group's interest, of course, and the elected agent is subject to replacement should he be found to have exercised this power unwisely or corruptly.

Do you think anyone will agree? Would YOU agree to this? I didn't think so.

You might be willing to create a commonly-owned entity, to which you and others in your group grant ownership of some specific portion of your existing resources. An elected representative or agent of the group as a whole can then use these invested resources, which now belong to the new entity, as a revenue source for routine expenses deemed to be in the common interest. You might also equip the new "corporate" entity with a means for seeking infusions of additional resources from members of the group in times of exceptional need.

The disposition of the initially-granted and/or subsequently-invested resources in such an arrangement would be within the control of the representative elected to manage the new entity, of course. Those resources might consist of productive land and other physical property. Or they might take the form of exploitable prerogatives, such as granting the entity the authority to charge fees in connection with the exercise of its delegated powers or to claim part of the profits from the economic use of its property or powers by others. All of these resources, of whatever character, would now be the property of that new entity, just as the money you spend to buy a share of a private company becomes the property of the company, to do with what its managers wish (including investing them in order to acquire more resources).

You and others you approach might very well be willing to make this sort of arrangement, to the extent that each participant saw a personal benefit in doing so. But never in a million years would you or anyone else agree to any entity or agency, however constituted, asserting control over any part of your current or future property on its own call, and especially not over your contemporaneous objection!

You wouldn't do it; your friends wouldn't do it; and by the way, those who set up the United States federal government wouldn't-- and didn't-- do it, either (as you will discover in the reading of this book). What's more, never in a trillion years would you or any number of your friends acquire the right to grant or delegate such control of anyone else's property to any agent or entity, whether that of anyone alive at the time or of those yet unborn.

There IS a circumstance to which all of the foregoing does not apply, however...

I observed earlier that if the United States Constitution is the instrument by which a general government is established, and that Constitution specifies that, "Congress shall make no law abridging the freedom of speech," then any act of Congress abridging the freedom of speech is self-evidently not an act of that government as such, and is devoid of general authority. Such an act can impose no obligation or restraint on anyone as an expression or invocation of any general legal jurisdiction possessed by the Constitutionally-established government.

But such an act CAN have jurisdiction of a specialized character, extending to, and enforceable against, only the creations of the enactors-- that is, the creations of Congress. In other words, a Congressional act abridging speech can be, and can ONLY be, merely an internal rule governing the behavior of the federal government itself (and is enacted, at least theoretically, in order to accomplish or perfect some Constitutionally-mandated federal purpose). It is Congress acting not in its capacity as a government, but in its capacity as the administrator of its own organs. It can be nothing else.

After all, authority which has not been delegated and which is therefore inherently dictatorial, can only be lawfully exercised upon a creation of Congress. Only a Congressional creature has no right which would otherwise be violated by such exercise.

Thus, when a court upholds such an enactment as Constitutional, it is not declaring the prohibition against Congressional abridgment of speech to have somehow disappeared, or to not mean what it so plainly and unambiguously says. The court is, rather, simply confirming the limited, specialized character of the enactment's jurisdiction and scope.

Such a ruling CAN ONLY be saying that the enactment being tested does not impermissibly claim or assert general jurisdictional authority or general application, because if the enactment DID make such a claim, it would be plainly unlawful, and the court would be obliged to say so (or become complicit in an attempt at despotism). Therefore, judicial approval of an enactment which is contrary to the specifications or prohibitions within the Constitution can and must be taken as a definitive declaration that the challenged legislation makes no claim to general, unspecialized application.

> *LAW, PRIVATE. An act of the legislature which relates to some private matters, which do not concern the public at large.* Bouvier's Dictionary of Law, Sixth Edition

Returning to the example of taxation, just as a creation of Congress has no right to free speech other than as granted to it by Congress, so all property possessed by, or coming into the possession of, a creation of Congress can be held to be Congress's to dispose of. Similarly, any activity engaged in by non-Congressionally-created entities, but which involves the use of that which belongs to Congress, can be deemed subject to related claims by Congress.

For instance, if I use some of Congress's property to make money, I can be held to owe Congress a "piece of the action", to the extent specified by relevant statute. That kind of obligation is called an "excise". The obligation arises not because of who or what I am, or because Congress has somehow acquired the impossible authority to directly commandeer my property, but because I chose to use its stuff, and accepted the consequent obligation as the price of doing so.

When such an obligation is asserted by Congress (or its executive agents), and/or upheld by a court, it is on the basis that a contractual arrangement of the sort just described exists. It cannot, after all, be on the basis of any delegated authority of Congress to simply seize my property for its own disposition. There has been, and can be, no such delegation.

Of course, there is one-- and only one-- alternative to the reasoning above: The entire federal apparatus is flatly treasonous, with Congress enacting unconstitutional legislation which is then illegally enforced by the executive, aided and abetted by colluding federal courts. I suppose this is possible.

But which is more likely? This latter alternative, by which virtually all federal office-holders would be risking grievous criminal penalties? Or the possibility that legislation infringing on speech, and commandeering property and so forth is actually all specialized legislation, which the American people have been strongly encouraged to misunderstand as being otherwise by things like gratuitous talk about "living Constitutions" amongst the intellectual supporters of whoever's interest the misunderstanding might serve, a misunderstanding which those in control of the federal apparatus have happily exploited for political purposes?

Let me add another factor into the mix in regard to this question: The operation of federal law, for better or for worse, tolerates a reliance on presumptions. That is, in applying a given statute to a given case, courts routinely presume fundamental jurisdiction-establishing "facts" to be true, unless and until such presumptions are rebutted. By virtue of this practice, if one is sued or charged with a crime under a statute with application to specially-limited circumstances or a special class of persons, it will be presumed that those circumstances exist, or that one is within that class-- unless and until such presumptions are positively rebutted. (We'll leave the issue of this practice turning the key due-process doctrine of the burden of proof being on the complaining party for another day.)

Only the individual who is aware of this practice and of the presumptive elements involved in the relevant statutes will be capable of escaping this web, and few are aware. Consequently, the American public is routinely treated to examples of special, limited-jurisdiction statutes being constructively applied to undistinguished persons. Since that special, limited-jurisdiction character of these statutes goes unrecognized, the impression is left that these cases prove that Congress has slipped the traces of the Constitution and legislates in defiance of its provisions, with the cooperation of the courts.

The relatively rare occasions in which a defendant DOES understand these issues are the exceptions that prove the rule. For instance, the existence of federal gun control acts, and periodic (if not frequent) prosecutions under such acts leave the impression that Congress legislates in defiance of the Second Amendment to the United States Constitution, which prohibits federal legislation infringing on anyone's right keep and bear arms. However, the broadly overlooked or misunderstood reality is that all such legislation really only criminalizes certain behavior involving the *interstate commerce* of firearms, and relies entirely on the presumption that anyone charged under these acts has received or possessed the firearm involved "in interstate commerce"

Thus, when addressed by a knowledgeable defendant, we see language such as this from the United States Supreme Court in a case involving an American charged with illegal possession of a firearm:

> *"There remains for decision the question of the power of Congress to create the presumption which declares, namely, that, from the prisoner's prior conviction of a crime of violence and his present possession of a firearm or ammunition, it shall be presumed (1) that the article was*

> *received by him in interstate or foreign commerce, and (2) that such receipt occurred subsequent to July 30, 1938, the effective date of the statute."* Tot v. United States, 319 US 463 (1943)

Tot having rebutted the presumptions and argued that his being obliged to do so constitutes a due-process violation, the court not only reverses his improper conviction in a lower court but goes on to rebuke Congress in regard to the propriety of such presumptions. Because Congress has made clear its unrestrained enthusiasm for presumptions over the intervening years, the court has abandoned its efforts to stop them from being deployed entirely, but has made unambiguous its insistence that they remain amenable to remedy by a knowledgeable defendant:

> *"...irrebuttable presumptions have long been disfavored under the Due Process Clauses of the Fifth and Fourteenth Amendments."* Vlandis v. Kline, 412 U.S. 441 (1973)

Congress has grudgingly accepted this reality, as is, for instance, rather awkwardly expressed in the following language from the federal rules of evidence:

> ***Federal Rules of Evidence Rule 301. Presumptions in General Civil Actions and Proceedings***
> *In all civil actions and proceedings not otherwise provided for by Act of Congress or by these rules, a presumption imposes on the party against whom it is directed the burden of going forward with evidence to rebut or meet the presumption, but does not shift to such party the burden of proof in the sense of the risk of nonpersuasion, which remains throughout the trial upon the party on whom it was originally cast.*

Federal rules of evidence for criminal cases contain a similar provision.

(The fact that gun control statutes reflect a grotesque misconstruction of the actual authority delegated under the "Interstate Commerce Clause" of the U.S. Constitution will not be addressed here-- the promiscuous abuse of that clause by Congress is very important in its own right, but is outside the scope of this discussion. Those interested in this subject should see my book, 'Upholding the Law And Other Observations'.)

The point, of course, is to ensure that as you proceed through the critical inquires that follow, you do so with the "rules of the road" firmly in mind. These rules will shed a great deal of light on what an all-too-often manipulative and exploitive entrenched political class very much would prefer to leave murky, to its advantage and your disadvantage.

Looking after your own interests is your responsibility-- certainly no one else can be counted on to do it for you. Meeting this responsibility requires knowledge and understanding, as well as courage and will. It is my hope that this collection will help equip you with the former, which will then fortify the latter, in turn.

***

By the way, nothing in this book should be construed or relied upon as particular advice or instructions for any particular reader. Each reader must make his or her own independent determination of how the nature, meaning and application of any law, policy or perspective affects or concerns himself or herself.

Searchable federal codes can be found at www4.law.cornell.edu/uscode/26/, and elsewhere. Federal statutes from the years 1789 - 1875, can be found at memory.loc.gov/ammem/amlaw/lwsl.html; others can be seen at any decent law library. The text of most Supreme and lower court rulings can be found at www.findlaw.com and other sites.

Additional material on the subject of taxes and other matters of law and public policy can be found on my website: www.losthorizons.com.

Was Grandpa Really A Moron?

or have you just been lied to, as usual...

Suppose that you were a member of a state legislature which had been presented with a proposed Constitutional amendment of great significance. This proposed amendment would undo one of the most fundamental elements of the then 120-year-old Constitution-- the existing limitation on federal authority to seize revenue from the citizenry at its pleasure.

Authority of this sort had been entirely denied to the federal government under the Articles of Confederation. During the reforming of the Articles which resulted in our current Constitution only an extremely restricted relaxation of this total denial had been adopted, and with such reluctance, and such recognition of the significance of the issue, that the Framers duplicated the restrictive clause imposed on the exercise of this limited authority-- making it the only prohibition incorporated into the Constitution twice.

The particular and explicit effect of this draconian amendment would be to authorize the federal government to seize an undefined (and therefore unlimited) portion of any payment made to anybody-- including you, other than the insignificant portion of your overall earnings being paid by the state government (one government can't impose a tax on the activities of another). This power would threaten the receipts of all of your constituents, as well.

Even while this dramatic transformation was being proposed, Congress already had an unlimited ability to raise revenue through the imposition of apportioned direct taxes. This sort of tax, although deliberately encumbered with a degree of political accountability inconvenient to federal politicians, had long-since proven itself both capable of raising enormous amounts of revenue and of being selective in its application to the various economic strata through the choices of objects of the tax and the provision of exemptions. In other words, apportioned direct taxes were fully capable of being laid exclusively on "the rich", if political considerations prompted such a preference.

On the other hand, the proposed amendment by which the existing Constitutional structure is meant to be undone contains no language limiting its application to the rich, or limiting it in any fashion whatever. The amendment offers no benefit or increased authority to the state government of which you were a part-- indeed, your state government is already subject to no limit on its ability to impose taxes, other than being unable to tax federal government activities taking place within its borders (something this amendment doesn't purport to change).

Furthermore, by the time this extraordinary amendment is presented to you, your colleagues and your constituents, the long-standing existing structure has already allowed America to become the most prosperous country on the planet.

SO,

- This proposed amendment offers no benefit to you personally, your state or your constituents. Quite the contrary, in fact-- it would convey a massive new power to another political entity which is, however congenially, in competition with you and your state for influence and resources nonetheless.

- The amendment would hang a new, unpredictable and inherently unlimited threat over the control you and every single one of your constituents currently enjoy over your own wealth and well-being, and have always jealously guarded.
- There is no demonstrable need for this fundamental and self-evidently dangerous transfer of power from you and your constituents to the federal government. Instead, the status quo is performing phenomenally well.
- The Founders, still revered and respected by an American population equipped with a high-grade 98% literacy rate*, had broadly warned (and taken pains to provide) against any such transfer.

What would you do, if this were really the choice you faced? Ratify? You, your colleagues and your constituents would have to be morons to do so. And yet, our grandparents DID ratify the Sixteenth Amendment (albeit, sloppily).

So, were they really all morons? Those who want you to believe that the Sixteenth Amendment accomplished the dire and dramatic transformation I've described here expect you to buy into that unlikely proposition (in lieu of suspecting that they themselves completely misunderstand-- or are lying about-- the amendment).

They also want you to overlook the repeated and explicit words of the United States Supreme Court and myriad other authorities to the contrary:

> *"We are of opinion, however, that the confusion is not inherent, but rather arises from the conclusion that the 16th*

Amendment provides for a hitherto unknown power of taxation; that is, a power to levy an income tax which, although direct, should not be subject to the regulation of apportionment applicable to all other direct taxes. And the far-reaching effect of this erroneous assumption will be made clear by generalizing the many contentions advanced in argument to support it..."

...

"[Taxation of "income" is] *in its nature an excise entitled to be enforced as such unless and until it was concluded that to enforce it would amount to accomplishing the result which the requirement as to apportionment of direct taxation was adopted to prevent, in which case the duty would arise to disregard form and consider substance alone, and hence subject the tax to the regulation as to apportionment which otherwise as an excise would not apply to it."* (That is, if the "income" tax ever comes to be administered as something other than an excise, or on something unsuited to an excise, the rule of apportionment must be applied.)
United States Supreme Court, Brushaber v. Union Pacific R. Co., 240 U.S. 1 (1916)

"The provisions of the Sixteenth Amendment conferred no new power of taxation . . ."
United States Supreme Court, Stanton v. Baltic Mining Co., 240 U.S. 103 (1916)

"The Sixteenth Amendment, although referred to in argument, has no real bearing and may be put out of view. As pointed out in recent decisions, it does not extend the taxing power to new or excepted subjects..."
United States Supreme Court, Peck v. Lowe, 247 U.S. 165 (1918)

"The Revised Statutes of the United States and the Statutes at Large of the United States are the sources of the law codified. The Revised Statutes cover the period ended December 1, 1873. The Statutes at Large codified cover the period following December 1, 1873, and are published in the 35 volumes numbered 18 to 52, inclusive. The separate

enactments carried into the internal revenue title, wholly or in part, from the Statutes at Large are 143 in number, exclusive of 93 statutes involving express amendment, reenactment, or repeal. The 277 Revised Statutes sections codified were derived from 21 basic statutes. The whole body of internal revenue law in effect on January 2, 1939, therefore, has its ultimate origin in 164 separate enactments of Congress. The earliest of these was approved July 1, 1862; the latest, June 16, 1938."
Preamble to the 1939 Internal Revenue Code

"The Supreme Court, in a decision written by Chief Justice White, first noted that the Sixteenth Amendment did not authorize any new type of tax, nor did it repeal or revoke the tax clauses of Article I of the Constitution, quoted above. Direct taxes were, notwithstanding the advent of the Sixteenth Amendment, still subject to the rule of apportionment and indirect taxes were still subject to the rule of uniformity."
Howard M. Zaritsky, Legislative Attorney, American Law Division of the Library of Congress, Report No. 80-19A, entitled "Some Constitutional Questions Regarding The Federal Income Tax Laws", page CRS-5 (1979)

"[T]he amendment made it possible to bring investment income within the scope of the general income-tax law, but did not change the character of the tax."
F. Morse Hubbard, legislative draftsman for the United States Treasury Department, testifying before Congress on March 27, 1943

"The legislative history merely shows... ...that the sole purpose of the Sixteenth Amendment was to remove the apportionment requirement for whichever incomes were otherwise taxable. 45 Cong. Rec. 2245-2246 (1910); id., at 2539; see also Brushaber v. Union Pacific R. Co., 240 U.S. 1, 17 -18 (1916)."
United States Supreme Court, South Carolina v. Baker, 485 U.S. 505 (1988)

***

Of course, our grandparents WEREN'T all morons, because the Sixteenth Amendment WASN'T a transformational event at all, as they understood full well.

Instead, the Sixteenth Amendment accomplished nothing more dramatic than closing a minor loophole "discovered" by the Supreme Court in the case of Pollock v. Farmer's Loan & Trust which prevented the application of the already 51-year-old "income" tax to dividends otherwise qualifying as taxable, due to their being derived from personally-owned stock. We'll look at the details of this ruling and the narrow effect of the amendment in the next few chapters.

*As recently as 1920, fewer than a third of American children were subjected to mis-education in government schools for more than a few years. Unfortunately, this didn't last. Compulsory attendance requirements, and tax extractions causing unsuspecting parents to favor the government schools they were being made to pay for whether they used them or not, steadily increased over the years. The combination caused a corresponding increase in both the portion of American children in those schools and the average term of attendance. Consequently, by 1952, only 81% of the adult American population could read at a nominal fourth-grade level; by 1973, the percentage had dropped to 73% (according to U.S. Army inductee testing data). It has only gotten worse since then. The Educational Testing Service reports in its analysis of its 1993 National Adult Literacy Survey that:

1. *Forty-two million Americans over the age of sixteen can't read. Some of this group can write their names on Social Security cards and fill in height, weight, and birth spaces on application forms.*

2. *Fifty million can recognize printed words on a fourth- and fifth-grade level. They cannot write simple messages or letters.*

3. *Fifty-five to sixty million are limited to sixth-, seventh-, and eighth-grade reading. A majority of this group could not figure out the price per ounce of peanut butter in a 20-ounce jar costing $1.99 when told they could round the answer off to a whole number.*

4. *Thirty million have ninth- and tenth-grade reading proficiency. This group (and all preceding) cannot understand a simplified written explanation of the procedures used by attorneys and judges in selecting juries.*

5. *About 3.5 percent of the 26,000-member sample demonstrated literacy skills adequate to do traditional college study, a level 30 percent of all U.S. high school students reached in 1940, and which 30 percent of secondary students in other developed countries can reach today. This last fact alone should warn you how misleading comparisons drawn from international student competitions really are, since the samples each country sends are small elite ones, unrepresentative of the entire student population. But behind the bogus superiority a real one is concealed.*

6. *Ninety-six and a half percent of the American population is mediocre to illiterate where deciphering print is concerned. This is no commentary on their intelligence, but without ability to take in primary information from print and to interpret it they are at the mercy of commentators who tell them what things mean. A working definition of immaturity might include an excessive need for other people to interpret information for us.*

(Army statistics and summary of the NALS analysis as presented by John Taylor Gatto in 'The Underground History of American Education')

By the way, don't let me hear anything about these schools just needing more money in order to do a better job! Even while the level of educational output was plummeting, expenditures in government schools were skyrocketing. Measured in constant

1992 dollars, per pupil spending in government schools leapt from $867 in 1930 to a whopping $6,043 by 1993!

It's Time To Stand, Or Fall

"As nightfall does not come at once, neither does oppression. In both instances, there is a twilight when everything remains seemingly unchanged. And it is in such twilight that we all must be most aware of change in the air-- however slight-- lest we become unwitting victims of the darkness."
– Justice of the Supreme Court, William O. Douglas

In October of 2007, the House of Representatives passed, 404 to 6, the first version of what is intended to be the next-- and perhaps, final-- weapon in the growing arsenal being assembled by the state in its program of binding the bulk of the American people into the status of livestock. The name given to the test-run version of this weapon against American liberty is 'The Violent Radicalization And Homegrown Terrorism Prevention Act Of 2007' (VRHTPA). Although this first roll-out failed in the Senate, the purpose behind the VRHTPA is not going to go away. Like the 'USA PATRIOT Act', much of which was written several years before finally being enacted in 2001, the now written-and-ready VRHTPA will be back.

Simply put, this bill is intended to create an institutional mechanism by which American critics of government policy can be silenced, and by which the dissemination of information and views not originating with, or approved by, the state will be effectively suppressed. The mechanism in the bill is a formal commission whose portfolio is the "identification" (read: designation) of American citizens as "terrorists", and the designation of sources of disfavored information as "terrorist" "facilitators". These designations can be based upon nothing more than the target having challenged or disputed an official, government-generated version of reality, or having facilitated the dissemination of such challenges or disputes.

The bill defines the "violent radicalization" against which it is deployed as,

> *(2) VIOLENT RADICALIZATION- The term 'violent radicalization' means the process of adopting or promoting an extremist belief system for the purpose of facilitating ideologically based violence to advance political, religious, or social change.*

More malleable language would be hard to come by. Indeed, a more malleable concept would be hard to come by. "Adopting" "an extremist belief system"? "Promoting" "an extremist belief system"?! "For the purpose of facilitating"??!!

We need not wrestle with what these deliberately vague and spinnable phrases really mean to see the impropriety of this legislation. Even just taking this language on its face, it is self-evident that "belief systems"-- whatever they might be-- are outside of governmental jurisdiction; and that this legislation is nonetheless intended to facilitate government promotion of the extremist belief that citizens cultivating the "belief system" of their choice is both a bad thing and IS within the government's proper purview.

However, a brief analysis makes clear that the reference to "belief systems" is just a red herring. Inconvenient information and opinions are the real target of this bill.

Indeed, there really is no such thing as a belief "system". The very use of this phrase is for the purpose of generating confusion as to the target of the legislation, and to protect the VRHTPA from the charge that it seeks to attack beliefs-- an attack which would be readily recognized as illegal even by the heavily-conditioned American "mainstream" without further ado.

What there actually ARE are simply beliefs, and the information and opinions upon which those beliefs are based. The only sense in which this combination is a "system" is the sense in which all reasoning is a system: a given conclusion (belief)-- and possible associated action-- arises only after consideration of a given body of information and analysis.

The conclusion arrived at in any given case (like the response that it might call forth) is discreet from the information upon which it is based. This bill, however, wishes to conflate the discreet elements into a "system", so that if the response of any given individual to a certain body of information is violent, or even can merely be expected to be passionate (and therefore "potentially violent"), any body of information upon which the related conclusion might be based can also be condemned, and made inaccessible to EVERYONE.

Here's an example: Suppose someone were to write an editorial criticizing a piece of federal legislation as an illegal effort by the government to hinder the free flow of information, so as to ensure its ability to "engineer consent" to policies favored by its clients. This editorial persuasively characterized the effort as a grim usurpation of authority for the purpose of binding the sovereign people into blind servitude.

Now, suppose someone reading the editorial were to then engage in a violent, or even merely "threatening" (that is, impassioned) protest of the legislation (or the federal perpetrator). Under the VRHTPA, the protest would be condemned as "homegrown terrorism":

> *(3) HOMEGROWN TERRORISM- The term `homegrown terrorism' means the use, planned use, or threatened use, of force or violence by a group or individual born,*

> *raised, or based and operating primarily within the United States or any possession of the United States to intimidate or coerce the United States government, the civilian population of the United States, or any segment thereof, in furtherance of political or social objectives.*

So would the editorial itself (since it would be accused of, *"promoting an extremist belief system for the purpose of facilitating ideologically based violence to advance political, religious, or social change."*)!

Here's another example: Suppose a website were to offer detailed information and analysis of what might have been a massive crime against the American people of a very immediate (and even ongoing) sort-- information that large and growing segments of the population were already closely studying, while simultaneously being reminded (on that site or elsewhere) of the principle that, *whenever any Form of Government becomes destructive of these ends* [assisting individuals in securing their rights, by means to which those individuals consent]*, it is the Right of the People to alter or to abolish it, and to institute new Government, laying its foundation on such principles and organizing its powers in such form, as to them shall seem most likely to effect their Safety and Happiness."*. Suppose that website (or others) also took note of the fact that the Second Amendment is explicitly provided in the federal Constitution in recognition of the fact that democratic processes might not suffice to reign in a rogue government, and that violent resort to the bayonets of the militia might be necessary in such cases.

Need I say it? Under the VRHTPA, the website offering the information about the possible crime (and those quoting the Declaration of Independence and the Second Amendment) would be designated as contributing to "homegrown terrorism". The VRHTPA actually announces its particular interest in suppressing troublesome websites, declaring the "finding of Congress" that:

> *"(3) The Internet has aided in facilitating violent radicalization, ideologically based violence, and the homegrown terrorism process in the United States by providing access to broad and constant streams of terrorist-related propaganda to United States citizens."*

I know. All of this sounds rather far-fetched at this point.

Surely, the VRHTPA is directed only at the dangerous "Islamofascism" manifesting itself in America today-- that is, all the wild-eyed "jihadists" constantly blowing things up around the country, marching in threatening protests in our big cities, and so on. It is mere stridency to propose that a bill such as this is intended to stifle critical inquiry inconvenient to the state... right? It has to be. It can't happen here...

Anyway, here's one final example of what can be expected under the VRHTPA: Suppose someone relentlessly promoted the notions that a particular foreign country was responsible for an attack on American soil leading to a substantial loss of life; that the country's ruler was facilitating the training and organization of terrorists in order to do more of the same; and that this ruler was even seeking to acquire nuclear weapons in connection with this purpose. The plain purpose of this promotion, and its direct consequence, has been to inflame large numbers into supporting, and even participating in, massive violence resulting in an ongoing loss of life already comparable to that of the deadliest war ever fought on American soil, and with no end in sight. (In this particular example, by the way, every single element of the information on which the violence is based has long-since been proven to have been not only false but deliberate lies.)

Under the provisions of the VRHTPA, the purveyors of this information would... continue to enjoy steady career advancement, lucrative benefits from their investments, and eventual settlement into well-cushioned positions in, or lobbying for, the industries whose bottom-lines have been fattened by the project. Critical investigations or revelations concerning the lies involved would be firmly suppressed. Everything would freeze into a nice, comforting, predictable stasis into the foreseeable future...

***

It need hardly be spelled-out that in addition to chilling information-providers directly, the terms of the 'Violent Radicalization And Homegrown Terrorism Prevention Act' will enlist the voluntary censorship of information and opinions susceptible to the attentions of the commission established by the legislation by otherwise disinterested telecomm service-providers, as well. It will escape no one that being the ISP or telecomm by which targeted information is disseminated could itself serve as a pretext for those same attentions, and these businesses, even when they don't consider their interests aligned with the statist quo, will be readily swayed by what has become a standard calculation in recent years:

> *"Now, let's see. Leviathan has made clear its disfavor of this customer's material, and its willingness to completely disregard all principles of due process, honesty and fairness in seeking to have its way. My customer has no legal means of forcing me to keep him, and he's only worth $XX to me. Leviathan, on the other hand, can and will impose huge costs on me for defying it-- heck, it even put that Qwest guy in prison for refusing to do illegal spying for it! What should I do..."*

I think the agonizing indecision will be short-lived.

Clearly then, the VRHTPA is a multi-faceted end-run around the First Amendment, intended to silence dissent and criticism of the government and its policies without overt state infringement of speech rights. But it's also much worse that just that...

IT HAS BEEN WELL SAID that those who permit themselves to be made ignorant of history are doomed to repeat the harsh lessons of the past. The VRHTPA will furnish a perfect example of this wisdom.

Americans ARE grossly ignorant of history-- vast numbers of American parents have blindly turned the education of their children over to the state for several generations now, and the state has (unsurprisingly) been lax at educating those children as to its own predispositions and past offenses against the citizenry. Happy to take advantage, our homegrown Leviathan and its clients-- who are feeling VERY threatened by the free exchange of ideas and information right now-- are reviving one of the worst of those past offenses, and appear likely to succeed with little notice being paid by the general public.

The fact is, the 'Violent Radicalization and Homegrown Terrorism Prevention Act' is actually a just the last step in a modern revival of the obscene 'Alien and Sedition' acts suffered by early Americans of the late 18th century until overwhelmingly rejected with the election of Thomas Jefferson. (See 'Strolling Down Memory Lane' in 'Upholding the Law And Other Observations' to learn more about these previous offenses, and the cold-eyed and deadly-serious reactions they prompted from Jefferson and James Madison.)

But this is a "revival" on steroids. This modern version of criminal state censorship and practical prior restraint will not only silence dissenters and other troublesome voices. It will be used to permanently "disappear" Americans who refuse to be silent, do what they're told, and believe what they're told, while their betters do what they wish and operate the "memory hole" unhindered whenever political expediency suggests its use.

Understand: the VRHTPA equates challenging the state in any way-- ranging from merely questioning its approved version of facts, all the way to enforcing the primacy of the people over the government-- with "terrorism". Under the provisions of the 'Military Commissions Act of 2006', those accused of "terrorism" are candidates for simply being black-bagged into the gulag for an indefinite stay without recourse or appeal.

I realize that to some this will all sound quite hyperbolic, of course. This is unavoidable, despite the fact that I am actually being quite dispassionate here. It is impossible to analyze and discuss this very real, immediate, comprehensive and ever-more-unmistakable effort to lock down America without appearing to be exercised. Simply to recite the words of enactments like this 'Homegrown Terrorism' act, the 'Military Commissions Act of 2006', the 'John Warner Defense Reauthorization Act of 2007' and others in this web is to paint a picture which is starkly alarming to anyone with an ounce of active brain tissue. Those to whom such a recitation seems hyperbolic are projecting into my expressions the clanging alarm very appropriately going off in the backs of their own minds.

***

It is important that what is going on be clearly understood-- because we are on the cusp of transformation, for good or for ill. Beginning in earnest in the late 1990s, the 'information revolution' has suddenly, unexpectedly and very inconveniently (for those who prefer that their machinations remain concealed) allowed us commoners to discover the degree to which we are being (and have been) fed upon by the parasitic kleptocracy that has long since established itself in control of the mechanisms of the state. That kleptocracy is scrambling to close the barn door.

Mere manipulation of the education establishment and the wholly-owned (or co-opted) "mainstream media", which used to suffice in dealing with the occasional penetration of disquieting sunlight into the barn, isn't good enough anymore. We now have our own media and our own teachers, and we're discovering things that have been carefully kept from us for many years.

To put it simply, we're discovering the degree to which our consent has been "engineered", and that the engineering was NOT benevolently done because we're just too dumb to look out for our own interests, and would have made bad choices if fairly left to make them. It was done for the purpose of viciously exploiting us.

Thanks to our unique and still fragile access to uncontrolled information, we're awake now, we're angry, and we're withdrawing our consent. Millions of us. We will now-- right now-- either seize and defend this opportunity, or we will go down into a long, dark night.

"I have sworn upon the altar of God, eternal hostility against every form of tyranny over the mind of man."
-Thomas Jefferson

I stand with Jefferson on this one. How about you?

The kleptocracy has one thing going for it, for a while, having successfully conditioned a lot of Americans to just ask, "How high?" when its institutionally-embedded tools say, "Jump!". Thus, at this point, if some institutional actor-- that is, a member of the governmental apparatus-- orders the suppression of inconvenient speech by one means or another under the alleged authority of one of the unconstitutional (and therefore entirely illegitimate) acts discussed above, it is likely to enjoy mindless cooperation.

Therefore, one of the important tasks before the rest of us is to relentlessly educate our fellows. I suggest that it is enough, and perhaps best, if the focus of that education effort be confined to these two simple lessons: Unquestioning obedience to "authority", and acceptance of its pronouncements, is inherently un-American-- indeed, un-human-- (and pathetically stupid, to boot); and any act or command by government that conflicts with what YOU find in the relevant state or federal Constitution-- not what the government says is there, or is meant by what is there, but what you personally read there yourself-- <u>is entirely without authority</u>.

Constitutions are the laws WE write, and they mean what WE intend them to mean-- nothing more and nothing less. But they don't mean anything if we don't stand up and enforce them.

Another important task for each of us, and one that requires the cooperation of no one, is taking control of our own contributions to Leviathan's health, and thus making use of one of the key mechanisms of provided by the Founders for the preservation of our liberties. Toward that end, please visit www.losthorizons.com/It'sTime.htm and view (and share) the film you'll find there. Then act.

It is the eleventh hour, people. It's time to get up.

***

And when at last this rebellion compelled the British Government to use the only power that any Government has -- force, used with general consent -- and British troops moved into Boston to restore order, Americans did not consent. They stood up and fought the British Regulars.

One man began that war. And who knows his name?

He was a farmer, asleep in his bed, when someone pounded on his door and shouted in the night, 'The troops are coming!'

What could he do against the King's troops? One man. If he had been the King, that would have been different; then he could have done great things. Then he could have set everything to rights, he could have made everyone good and prosperous and happy, he could have changed the course of history. But he was not a King, not a Royal Governor, not a rich man, not even prosperous, not important at all, not even known outside the neighborhood. What could he do? What was the use of his trying to do anything? One man, even a few men, can not stand against the King's troops. He had a wife and children to think of; what would become of them, if he acted like a fool?

Most men had better sense; most men knew they could do nothing and they stayed in bed, that night in Lexington. But one man got up. He put on his clothes and took his gun and went out to meet the King's troops. He was one man who did not consent to a control which he knew did not exist.

The fight on the road to Lexington did not defeat the British troops What that man did was to fire a shot heard around the world, and still heard...

That shot was the first sound of a common man's voice that the Old World ever heard. For the first time in all history, an individual spoke, an ordinary man, unknown, unimportant, disregarded, without rank, without power, without influence.

Not acting under orders, not led, but standing on his own feet, acting from his own will, responsible, self-controlling, he fired on the King's troops. He defied a world-empire.

The sound of that shot said: Government has no power but force; it can not control any man.

No one knows who began the American Revolution. Only his neighbors ever knew him, and no one now remembers any of them. He was an unknown man, an individual, the only force that can ever defend freedom."

-Rose Wilder Lane, 'THE DISCOVERY OF FREEDOM: Man's Struggle Against Authority'

A Brief Introduction To The Fascinating Truth About The Income Tax

PART ONE

The purpose of this brief study is to introduce a couple of key facts that must be known by anyone hoping for a clear understanding of the legal character of the United States federal income tax (and the state and local impositions of the same tax). We're going to start by:

> *1. Examining the meaning of the Constitutional term "capitation" (a tax effectively falling on revenue generally-- that is, a tax on "what comes in", either in its entirety, or on any part, of otherwise undistinguished revenue); and*
>
> *2. Establishing that the income tax is, and always has been, an exercise-of-privilege-based "piece of the action" excise tax on distinguished activity, rather than a capitation, and that "income" as meant in the context of the tax refers only to that distinguished activity (the amount of which is measured by the dollar value it produces).*

The Meaning of "Capitation"

There is a persistent misunderstanding in America about the meaning of one of the key terms in our own federal Constitution. That term is "capitation", and it is the sole specifically-listed type of direct tax in the Constitution.

It's a funny thing that this term should be so poorly understood, and has seen little effort in the past to discern its meaning. Under the utterly explicit and still-controlling prescription of the Constitution, anything which qualifies as a capitation is subject to the rule of apportionment (by which the total to be collected with each imposition of the tax is divided among the states in proportion to their shares of the national population, and is then collected and remitted by the state governments). The reciprocal of this, of course, is that in order for the income tax we know and love (or any other tax, for that matter) to be administered WITHOUT apportionment, and yet still be valid, it CANNOT be a capitation. Before we discuss what the tax IS then, let's have a close look at what it CANNOT be...

> *"CAPITATION, A poll tax; an imposition which is yearly laid on each person according to his estate and ability. 2. **The Constitution of the United States provides that "no capitation, or other direct tax, shall be laid, unless in proportion to the census, or enumeration, therein before directed to be taken." Art. 1, s. 9, n. 4. See 3 Dall. 171; 5 Wheat 317**."* Bouvier's Law Dictionary, 6th Ed. (1856). (Emphasis added.)

In a way, this simple definition from what was, in its time, the Congressional law dictionary of record more-or-less tells us all that we need to know. A capitation is an annual imposition on each person measured by his estate and ability. Some may split hairs on the meaning of "estate", but "ability" pretty clearly refers to ability to pay, and that pretty clearly means "revenue". On the other hand, the reference to a "poll tax" leads to some confusion as well, especially when more modern references are relied upon.

For instance, the entire definition of "capitation" offered by Black's Law Dictionary (fifth edition) is as follows:

> "***Capitation tax.*** *A poll tax (q.v.). A tax or imposition upon the person. It is a very ancient kind of tribute, and answers to what the Latins called "tributum", by which taxes on persons are distinguished from taxes on merchandise, called "vectigalia"."*

Not very illuminating.

Turning to the definition of "poll tax" in the same collection, we find:

> "***Poll-tax.*** *A capitation tax; a tax of a specific sum levied upon each person within the jurisdiction of the taxing power and within a certain class (as, all males of a certain age, etc.) without reference to his property or lack of it.*
>
> *Poll taxes as a prerequisite to voting in federal elections are prohibited by the 24th Amendment and as to state elections such were held to be unconstitutional in Harper v. Virginia Bd. of Elections, 383 U.S. 663, 86 S. Ct. 1079, 16 L.Ed2d 169."*

If one makes no further study of this subject, and relies on Black's definitions, one would conclude that a "capitation" is just a "poll tax" (that is, a "head tax"), and might even confuse it with a "voting tax"-- that is, a tax taken at the polling place before the right to vote can be exercised.

However, Black's definitions are woefully incomplete and misleading. A capitation is NOT simply a "poll tax", and a "poll tax" is not a "voting tax" (as is self-evident when the Constitution's "apportionment" clause is considered, since apportionment can't apply to a "voting tax", and is superfluous in regard to "head tax"). Nonetheless, since most have never made a study of this subject, sloppy presentations in prominent sources such as Black's have muddied the subject enough to make "capitation" a cognitive 'hiccup' term. Far too many who encounter the term, even while poring over the language of our fundamental law, simply skim past with no registration of its meaning or import.

So, just to clear up (or forestall) such confusion, let's examine the relevant observations of a couple of fellows who were inarguably in a position to know what they were talking about. We'll start with Alexander Hamilton, one of the chief authors of the Constitution itself, who discussed direct and indirect taxes in the first tax case argued before the United States Supreme Court, observing that:

> *"The following are presumed to be the only direct taxes. Capitation or poll taxes. Taxes on lands and buildings. General assessments, whether on the whole property of individuals, or on their whole real or personal estate; all else must of necessity be considered as indirect taxes."*

In addition to his inclusion of general assessments on personal estates as being in the class of direct taxes, note also that Hamilton does NOT characterize "poll tax" as just an alternative name for "capitation"; more important still, as will become clearer in a moment, he specifically declares "poll taxes" to also be among the direct taxes subject to the apportionment rule.

Now let's turn to the singular expert on this subject, and the one whose work guided the framers in their use of terms in the taxing clauses, Adam Smith, author of 'The Wealth Of Nations', perhaps the most important work ever written about economics and taxation:

> *"The taxes which, it is intended, should fall indifferently upon every different species of revenue, are capitation taxes,"... "Capitation taxes, if it is attempted to proportion them to the fortune or revenue of each contributor, become altogether arbitrary. The state of a man's fortune varies from day to day, and without an inquisition more intolerable than any tax, and renewed*

> *at least once every year, can only be guessed at."..."Capitation taxes, so far as they are levied upon the lower ranks of people, are direct taxes upon the wages of labour, and are attended with all the inconveniences of such taxes."..." In the capitation which has been levied in France without any interruption since the beginning of the present century, the highest orders of people are rated according to their rank by an invariable tariff; the lower orders of people, according to what is supposed to be their fortune, by an assessment which varies from year to year."* (Bear in mind that Smith is using the common word 'wages', not the custom-defined legal term of the same spelling found in the modern revenue laws.)

Smith goes on to discuss the version of capitations imposed under the name of "poll taxes", as well, observing that in the first poll tax, for instance, many were taxed according to their supposed fortune, being *"assessed at three shillings in the pound of their supposed income"*.

Clearly, a general, indiscriminate tax on income read as "all that comes in", or on "every species of revenue", qualifies as either a "capitation" or a "poll tax" (or both) as each term is properly understood. Consequently, we know that any such tax must, under the provisions of the Constitution, be administered exclusively by the rule of apportionment.

I'll close this introductory discussion of "capitations" with the acknowledgment by the United States Supreme Court, in the case of Pollock v. Farmer's Loan & Trust, 157 U.S. 429 (1895), that the understanding of the term that I have presented here is precisely the one which informed the Framers of the Constitution when choosing the wording "capitations and other direct taxes" in laying down the rule of apportionment. Declaring the meaning of the phrase "capitations and other direct taxes" in its ruling in the case, the court resorts to the authority of Albert Gallatin, Pennsylvania state congressman, United States Representative and Senator, United States

Minister to England and France, respectively, and the longest serving Secretary of the Treasury in American history, and says:

> *"...Albert Gallatin, in his Sketch of the Finances of the United States, published in November, 1796, said: 'The most generally received opinion, however, is that, by direct taxes in the constitution, those are meant which are raised on the capital or revenue of the people;...'*
>
> *...*
>
> *"He then quotes from Smith's Wealth of Nations, and continues: 'The remarkable coincidence of the clause of the constitution with this passage in using the word 'capitation' as a generic expression, including the different species of direct taxes-- an acceptation of the word peculiar, it is believed, to Dr. Smith-- leaves little doubt that the framers of the one had the other in view at the time, and that they, as well as he, by direct taxes, meant those paid directly from the falling immediately on the revenue;...'"*

The Origin of the Tax; Its Character as an Excise; and the Meaning of "Income"

"The name by which the tax is described in the statute is, of course, immaterial. Its character must be determined by its incidents..." Dawson v. Kentucky Distillers & Warehouse Co., 255 U.S. 288 (1921)

The Lincoln administration was aware of all that we have just discussed when, in 1862, it instituted the income tax we've since come to know so poorly, but loathe so well. The Lincoln administration knew the Constitution prohibits capitations and other direct taxes unless apportioned; it knew a tax that actually touched upon the "all species of revenue" which constitute the broad class of receipts known as "income" in the common usage of that word WOULD be a capitation, and had under various names always been recognized and designated as a direct tax throughout history; and it also knew that apportioned direct taxes were really only suited to one-time debt-retirements and had traditionally been used exclusively for that purpose.

One-time debt-retirement was not what the Lincoln administration needed or wanted. Lincoln was looking to finance an ongoing war effort, and he needed the kind of tax that, once instituted, keeps on giving and giving without the inconveniences of repeated legislation and voting. In short, he wanted an excise, and that's what he imposed-- an excise on certain activities, measured by (and typically paid out of) the revenue they produced.

> *"...in Springer v. U. S., 102 U.S. 586 (1880), it was held that [the] tax upon gains, profits, and income was an excise or duty, and not a direct tax, within the meaning of the constitution, and that its imposition was not, therefore, unconstitutional."* United States Supreme Court, Pollock v. Farmer's Loan & Trust, 158 U.S. 601, (1895);
>
> *"...taxation on income was in its nature an excise entitled to be enforced as such,"*
> United States Supreme Court, Brushaber v. Union Pacific R. Co., 240 U.S. 1 (1916), quoting and reiterating language used in its ruling in Pollock v. Farmer's Loan and Trust.
>
> *"I hereby certify that the following is a true and faithful statement of the gains, profits, or income of _____ _____, of the _____ of _____, in the county of _____, and State of _____, whether derived from any kind of property, rents, interest, dividends, salary, or from any profession, trade, employment, or vocation, or from any other source whatever, from the 1st day of January to the 31st day of December, 1862, both days inclusive, and subject to an income tax* ***under the excise laws*** *of the United States."*
> (from the first income tax return form, emphasis added).

As legislative draftsman for the United States Treasury Department F. Morse Hubbard put it in no uncertain terms while testifying before Congress in 1943:

> *"The income tax... ...is an excise tax with respect to certain activities and privileges which is measured by reference to the income [earnings] which they produce."*
> House Congressional Record, March 27, 1943, page 2580

***

Perhaps because the tax can easily be mistaken for a tax on the revenue itself (due to the fact that the amount of activity being taxed is measured by the dollars produced, and the amount of tax-due is determined by applying the rate of tax to that amount of dollars), the name "income tax" recommended itself to Congress; nonetheless, the tax is not, for reasons we have observed, any kind of general tax on income read as "all that comes in". Instead, it is a tax on only a *specialized subset* of the larger class of income, <u>consisting exclusively of revenues attributable to the voluntary, profitable use of federal privilege, property or powers</u>-- that is, revenues in which the federal government has a direct ownership interest, and to which it can therefore exercise a direct claim as a matter of right.

(As an aside, it is worth noting that <u>within the realm of federal privilege</u>, and <u>within the context of the tax</u>, though, "income" COULD be described as effectively meaning "all that comes in", and sometimes is so described by courts and government agencies. This is because <u>every</u> activity involving the use of federal privilege, property or prerogative measurable by dollars (or dollar-value) produced qualifies as the "income" subject to the tax:

> *""(a) GENERAL DEFINITION. 'Gross income' includes gains, profits, and income derived from salaries, wages, or compensation for personal service . . . of whatever kind and in whatever form paid, or from professions, vocations, trades, businesses, commerce, or sales, or*

> *dealings in property, whether real or personal, growing out of the ownership or use of or interest in such property; also from interest, rent, dividends, securities, or the transaction of any business carried on for gain or profit,* or gains or profits and income derived from any source whatever. . . ." *(emphasis added)"* Commissioner v. Glenshaw Glass Co., 348 U.S. 426 (1955)

So, to the extent that one operates within the federal universe (so to speak), "income" DOES mean "all that comes in", and may be described that way within the appropriate context. But this doesn't extend the reach of the tax to activities outside of that universe. Thus, even within that universe and context, the more accurate and complete definition of the term "income" is "all that comes in here".)

The language of the original income tax enactment is helpful in illuminating the true character of the tax and the "income" to which it applies:

> *'An Act to provide Internal Revenue to support the Government and to pay interest on the Public Debt'*
> *Sec. 86. And be it further enacted, That on and after the first day of August, eighteen hundred and sixty-two, there shall be levied, collected, and paid on all salaries of officers, or payments to persons in the civil, military, naval, or other employment or service of the United States, including senators and representatives and delegates in Congress, when exceeding the rate of six hundred dollars per annum, a duty of three per centum on the excess above the said six hundred dollars; and it shall be the duty of all paymasters, and all disbursing officers, under the government of the United States, or in the employ thereof, when making any payments to officers and persons as aforesaid, or upon settling and adjusting the accounts of such officers and persons, to deduct and withhold the aforesaid duty of three per centum, and shall, at the same time, make a certificate stating the name of the officer or person from whom*

> *such deduction was made, and the amount thereof, which shall be transmitted to the office of the Commissioner of Internal Revenue, and entered as part of the internal duties;...* ("Income" derived from less formalized federally-connected activities, such as investment in, or contracts with, federal entities is also taxed under other provisions in the act.)

It is because the tax confines itself solely to revenue-generating federal activities as listed in part in this section of law that it is NOT a capitation-- that is, a tax on revenue generally. This limited scope also prevents the "income" tax from amounting to a tax burdening the exercise of individual rights, by the way-- a transgression which by itself would drop the tax squarely into the category of "direct" even without regard to the capitation issue. As the Supreme Court observes in the case of Knowlton v. Moore, 178 U.S. 41 (1900), quoting the long-standing official French tax law definition as being illustrative of the distinctions drawn in the U. S. Constitution:

> *"Direct taxes bear immediately upon persons, upon the possession and enjoyments of rights;"*

Many other rulings make the same, utterly fundamental point, which is self-evident, in any case. To tax undistinguished revenue simply as an exercise of power is to tax a person's exercise of the fundamental individual right to work or trade.

> *"The right to follow any of the common occupations of life is an inalienable right...*
>
> *It has been well said that 'the property which every man has in his own labor, as it is the original foundation of all other property, so it is the most sacred and inviolable. The patrimony of the poor man lies in the strength and dexterity of his own hands, and to hinder his employing this strength and dexterity in what manner he thinks proper, without injury to his neighbor, is a plain violation of this most sacred property'."* United States Supreme Court, Butcher's Union Co. v. Crescent City Co., 111 U.S. 746 (1883);

> *"Included in the right of personal liberty and the right of private property- partaking of the nature of each- is the right to make contracts for the acquisition of property. Chief among such contracts is that of personal employment, by which labor and other services are exchanged for money or other forms of property"* United States Supreme Court, Coppage v. Kansas, 236 U.S. 1 (1915).

On the other hand, to tax revenue proceeding from the voluntary, profitable exercise of the government's own property or powers (whether directly or by proxy through investment) is to impose an indirect tax having nothing to do with the tax-payer's rights. Instead, such a tax merely involves an ownership-related claim to a piece of the privileged "action".

> *"PRIVILEGE: A particular benefit or advantage enjoyed by a person, company, or class beyond the common advantages of others citizens. An exceptional or extraordinary power of exemption. A particular right, advantage, exemption, power, franchise, or immunity held by a person or class, not generally possessed by others."* Black's Law Dictionary, 6th Edition.

> *...the requirement to pay* [excise] *taxes involves the exercise of privilege."* United States Supreme Court, Flint vs. Stone Tracy Co. 220 U.S. 107 (1911);

> *"The terms 'excise tax' and 'privilege tax' are synonymous. The two are often used interchangeably."* American Airways v. Wallace, 57 F.2d 877, 880 (Dist. Ct., M.D. Tenn., 1937)

> *"The 'Government' is an abstraction, and its possession of property largely constructive. Actual possession and custody of Government property nearly always are in someone who is not himself the Government but acts in its behalf and for its purposes. He may be an officer, an agent, or a contractor. His personal advantages from the relationship by way of salary, profit, or beneficial personal use of the property may be taxed..."* United

States Supreme Court, United States v. County of Allegheny, 322 US 174 (1944)

Its confinement to activities distinguished by privilege-dependence is what keeps the "income" tax from crossing the line into being both a capitation and a burden on the exercise of natural rights.

For the sake of clearing away possible cognitive stumbling blocks it is necessary to point out that while the realm in which the tax operates is limited, within that realm the tax is quite comprehensive. As was noted previously, within the federal universe, EVERY gainful activity qualifies as "income"-producing, because every such activity is "privileged" in the relevant sense. While working for the Post Office might not seem like the exercise of a "privilege" as we are accustomed to think of that word (as opposed to, say, the privilege involved in profiting from investment in a railroad running on federally-granted or -subsidized land, or owning or investing in a national bank or other federal instrumentality), in a legal sense it very much is. ANYTHING one does that requires the permission of another is the exercise of a privilege, and can properly be subject to conditions such as taxes.

In fact, legally speaking, even something as mundane as being allowed to borrow my lawnmower for use in your landscaping business is a privilege-- something to which you have no inherent right and which I can withhold from you-- or tax-- at my pleasure. Opening and operating "Joe's Delivery Service" is a matter of right, and anyone can do it without anyone else's permission. Working for the United States Post Office, on the other hand, can only be done with the permission of the United States. By confining itself exclusively to receipts proceeding from such voluntarily-engaged-in, but federal-privilege-dependent activities-- whether those of a federal worker, investor, office-holder or cash-grant beneficiary-- the "income tax" as practiced in America does not cross the line from an indirect tax to what would otherwise inescapably be a direct tax, and one which would require the mechanism of apportionment in its administration.

It is true that the external appearance of many of these activities is indistinguishable from those conducted as matters of private right. A doctor working for the federal government practices medicine in the same manner as a doctor in private enterprise does. A plumber in the civil service uses the same tools and skills as the one that comes to your home. An investor buying stock in a national bank or railroad, or other federal corporation or instrumentality, places those orders with his broker at the same time that he buys stock in Sears, and his dividend check may even combine the profits from all of these investments.

However, the superficial similarity of private and privileged activities masks a fundamental difference between them, which is that those in the subset to which the tax applies are made possible only due to the existence, and with the cooperation, of the federal government. In a very real and explicit sense, the aptly-named "income" tax in this country is, in fact, a "FEDERAL income tax". A detailed, accurate and comprehensive study of the income tax law-- such as that presented exclusively in 'Cracking the Code- The Fascinating Truth About Taxation In America' (CtC)-- makes clear that this distinction is thoroughly embedded in that law. In no respect whatsoever does the federal income tax purport to be anything but the limited, specialized tax that it must be, or to touch upon any revenue not distinguished as noted here-- decades of diligent efforts to obscure that fact in the public mind notwithstanding.

For instance, a close examination of the current statutory structure defining "wages"-- a term central to the measurement and reporting of "income"-taxable activities by paid-performers-of-services-- illustrates that the tax remains scrupulously adherent to its proper Constitutional limits. The term confines itself to remuneration paid to:

> *"...an officer, employee, or elected official of the United States, a State*, or any political subdivision thereof, or the District of Columbia, or any agency or instrumentality of any one or more of the foregoing."*
> *"State", as used in this statute, has its own custom definition in the law.

This definition also explicitly covers remuneration paid for service as officers of federal corporations, and implicitly covers other federal workers/office holders not listed, by virtue of the "includes" mechanism discussed briefly below and in detail in CtC. (NOTE: The language presented above is from the general "wage withholding" section of the internal revenue laws. The more narrowly focused FICA "income" surtaxes are also measured and reported using the term "wages", but deploy a somewhat more elaborate structure to define the term, which is also discussed in detail in CtC.) Similarly, the statutory definition of the conduct of a "trade or business", the receipts from which are to be reported and taxed as "income", is:

> *"...the performance of the functions of a public office."*

By virtue of the statutory rule of construction concerning "includes"-- another custom legal term deployed in the definitions of both of "wages" and "trade or business", these terms are amenable to a narrowly limited potential expansion to cover other things of the same class (legal character) as those already listed, but nothing else.

"Includes" and "including" are deployed in a number of key statutes by which the "income" tax is laid, and the terms have been a source of confusion in some quarters, even within the legal profession. Thus, they merit an extended discussion.

Normally, "includes" and "including" are flatly restrictive. As United States Supreme Court Chief Justice John Marshall derisively observed when presented with a strained argument to the contrary in an 1808 case:

> *"It [is argued that] the word "including" means "moreover", or "as well as"; but if this was the meaning of the legislature, it was a very embarrassing mode of expressing the idea."* United States v. The Schooner Betsey and Charlotte, 8 U.S. 443 (1808).

Marshall goes on to declare that the proposition that "moreover" or "as well as" is, in fact, what is meant by the legislative use of "including" (or, by extension, "includes") is nonsense. The court re-iterates this rule a century later:

> *"The [state supreme] court also considered that the word 'including' was used as a word of enlargement, the learned court being of the opinion that such was its ordinary sense. With this we cannot concur."* Montello Salt Co. v. Utah, 221 U.S. 452 (1911)

In federal tax law, though, "includes" and "including" are permitted a little bit of latitude, being controlled by the following rule:

> *"Includes and including: The terms "includes" and "including" when used in a definition contained in this title shall not be deemed to exclude other things otherwise within the meaning of the term defined."* Rev. Act of 1938 §901(b) (Codified at 26 USC 7701(c).)

The Department of the Treasury has helpfully clarified the meaning of this provision with the following regulatory language:

> *"The terms "includes and including" do not exclude things not enumerated which are in the same general class;"* 27 CFR 26.11 and 27 CFR 72.11

The United States Supreme Court has been even more helpful:

> *"[T]he verb "includes" imports a general class, some of whose particular instances are those specified in the definition. This view finds support in § 2(b) of the Act, which reads: "The terms 'includes' and 'including,' when used in a definition contained in this title, shall not be deemed to exclude other things otherwise within the*

> *meaning of the term defined.""* Helvering v Morgan's, Inc, 293 U.S. 121, 126 fn. 1 (1934)

The court refers to and re-iterates this observation in Federal Land Bank of St. Paul v. Bismarck Lumber Co. 314 U.S. 95, 62 S.Ct. 1 U.S. (1941):

> *"[I]ncluding... ...connotes simply an illustrative application of the general principle."*

(That is, the enumerated items in a definition in which "including" is deployed "illustrate"-- identify, and thus establish-- the contours of the class which the defined term represents-- the "general principle" of its application). In Massachusetts v. EPA, 549 U.S. 497 (2007), the court re-iterates this doctrine concerning the meaning of "includes" and "including" in a dissent on other grounds authored by Justice Scalia and joined by Chief Justice Roberts and Justices Thomas and Alito:

> *"The word "including" can indeed indicate that what follows will be an "illustrative" sampling of the general category that precedes the word. Federal Land Bank of St. Paul v. Bismarck Lumber Co., 314 U.S. 95, 100 (1941)."* (Internal quote marks in the original.)

The reference to the Federal Land Bank ruling, which itself drew on the Helvering v. Morgan ruling, makes clear that the circumstances under which the 2007 court recognizes that the use of "including (or "includes") indicates that what follows is an illustrative sampling of a general category being defined is when their use is under the influence of the language of 26 USC 7701(c).

The principle involved in the "includes" mechanism is largely that described by the Supreme Court in Gustafson v. Alloyd Co. (93-404), 513 US 561 (1995):

> *"...a word is known by the company it keeps (the doctrine of noscitur a sociis). This rule we rely upon to avoid ascribing to one word a meaning so broad that it*

> *is inconsistent with its accompanying words, thus giving "unintended breadth to the Acts of Congress."*

The 1st Circuit Court of Appeals puts it this way in Brigham v. United States, 160 F.3d 759 (1st Cir. 1998):

> *"[T]he terms 'includes' and 'including' . . . shall not be deemed to exclude other things otherwise within the meaning of the term defined." 26 U.S.C. § 7701(c). In light of this we apply the principle that a list of terms should be construed to include by implication those additional terms of like kind and class as the expressly included terms. *fn2: This follows from the canon noscitur a sociis, "a word is known by the company it keeps." Neal v. Clark, 95 U.S. 704, 708-09 (1878)."*

The principle is clarified by these additional, related rulings:

> *"When a statute includes an explicit definition, we must follow that definition, even if it varies from that term's ordinary meaning."* Stenberg v. Carhart, 530 U.S. 914 (2000)
>
> *"It is axiomatic that the statutory definition of the term excludes unstated meanings of that term."* Meese v. Keene, 481 U.S. 465 (1987)
>
> *"Of course, statutory definitions of terms used therein prevail over colloquial meanings. Fox v. Standard Oil Co., 294 U.S. 87, 95, 55 S.Ct. 333, 336."* Western Union Telegraph Co. v. Lenroot, 323 U.S. 490 (1945)

These rulings reflect the fact that when a word becomes a statutorily-defined "term", its original meaning is entirely stripped away and replaced with the new meaning described. This is why, for instance, the definition of "employee" at which we looked earlier explicitly lists "federal employees". Despite being identically spelled and pronounced, the statutorily-defined-term doesn't mean "anyone who works for a boss", or whatever dictionary definition you might find for the common word 'employee'; nor does it mean 'employee' as commonly-defined plus the additional listed persons or types (by virtue of which federal employees would have been encompassed without being listed). When the former understanding and usage is intended, no statutory definition is provided; and when the latter construction is intended qualifying phrases such as, "includes, but is not limited to..." and "including, but not limited to..." are deployed, as can be found in dozens of places within the body of federal tax law.

If a definition IS provided, and "includes" is used without additional qualifying language (as in the definition of "employee" discussed above) the term only means what the enumerated list describes-- in this case, persons working for the federal government or its subordinate entities, under a variety of different labels and in a variety of different capacities. Thanks to the limited-expansion rule provided at 7701(c), the meaning of the defined-term "employee" can be considered to cover others not listed who also work for the federal government or its subordinate entities (and who are thus within the class established by the existing list), <u>but no one else</u>. These rules and statutory practices play an important role in preventing the "income" tax from functioning as a de facto capitation or other direct tax.

PART TWO

OK, now we've seen that the income tax is, always has been, and can only be, an exercise-of-privilege-based "piece of the action" excise tax on distinguished activity, rather than a capitation, and that "income" as meant in the context of the tax refers only to that distinguished activity (the amount of which is measured by the dollar value it produces).

Now we'll look at what the 16th Amendment was all about, and discover that, rather than instituting, or authorizing the "income" tax, the amendment concerned nothing more than closing a loophole opened by a late-nineteenth-century Supreme Court ruling that briefly impeded the application of the tax to a particular kind of "income", which is distinguished from the larger subclass of distinguished, revenue-measured taxable activity by virtue of its connection to personal property.

"The whole body of internal revenue law in effect on January 2, 1939... ...has its ultimate origin in 164 separate enactments of Congress. The earliest of these was approved July 1, 1862; the latest, June 16, 1938."
-Preamble to the 1939 Internal Revenue Code

It is clear that were the distinct, limited meaning of the "income" subject to the "income tax" to be eroded away, and the tax come to be applied to "all that comes in", it would be, and would have to be recognized as, a capitation or other direct tax. The United States Supreme Court explicitly declares in its 1916 ruling in Brushaber v. Union Pacific R. Co., 240 U.S. 1 (while specifically considering the limited meaning and effect of the 16th Amendment) that should the tax ever come to exceed its proper boundaries,

> *"the duty would arise to disregard form* [that is, any pretense by which it is made to appear that the tax is being confined to its proper limits when it is not, such as by creatively construing the meaning of "income", or the use of any pretense, scheme or construction by which non-specialized revenue or activities are made to appear otherwise so as to be subjected to the tax] *and consider substance alone* [that is, what the tax is actually falling upon as a practical reality]*, and hence subject the tax to the regulation as to apportionment which otherwise as an excise would not apply to it."*

But, of course, the law behind the tax never has exceeded those boundaries. This is why the very tax which is administered today, on the same activities as it is administered today-- without apportionment, and without any pretense of relief of the apportionment rule, such as is inaccurately ascribed to the 16th Amendment-- could be laid and administered for decades BEFORE that amendment, and yet be upheld by the United States Supreme Court.

For example, in Gray v. Darlington, 82 U.S. 63 (1872), the court had occasion to rule on a "capital gains" application of the tax, citing the following language from the 1867 statute,

> *"'There shall be levied, collected, and paid annually upon the gains, profits, and income of every person, . . . whether derived from any kind of property, rents, interest, dividends, or salaries, or from any profession, trade, employment, or vocation, . . . or from any other source whatever, . . . a tax of five per centum on the amount so derived over $ 1000 . . .. And the tax herein provided for shall be assessed, collected, and paid upon the gains, profits, and income for the year ending the 31st of December next preceding the time for levying, collecting, and paying said tax.'"*

The court finds no issue with the tax generally, but merely holds that,

> *"The rule adopted by the officers of the revenue in the present case would justify them in treating as gains of one year the increase in the value of property extending through any number of years, through even the entire century. The actual advance in value of property over its cost may, in fact, reach its height years before its sale; the value of the property may, in truth, be less at the time of the sale than at any previous period in ten years, yet, if the amount received exceed the actual cost of the property, the excess is to be treated, according to their views, as gains of the owner for the year in which the sale takes place. We are satisfied that no such result was intended by the statute."*

Again, in Springer v. U. S., 102 U.S. 586 (1880), a test case of which the Supreme Court declares that:

> *"The central and controlling question in this case is whether the tax which was levied on the income, gains, and profits of the plaintiff in error, as set forth in the record, and by pretended virtue of the acts of Congress*

> *and parts of acts therein mentioned* [the act of June 30, 1864, as amended by the act of March 3, 1865-- the relevant language of which duplicated that quoted above in the Gray case], *is a direct tax;"*

and that:

> *"The plaintiff in error advises us by his elaborate brief 'that on the trial of the case below the proceedings were merely formal,' and that 'no arguments or briefs were submitted, and only such proceedings were had as were necessary to prepare the case for the Supreme Court'";*

the court ultimately concludes (as summarized in a later case) that,

> *"[The] tax upon gains, profits, and income [is] an excise or duty, and not a direct tax, within the meaning of the constitution, and that its imposition [is] not, therefore, unconstitutional."* United States Supreme Court, Pollock v. Farmer's Loan & Trust, 158 U.S. 601, 1895.

In the Pollock ruling itself, the most exhaustive judicial consideration of the federal taxing power undertaken in American history (and another ruling preceding the 16th Amendment), the Supreme Court observes first that when used in the generic sense of "all that comes in", a tax on income is inherently a direct tax:

> *"In England, we do not understand that an income tax has ever been regarded as other than a direct tax. In Dowell's History of Taxation and Taxes in England, admitted to be the leading authority, the evolution of taxation in that country is given, and an income tax is invariably classified as a direct tax."*

and,

> *"At the time the constitution was framed and adopted, under the systems of direct taxation of many of the states, taxes were laid on incomes from professions, business, or employments..."*

The court then proceeds to distinguish the tax laid by the federal income tax statutes as being only on a special class of receipts amenable to taxation by excise (that is, the class we have been referring to as "income"):

> *"We have considered the act only in respect of the tax on income derived from real estate, and from invested personal property, and have not commented on so much of it as bears on gains or profits from business, privileges, or employments, in view of the instances in which taxation on business, privileges, or employments* ***has assumed the guise of an excise tax and been sustained as such."*** (Emphasis added)

(Remember, as noted in the Brushaber decision, a tax does not qualify as an excise because the government chooses to call it one [form], but because its character-- both as to object and application-- is, in every particular, such a tax [substance].) The court goes on to point out that this excise on "income" is, in fact, what is taxed as such under the federal income tax structure:

> *"If [the portion of the 1894 Revenue Act laying the tax on income from real estate] be stricken out, and also the income from all invested personal property, bonds, stocks, investments of all kinds, it is obvious that by far the largest part of the anticipated revenue would be eliminated, and* ***this would leave the burden of the tax to be borne by professions, trades, employments, or vocations****; and in that way what was intended as a tax on capital would remain, in substance, a tax on occupations and labor. We cannot believe that such was the intention of congress. We do not mean to say that an act laying by apportionment a direct tax on all real estate and personal property, or the income thereof, might not also lay excise taxes on business, privileges, employments, and vocations. But this is not such an act [because the real estate and personal property exactions were not, in fact, laid by apportionment in the act], and the scheme must be considered as a whole."* (Emphasis added)

The continued strict and scrupulous adherence of the "income" tax to the same proper and necessary boundaries by which it has been confined since its inception in 1862 is why the Supreme Court is able to repeatedly declare over the years SINCE the 16th Amendment that the amendment did not create a new tax:

> *"The provisions of the Sixteenth Amendment conferred no new power of taxation..."* Stanton v. Baltic Mining Co., 240 U.S. 103 (1916);

did not extend the tax to anything it had not embraced before:

> *"The Sixteenth Amendment, although referred to in argument, has no real bearing and may be put out of view. As pointed out in recent decisions, it does not extend the taxing power to new or excepted subjects..."* Peck v. Lowe, 247 U.S. 165 (1918);

did not create authority for some hybrid tax which could fall upon any traditional or inherent object of a direct tax (such as a general income tax) but which was now simply not subject to the rule of apportionment:

> *"We are of opinion, however, that the confusion is not inherent, but rather arises from the conclusion that the 16th Amendment provides for a hitherto unknown power of taxation; that is, a power to levy an income tax which, although direct, should not be subject to the regulation of apportionment applicable to all other direct taxes. And the far-reaching effect of this erroneous assumption will be made clear by generalizing the many contentions advanced in argument to support it..."* Brushaber v. Union Pacific R. Co., 240 U.S. 1 (1916);

and cannot be otherwise construed, since to do so would cause:

> *"...one provision of the Constitution [to] destroy another; that is, [it] would result in bringing the provisions of the Amendment [supposedly] exempting a direct tax from apportionment into irreconcilable conflict with the general requirement that all direct taxes be apportioned."* Id;

and yet continue to find the unapportioned "income" tax Constitutional. The tax didn't need any of these changes in order to be Constitutional, because it didn't become anything it hadn't previously been upon the advent of the 16th Amendment. It still is not, and cannot be, a tax on undistinguished, unspecialized activities (or the revenue produced thereby).

This point bears repeating, due to the pervasiveness of tax-agency-cultivated misunderstanding about the 16th Amendment: All these observations by the Supreme Court are simultaneously true and in harmony with each other **because the limited nature of the tax has never changed**, the 16th Amendment notwithstanding; in fact, these observations CAN ONLY be simultaneously true and in harmony with each other because the limited nature of the tax has never changed:

> *"[T]he settled doctrine is that the Sixteenth Amendment confers no power upon Congress to define and tax as income without apportionment something which theretofore could not have been properly regarded as income."* Taft v. Bowers, 278 US 470, 481 (1929) (Emphasis added.)

In 1988, in South Carolina v. Baker, 485 U.S. 505, the Supreme Court revisits the subject and observes that,

> *"The legislative history merely shows... ...that the sole purpose of the Sixteenth Amendment was to remove the apportionment requirement for whichever incomes were otherwise taxable."* (Emphasis added.)

The court is (again) recognizing that the 16th Amendment operates only on those "incomes" which already were, and always have been, inherently taxable under the "income" excise, and which had been so taxable-- without apportionment-- BEFORE the 16th amendment, until the application of the tax in certain cases was briefly thwarted by the Pollock loophole in 1895. Howard M. Zaritsky, Legislative Attorney of the American

Law Division of the Library of Congress, helpfully summarizes all of this in his 1979 Report N0. 80-19A entitled "Some Constitutional Questions Regarding The Federal Income Tax Laws":

> *"The Supreme Court, in a decision written by Chief Justice White, first noted that the Sixteenth Amendment did not authorize any new type of tax, nor did it repeal or revoke the tax clauses of Article I of the Constitution, quoted above. Direct taxes were, notwithstanding the advent of the Sixteenth Amendment, still subject to the rule of apportionment..."*

***

So, what exactly DID the 16th Amendment do? It simply closed a "loophole" introduced into the administration of the federal income tax by the Supreme Court in its ruling regarding the taxation of "income" from invested personal property in the case of Pollock v. Farmer's Loan & Trust discussed above.

The Pollock ruling held that the application of the tax to the proceeds of investments and real estate leases functioned as a property tax rather than a federal income tax. The reasoning was that to tax such gains-- even when the investments and leases were in, or to, federal entities, as was involved in the case-- is to effectively tax the stock and land itself. Since both are personal property, such a tax was really a property tax and not, in this respect, an excise which could be applied without apportionment. With this ruling the court struck down ten sections of the recently reactivated federal income tax, which had been dormant since its last two-year implementation had expired in 1873.

The effect of this reasoning was to relieve the Robber-Baron class, which was heavily invested in money-making federal instrumentalities such as national banks and railroads and had numerous sweet-heart deals leasing property to the feds, from the burden of the tax. This didn't sit well with the growing and reactionary populist movement, which had little patience with the idea that a cadre of coupon-clipping fat cats--widely, and accurately, perceived as pulling Washington's strings and benefiting handsomely thereby-- should escape the tax, while revenue tariffs, by which even the poorest Americans were affected, stood relatively high in order to make up the loss.

The populists demanded an amendment to the Constitution to close the loophole, and eventually succeeded with the 16th Amendment, which declares that what is otherwise inherently taxable under the federal income tax cannot be shielded therefrom by a resort to the source of the revenue involved. Treasury Department legislative draftsman F. Morse Hubbard usefully summarizes this sole and exclusive effect of the amendment in his 1943 testimony:

> *"[T]he amendment made it possible to bring investment income within the scope of the general income-tax law, but did not change the character of the tax. It is still fundamentally an excise or duty with respect to the privilege of carrying on any activity or owning any property which produces income."* (that is, "income otherwise taxable", as the Supreme Court reminds us some four-and-a-half decades later in the South Carolina v. Baker decision...)

Remember, as soon as Lincoln's 1862 act was passed, "income" acquired a fixed, limited and specialized definition for purposes of federal tax law (without which it would have been ruled unconstitutional for lack of apportionment in several cases arising before Pollock). Thus:

- The 1894 act that Pollock challenged only sought to tax "income" so defined.
- The Supreme Court ruling in that case only addressed the application of the tax to "income" so defined.
- The 16th Amendment only removed the apportionment

> requirement to "income" so defined-- and only that part of it comprising gains from invested personal property and real estate, because it was only that form of "income" that the Pollock court had concluded couldn't be taxed other than by apportionment. All other forms of "income" have always been able to be taxed without apportionment, because of the particular legal character of the receipts which qualify for the tax and which were (and are) the only variety which the tax attempts to reach.

That is why the court can say that direct taxes remain subject to the rule of apportionment even after the amendment; that the provisions of the amendment conferred no new power of taxation; that the amendment does not extend the taxing power to new or excepted subjects; that the sole purpose of the amendment was to remove the apportionment requirement for whichever "incomes" were otherwise taxable; and that the "income" tax remains Constitutional even though capitations still require apportionment.

(A few lower courts have made confusing-- or confused-- declarations over the years to the effect that the 16th Amendment authorized a direct tax without apportionment. What they mean is that in the context of the Pollock court's reasoning, the amendment removed the apportionment requirement from what is really a property-- and therefore inherently direct-- tax, because that's what the Pollock court saw the tax on dividends to be.

However, since the "property tax" involved only applies to gains which otherwise qualify as "income" by virtue of their federal connections, such declarations are misleading when offered without context. Property which is taxable "directly" under the new protocol is not just any property, but only that producing benefits from a voluntarily-undertaken federal linkage. That's why we don't all get federal property-tax bills every year. In reality, the 16th Amendment resulted in an unapportioned "direct" tax only on receipts which are within the class of those IN-directly taxed.)

PART THREE

We're going to conclude this introduction to the truth about the income tax with a look at how general American understanding of all of the foregoing was lost over the course of the twentieth century, but also at how the means of individually correcting misapplications of the "income" tax are inherent within the very structure of the tax itself...

So how did all of this slip away from the American consciousness? Slowly, for one thing. At no time prior to 1942, eight decades after the federal income tax was first introduced, did more than 8% of American households ever file federal income tax returns in any given year. In most of those years, the percentage was far lower than even that small figure. As recently as 1936, only 3.9% of the entire American population filed returns, according to the Treasury Department's Division of Tax Research (Division Staff Memo: "Collection at Source of the Individual Normal Income Tax", 9 January, 1941).

Nonetheless, by 1943, thanks to the distractions of a world war, the exhortations of Donald Duck™ (see www.losthorizons.com/NewSpiritExcerpt.wmv and ask yourself: how many MANDATORY obligations must be sold to the public by cartoon animals?), and the adoption of a vague and confusingly-worded temporary measure called "The Victory Tax", the percentage of households sending in payments declared to be of "income" taxes rose to 38. That same year, the Treasury Department introduced its masterwork: 'The Current Tax Payment Act of 1943', by which the practice of withholding tax deposits from "wages", which had been a feature of the very first federal income tax acts but had been abandoned early in the 20th Century, was re-introduced. The new version was a rare work of lawyerly art, and contributed enormously to the ongoing erosion of general understanding of the nature of the tax-- already well advanced at that point, thanks to the extended passage of time since the initial adoption of the vast bulk of the relevant law. In short, the understanding of the limits of the federal income tax also slipped away from American consciousness organically.

We have suffered heavily for our carelessness ever since, to the tune of trillions of dollars of wealth improperly extracted from us over the years. The fact that the tax is limited as it is, and doesn't actually apply to most receipts, doesn't mean that it does not, or cannot, affect most Americans. In fact, there is an elaborate bureaucratic and legal structure in place which inadvertently leads to the application of the tax outside its proper scope, by encouraging everyone making payments to others to substantively allege that the payments were connected with the conduct of a taxable activity, whether this is actually true or not.

By way of this structure, most UN-taxable receipts become presumptively taxable in the eyes of the law, and the recipients become presumptively required to file a tax return and pay a resulting tax. Of course, false presumptions can be corrected, and in this case, a quirky idiosyncrasy of the relevant law provides that the means by which an inaccurate presumptive transformation of untaxable receipts into taxable receipts is corrected itself involves the filing of a tax return.

Although this appears strange-- even contradictory-- at first glance, it really is not. Every legal action involves an allegation and an answer. The only way to prove that there is nothing to be answered for is by the making of the answer-- however much that dynamic has the character of a "Catch-22". There is simply no other way for the law to work, since to make no rebuttal in the face of an allegation is to admit to what is alleged, by default. So, Congress, recognizing the need, has specified that the making of the same type of tax return used to acknowledge the receipt of "income" when, and to the degree that, allegations to that effect are true is also the formal means of rebutting such allegations when they are not:

> *"And be it further enacted,...that any party, in his or her own behalf,...shall be permitted to declare, under oath or affirmation, the form and manner of which shall be prescribed by the Commissioner of Internal Revenue,... ...the amount of his or her annual income,... liable to be assessed,... and the same so declared shall be received as the sum upon which duties are to be assessed and collected."* Section 93 of The Revenue Act of 1862.

Knowing how these allegations are made, the details of the related provisions and specifications made by Congress, and the underlying principles of law involved in properly answering them requires a careful and thorough reading of 'Cracking the Code- The Fascinating Truth About Taxation In America'. However, a general sense of these things, and of the manner in which the exploitive and obnoxious structure needing to be pro-actively addressed each year by most Americans came to be, can be had by reading the little parable in the following chapter.

Bob's Bicycles
or
Getting Free Of The "Income" Tax Scheme Is As Easy As Falling Off A Bike

To get an idea of how today's "income" tax scheme works, try this little exercise:

Keeping in mind the Constitutional limitations on the federal taxing power that we've just discussed in the last chapter, think of the federal government like a guy named Bob, who lives down the street from you in a town that is really big on bicycles. Bikes get used for commuting, deliveries, shopping, etc.. In fact, other than walking, bicycles are the exclusive form of transportation in your town.

Your neighbor Bob has a by-the-mile bicycle-renting business-- "Bob's Bicycles". Bob's Bicycles is far and away the biggest business in town.

Part of Bob's success is because he does a lot of contract business. However, Bob doesn't just get paid by riders who have signed an agreement with him, or even just those using Bob's bikes. Bob gets something every time anybody in town does any riding at all, through an odd combination of circumstances that took many years to come together.

Here's how it happened...

Bob's Bicycles was launched long ago by the great grandfather of the present Bob (Bob IV). Great Grandpa Bob started out not only with a main location for his contract business-- he also had the bright idea of setting up spots around town where he parked some of his bikes for use by the more occasional rider, on an "honor system". Anyone could take and use one of these bikes, but they were expected to keep track of their mileage, and send Bob a "1040 Mileage Ridden/Rent Due Form" (and the appropriate rent), periodically. The initial design of the form was like this:

> *I, ___________, rode a Bob's Bicycle a total of _____ miles this year.*
>
> *At Bob's rental rate of $.15 per mile, I owe Bob $_____*

I said that Great Grandpa Bob planned to deal with these occasional riders on the "honor system", and that's true. But he liked his money, too, and didn't want to miss anything that was due him. So, after setting up the "self-serve" locations, Great Grandpa Bob went around handing out "W-2, 1099 or K-1 Rider Reporting Forms" to every other business in town. The forms-- accompanied by notices that if Bob didn't get his rent from someone riding a bicycle in connection with any business, he would sue the company involved-- said:

> *I, _________, saw _________ riding a bicycle*
> *from _______ to _______ on __/__/__*
>
> *I swear this to be true to the best of my knowledge and belief under penalties of perjury,*
> *__________________ __/__/__*

***

To begin with, everybody understood that where it says "bicycle" on one of Bob's "W-2, 1099 or K-1 Rider Reporting Forms" or notices, it means "one of Bob's bicycles". For one thing, this was obvious. After all, what legitimate interest would Bob have in getting a report about someone riding a bike that wasn't his?

Indeed, what business would Bob have even *asking* for a report about someone riding a non-Bob's Bicycle? Everyone understood, and besides, on the back of the form, anyone who looked would find, *"When used on one of Bob's forms or notices, "bicycle" means "one of Bob's bicycles""*. So, these forms worked well enough, to begin with. Everyone understood what they were for, and Bob's "honor system" bicycles were all painted bright red, so mistakes were few.

Some mistakes DID happen though. So, Great Grandpa Bob provided that the same reporting process used to admit riding a "Bob's Bicycle" on the honor system would serve to correct any errors. All that a victim of an erroneous "W-2, 1099 or K-1 Rider Reporting Form" needed to do was fill out one of the "1040 Mileage Ridden/Rent Due" forms-- which could be conveniently found at the "Bob's Bicycles" locations all over town-- declaring the truth of the matter (with a specific rebuttal or correction of the erroneous "W-2, 1099 or K-1 Rider Reporting Form" assertions attached).

This might mean reporting that they had ridden '0' miles on one of Bob's bikes that year. Or it might mean acknowledging that they DID ride one of Bob's bikes for a certain number of miles, just not the number reported on the erroneous "W-2, 1099 or K-1 Rider Reporting Form". This particular use of the "1040 Mileage Ridden/Rent Due" form led to a little change in its design. Now it looked like this:

> *I, ___________, rode a Bob's Bicycle a total of _____ miles this year.*
>
> *Since Bob's rental rate is $.15 per mile, I owe Bob $_____*
>
> *Under penalties of perjury, I declare the foregoing to be true, complete and correct to the best of my knowledge and belief,*
>
> ___________ __/__/__

(Great Grandpa Bob was a nice guy, and he was comfortable with his "honor system". But Great Grandpa Bob wasn't born yesterday.)

Over the years, things got a bit more complicated, just by an unfortunate coincidence of several misunderstandings. For one thing, Bob Jr. stopped personally distributing the "W-2, 1099 or K-1 Rider Reporting Forms", and hired a company to take care of this for him. Now, folks who had never even met Bob, and didn't know anything about him or his business, started getting "W-2, 1099 or K-1 Rider Reporting Forms" in the mail.

Along with the forms came prominent instructions advising the recipient to, *"Use this form to report the use of a bicycle by any person".* The note that, *"When used on one of*

Bob's forms or notices, "bicycle" means "one of Bob's bicycles"", got reworded into more complex 'legalese', and buried in a whole lot of new fine print on the back of the form.

Later, that clarifying note moved off the form entirely--first being replaced by a cryptic reference to where the definition might be found in the "Bicycle Forms, Publications and Policies Guide" (conveniently available at each "Bob's" location around town), and then ultimately being dropped altogether under the principle that knowing what the forms are for is the responsibility of the person filling one out. Unsurprisingly, a lot of folks misunderstood, and began filling out and sending these reports to the address provided every time they saw anyone riding ANY bicycle.

Another thing contributing to complications with Great Grandpa Bob's program was Bob Jr's decision to stop painting his "honor system" bikes bright red. Pretty soon, even folks who remembered that "W-2, 1099 or K-1 Rider Reporting Forms" only related to Bob's bicycles were filling them out anytime they saw anyone riding a bike. This was only partly out of confusion.

"Bob's" had become a very successful business over the years, and was an important customer to every other company in town. People were eager to please Bob, and keep in his good graces; furthermore, although the fine print on the "W-2, 1099 or K-1 Rider Reporting Forms" had changed, those notices about Bob suing for his money hadn't. Bob maintained a really active PR department, and was well thought-of in the community in general, but he also had the most aggressive collections and legal operations in town. What with the subject of a report having a simple means of correcting any error, and in light of these other considerations, the simplest and safest course was just to fill out a report whenever anyone was seen on any bike.

It wasn't long before the town's kids were growing up with the impression that Bob had some kind of legal interest in bicycle usage in general. After all, once they got jobs, the company they worked for would automatically fill out a "W-2, 1099 or K-1 Rider Reporting Form" and send it to Bob, even when the kids rode their own bikes. If the rider didn't then send in the rent, Bob's collection agency would be all over them like ugly on an ape, with no questions asked.

By the time the grandkids of the first "Bob's Bicycles" customers were coming up, everyone had heard stories about riders who, having not paid Bob, were hauled into court and accused of "bicycle rent evasion". All that ever was alleged in these cases was that the accused rode a bicycle, and hadn't paid Bob. It appeared that if just these things alone were proven, dire consequences followed.

Bob, it seemed, could charge you rent for using your own stuff, and the legal system would back him up! By then it didn't occur to anyone-- including the defendants in these affairs-- that when used in a Bob's-bicycles-related legal action "bicycle" doesn't mean "any bicycle", but only means "one of Bob's bicycles", just as it does on a "W-2, 1099 or K-1 Rider Reporting Form". After all, by then almost no one alive could remember back to the beginning. By then, almost no one alive had ever read through Bob's "Bicycle Forms, Publications and Policies Guide", which had grown over the years to thousands and thousands of pages in length.

Further, by then Bob's Bicycles was so big, and so rich, and so diversified, that Bob III had a hand in everything that went on in town, and knew just how to spread all that rent money around. He had no trouble securing the support of the town fathers and other important and influential folks, and those movers and shakers-- just as ignorant of the truth as anyone else-- were happy to help Bob's PR department encourage everyone to just "pay their rent" without question. Paying rent to Bob became something to be done not only unselfishly, but with pride. Paying rent to Bob was good for the community!

Over the years, every "Bob" has carefully kept the overall rent-burden tolerable. The nominal rates have often been high, but a big list of discounts and credits has grown in pace with the misunderstanding about who really owes rent to Bob.

When everyone had understood, and all the business done with Bob was knowingly voluntary, one simple rental rate was enough, and no elaborate discounting was needed. But as more and more people found themselves seemingly beholden to Bob, he realized that if he tried to take the same rate from the less-well-off that he could get away with from the well-to-do, somebody-- faced with a bill they couldn't handle-- might just start actually reading his "Bicycle Forms, Publications and Policies Guide", however difficult that had been made. Then the good thing Bob has grown accustomed to might fall apart. So, Bob's rental rates have grown increasingly "progressive". Bob, no dummy, is content to sacrifice on margin and make it up in volume.

In his best move ever, Bob instituted a "payroll deduction" program, under which the townsfolk are encouraged to anticipate how much riding they're going to do over the year, and then have part of their pay sent to Bob each week against the annual rent bill they figure will result. By virtue of this program, most folks never even really notice how much they're sending to Bob! (Bob is still chortling over this one, decades after thinking it up...)

Needless to say, Bob's "1040 Mileage Ridden/Rent Due" forms have gotten rather complicated. But whole industries have sprung up in town just to help people fill them out (for a fee, of course). The average person doesn't directly deal with paying Bob at all, anymore-- in fact, most get a "refund" from Bob each year, of what had been "over-deducted" under the "payroll deduction" program, and view it like a birthday present. All-in-all, Bob has succeeded in creating the "perfect storm" of misunderstanding.

Well, that's the story of Bob's Bicycles. Today, everyone in town plans all their affairs with Bob's piece-of-the-action factored in. Indeed, big chunks of the population do nothing but handle Bob's Bicycle-related activities. Most of the rest can't imagine a time without the business Bob does with their own businesses, or the charitable "giving-back-to-the-community" grants Bob makes out of the rent money he collects.

Great Grandpa Bob rests; probably with a smile on his face, 'cause the kids are doing all right. And deep within Bob's "Bicycle Forms, Publications and Policies Guide", the long-forgotten truth rests, too-- waiting for anyone who'll bother to take it out for a spin.

So, How About You?

Who Gave You YOUR Wheels?

*****

Finally,

Complete your introduction to the truth about the "income" tax by viewing the short film you'll find at

'It's Time To Learn The Truth About The Income Tax'
(www.losthorizons.com/It'sTimeToLearnTheTruth.wmv)

"Although all men are born free, slavery has been the general lot of the human race. Ignorant--they have been cheated; asleep--they have been surprised; divided--the yoke has been forced upon them. But what is the lesson?...the people ought to be enlightened, to be awakened, to be united, that after establishing a government they should watch over it....It is universally admitted that a well-instructed people alone can be permanently free."

-James Madison

Regarding Tax "Reform"

An astonishing number of Americans continue to call for the enactment of a "national sales tax" (such as the so-called 'Fair Tax'). These poor folks have let themselves be suborned into thus endorsing the notion that the federal government has a legitimate claim on an unlimited portion of every American's personal property-- enforceable by one means or another-- in exchange for nothing more than being spared getting a headache filling out a bunch of tax forms each year (or going to the trouble to learn the truth about the law).

Understand, the sole "benefit" pitched by boosters of this shell-game "reform" is that the individual paperwork burden would diminish. Everyone would still have just as much of their property taken. What this is really all about is distracting Americans from consideration of the real issue-- that is, who actually has a lawful claim to all that money-- by dangling a minor symptomatic relief in front of them. It is with these folks in mind that I offer the following comments...

"Every reform is only a mask under cover of which a more terrible reform, which dares not yet name itself, advances."
-R. W. Emerson

Now that the current income tax structure has been deciphered and revealed to be benign in 'Cracking the Code- The Fascinating Truth About Taxation In America', it falls to all of us to actively and strenuously resist any attempt by the tax beneficiary crowd to replace that structure-- which they are coming to recognize as fatally compromised, for their purposes-- with an alternative, such as a national sales tax or value-added tax. Such alternatives-- all of which would seek to maintain spending at or near current levels-- would quickly be riddled with exceptions, special-interest pay-offs and so forth; as well as the subsidies and associated means-testing necessary to forestall what would otherwise be an intolerable burden for the poor. They would quickly become indistinguishable from the current regime in complexity, bureaucracy, and injustice. More importantly, depending upon how such an alternative was instituted, we might never be rid of it.

After all, a broad-based federal sales tax or VAT-- which would be functionally involuntary in nature (thus, direct), and would lack any effective connection between the federal government and the object of the tax as well-- is just as much prohibited by Article 1, Section 9 of the Constitution as is the general tax on receipts that most Americans misunderstand the income tax to be, and thus would be unconstitutional without an amendment. However, with the income tax having been broadly misunderstood-- and thus obnoxiously misapplied-- for so long that many Americans have reached an, *"Anything but this!"* attitude, there is every danger that the general public could take the position that if a Constitutional amendment would rid us of that current regime, then so be it.

Should that happen, not only would we abandon an existing statutory structure which, as actually written, is dramatically better than even the wildest promises made by those who tout "reform", but the evils we suffer under today-- by virtue of mere ignorance, something easily remedied-- will become evils we suffer from tomorrow with no remedy available at all. Thus, calls for such reforms really amount to efforts to better secure the benefits enjoyed by clients of the state under the current mis-administration of the existing law.

Some will argue that, since the income tax-- if administered as actually provided for in the law-- can't bring in nearly as much revenue as is delivered to government under the current reign of misunderstanding, a replacement such as one of those touted by the "reformers" is unavoidable, whatever its faults. This is simply not true.

Even if current levels of spending are deemed desirable or necessary, the Constitution has always provided perfectly adequate methods by which the money can be raised. There is no limit to the size of a lawful apportioned direct tax-- and such a tax can be sought as often as circumstances require. A revenue tariff is also available, and capable of bringing in very large amounts indefinitely. These are the methods provided for by the founders, and they are quite sufficient. They also happen to be far more accountable and politically rigorous than the open spigot of money into the federal coffers that the mis-administered income tax has become, and thus far less desirable to the political class.

In fact, one of the most pernicious political-accountability-evasion aspects of the mis-administered "income" tax enjoyed by the state under the current regime-- the concealment of the true tax burden by means of the "withholding" system-- would be exacerbated enormously by a national sales tax, or VAT. "Withholding" arranges things so that most Americans never really perceive the total amount being extracted from them by the state. Instead, most quickly become unconscious of the degree by which their earnings are incrementally diminished over the course of each year (precisely as was intended by the system's designers), and actually celebrate the return of a pittance each spring in the form of a "refund". Under a sales or VAT tax, the amount extracted is broken into vastly smaller incremental hemorrhages guaranteed to quickly slip under the radar screen and remain there.

One of the awkward realities of life is that the freedom of the people, and the convenience of the state, are generally mutually exclusive. We can provide for only one or the other. I know which one I choose, and with no second thoughts at all, even if inconveniencing the state should occasionally prove to inconvenience me as well. I have the benefit of the trenchant words of Thomas Jefferson to help me keep things in perspective: *"I would rather be exposed to the inconveniences attending too much liberty than those attending too small a degree of it."*

I hope that everyone will join me in vigorously opposing all efforts at "tax reform", and instead, dedicate themselves to the support of simple, lawful taxation, as provided for in the Constitution.

Poisonous "Pieties" Serve The Enemies Of The People

ONE OF THE FAVORITE PLOYS OF DESPOTS and would-be despots to pacify the masses they intend to exploit is through the corruption of scripture and religious doctrine.

The classic example of this is the recital of Jesus' words, "Render unto Caesar that which is Caesar's" in order to pacify an uncertain host so that a governmental parasite can more easily have its meal of taxes. This line is cited as though everyone is to take for granted that some percentage of the wealth they create or acquire is actually, and automatically, "Caesar's"!

This is nonsense, of course, both as to the matter of to whom any given wealth belongs, and that of what Jesus was really saying. All wealth (or a part of all wealth) DOESN'T belong to "Caesar", and Jesus DIDN'T say that it does. What Jesus said is, "Render unto Caesar THAT WHICH IS CAESAR'S..." The reality is that Jesus' admonition about "rendering unto Caesar" is a plain and straightforward endorsement of the principle behind legitimate excise taxation: an actor (such as the state) whose stuff was used to produce wealth has a legitimate claim against the wealth, and it is proper that "his" part should be "rendered unto" him.

This is precisely how the "income" excise works. It is a tax on gains realized through the use of privileges, prerogatives and/or property belonging to the federal government, to part of which that government therefore has a legitimate claim. As used in the context of the tax, "income" means gains so realized-- any and all of which, by virtue of that legal character, potentially "belong to Caesar".

By virtue of the same principle, of course, the federal government has NO claim by way of this type of tax to gains NOT created or acquired through the use of its privileges, prerogatives and/or property, and a thorough study of the federal "income" tax structure reveals that the tax scrupulously abides by this limitation. We don't actually have any "Caesar" in America and we've never authorized the State to act as though we do; in fact, we've explicitly prohibited the State from trying act that way.

Properly understood (rather than in a corruption intended to serve the voracious State), and as expressed in the principles of excise taxation, what Jesus said is, "Render unto Caesar [ONLY] that which is Caesar's..."

But the fit of Jesus' admonition to the American "income" tax is even handsomer still, because there is another part to those famous words: "...and unto God that which is God's". This instruction, too, is directly reflected in the "income" tax, because the application of the tax is intimately dependent on testimony.

Surely those who would refer to "rendering unto Caesar" in encouraging the payment of taxes would not deny that what "is God's"-- in the sense of what is owed, and must be rendered, to God-- includes our adherence to morality, and that our adherence to morality includes scrupulous honesty in testimony we make! Surely such honesty involves saying what we know and believe to be true, and NOT saying what we

DON'T know and believe to be true! Indeed, the latter actually has its own proscription in the core Judeo-Christian code: "Thou shalt not bear false witness against thy neighbor."

This moral obligation is called upon at the very heart of the "income" tax structure, in which payers of money are expected to report to the government payment of gains in which "Caesar's" stuff played a part (on the basis of which reports "Caesar" will then aggressively pursue his claim to a part of those gains). However, such payers are ALSO relied upon to scrupulously NOT report payments of gains in which "Caesar's" stuff was NOT involved (thus sparing the recipient from the improper burden of being obliged to suffer the effects of false testimony).

Similarly, the recipients of gains are relied upon to honestly report those receipts to which "Caesar" has a claim. But they, too, are just as much obliged morally (and legally) to NOT mischaracterize and report receipts to which "Caesar" DOESN'T have a claim.

In short, the "income" tax comprehensively requires us to adhere to both parts of Jesus' admonition to, "Render unto Caesar that which is Caesar's, and unto God that which is God's".

Unfortunately, there are those who would have Americans misunderstand the plain meaning of these words. Some are the direct operators of the parasitic State, whose interest needs no explanation.

Others are corrupt symbiotes of the parasitic State. They encourage everyone to imagine that "Caesar" has a legitimate claim to everything because part of what is "rendered unto" finds its way into their pockets; or because they imagine they will be aggrandized themselves by a "Caesar" grown ever more swollen with wealth and power.

Some of these corrupt symbiotes encourage everyone to imagine that "Caesar" has a legitimate claim to everything because they thereby curry "Caesar's" favor, and secure his beneficent attention to their policies and preferences; or because their policies and preferences can only be realized with the help of a swollen and powerful Caesar.

Some do it merely because they make a nice living helping everyone else do their "rendering".

Whatever their reasons, the "ignorance tax" despots and their accomplices can be marked by their habit of reciting the first three of Jesus' wise words, "Render unto Caesar..." and then just suggestively trailing off with a shrug and a smirk, in the hope that we'll all overlook the rest of those words and just "render up" (or stand silent in the face of false claims). Like the corrupt and cynical have always done, they encourage and exploit misunderstanding of the whole of the scriptural reference, just as they encourage and exploit misunderstanding of the "income" tax laws.

Let EVERY Soul Be Subject Unto The Higher Powers*

THE CORRUPT ABUSE of a scriptural reference discussed above is of a piece with another of even broader and more pernicious ill effect. The passage exploited in THIS sleazy ploy is a portion of chapter 13 of Paul's "Epistle to the Romans":

> *"Let every soul be subject unto the higher powers. For there is no power but of God: the powers that be are ordained of God. Whosoever therefore resisteth the power, resisteth the ordinance of God: and they that resist shall receive to themselves damnation.*

This passage is deployed to absurdly argue that it is the duty of every Christian to be the obedient and unquestioning subordinate of whatever political hack has most recently been granted an office by that same Christian and his neighbors!

Somehow those making this argument forget to mention that the hacks they mean to see worshipped and obeyed as though kings by divine right are actually mere delegates, temporarily granted a smidgeon of the authority belonging to those this argument would have abase themselves. Somehow they fail to observe that even this delegation of authority is strictly on a "good behavior" basis; and is subject to explicit, narrow written limits as to its range, depth and means of application.

Somehow, those making this "argument from scripture" for blind subordination to their favored political machine conveniently overlook just who is the "higher power" in America, and the fact that those who have temporarily been delegated some of the authority of that higher power have only been granted it after swearing an oath of faith and subordination to the law which formalizes that relationship.

Indeed, to the degree that Romans 13 has any meaningful application here in America, it is that any office-holder who violates any Constitutional provision-- even if only by acting on some creative, convenient interpretation, and even if that "creative interpretation" is endorsed by judges, lawyers, or anyone else-- is guilty of "resisting the power", and thus "resisting the ordinance of God" and has earned the appropriate sanction. It is sovereign individuals that are actually graced with power and authority-- not princes, and not politicians or political factions, however much it may have been princes who commanded the most swords in Paul's place and time.

Paul goes on to issue warnings of a more temporal character (in which we should appropriately substitute "they [are]" for "he [is]"):

> *"For rulers are not a terror to good works, but to the evil. Wilt thou then not be afraid of the power? do that which is good, and thou shalt have praise of the same: For he is the minister of God to thee for good. But if thou do that which is evil, be afraid; for he beareth not the sword in vain: for he is the minister of God, a revenger to execute wrath upon him that doeth evil.*

> *Wherefore ye must needs be subject, not only for wrath, but also for conscience sake."*

Taking these words as authoritative, it is clear that properly understood, Romans 13 puts we, the people, under a moral imperative to execute our office as the "higher power", and closely supervise and discipline our servant governments. In that regard, we find Paul's words remarkably harmonious with others of a more recent vintage and specifically relevant to our American structure of government, such as these, from United States Supreme Court Justice Joseph Story's discussion of the Second Amendment in his 'Commentaries on the Constitution' (1833) (in which "rulers" is clearly meant to be understood as "office-holders"):

> *"The right of the citizens to keep and bear arms has justly been considered, as the palladium of the liberties of a republic; since it offers a strong moral check against the usurpation and arbitrary power of rulers; and will generally, even if these [usurpations] are successful in the first instance, enable the people to resist and triumph over them."*

***

THE CORRUPTION OF OUR TIMES runs deep, and there are few expressions of it more telling than sleazy exploitations of sacred texts such as those discussed above. Unfortunately, that fact doesn't hinder the ambitious and powerful in their use.

It is widely reported that pastors across the country have been encouraged by government officials to prepare for the false teaching of Romans 13 in order to pacify and subvert their congregations in the event a "national emergency" is declared. Indeed, this is said to have already been done by pastors in New Orleans to discourage resistance while federal troops were moving through the city disarming and taking prisoner those in safe areas who had chosen to remain in their homes in the aftermath of Hurricane Katrina. I can't verify the truth of these reports from personal knowledge, but I can attest that this false teaching has long had a voice in places throughout our American community.

Everyone must look to his or her own conscience for guidance in these matters. For my part, if *I* hear this nonsense preached, I will conclude that I am in the presence of an enemy.

Are You Counting On The Constitution To Preserve Your Liberties? You've Got It Backwards...

"Liberty lies in the hearts of men and women; when it dies there, no constitution, no law, no court can save it; no constitution, no law, no court can even do much to help it."
-Justice Learned Hand

Everyone understands that despite the all-too-human tendency to avoid eye-contact with certain realities, what is, nonetheless, is. For instance, reluctance to face the facts under certain circumstances notwithstanding, a woman can't be "a little bit pregnant". A woman who is "a little bit pregnant" is as pregnant as she can get.

The same inflexible truth applies to freedom. It is not possible to be "mostly free", or only "a little bit enslaved". If one were involuntarily subordinate to the interests of another in some respect as a matter of law, one would be entirely a slave in that respect. Even if the exploitation of that relationship should be (relatively) insignificant at any given point, this would not reflect the slave's retention of a degree of freedom, but merely the owner's restraint. When a slave's burdens are light, it is not because the slave has exercised his will, but only because his owner has declined to exercise HIS will to the full measure of its authority.

For example, if, as a matter of law, one could not choose to stop subsidizing a government which has begun acting against one's own interests (or for any other reason), one would be every bit that government's slave.

(Actually, of course, if you can't elect to keep your resources from the hands of the government, you are not "the government's" slave, you are, in fact, the slave of whichever of your neighbors are giving the orders in the name of "the government"...

Although children are taught the fiction that "the government" is some kind of mystical creature with an existence, nature and will which are distinct in some fashion from the existence, nature and will of those who speak in its name, this IS nothing more than a childish fiction intended to confuse the simple-minded. The only degree to which "the government" is independent is insofar as it represents an enduring infrastructure of powers, property, and propaganda such as that being discussed here-- the command and exploitation of which fall into the hands of each succeeding batch of office-holders in turn.

Once in those hands, "the government" is nothing but the tool of those office-holder's individual or collective will, limited in its service of the personal ambitions and interests of those office-holders by nothing more than the will of the rest of us to resist their predations. See 'Fiat Money, And The Formless Fed' in '<u>Upholding the Law And Other Observations</u>' for a comprehensive discussion of this fiction.)

Here in America-- *"the Land of the Free"*-- it would never do to suggest or defend the idea that the people are the government's slaves in any respect, of course. Nonetheless, we are strongly encouraged to believe that we can't, in fact, choose to withhold our support from government practices and policies which we see as contrary or harmful to our own interests.

In service to this self-evident contradiction, we are invited by those who speak in the name of the government to imagine that subordination to their dictates somehow really can't qualify as slavery as long as we are given an opportunity to vote for one or another of such speakers every two, four and six years. However, unless *declining* to vote would serve to relieve one from the obligation to subordinate one's interests to the will of the victors in the electoral contest, this perception is complete nonsense. If there is no way to meaningfully elect to have *"None of the above!"*, as it were, then the reality of enslavement is unaffected by the mere possession of the franchise.

If universal subordination to the dictates of the electoral victors inescapably obtains, then at best the electoral process means merely that for any given period some segment of the population is enslaved by what it imagines to be its friends. While this segment might be arguably in a willing bondage, and thus not "enslaved" as such, there is no denying that the other segment is perforce in unwilling bondage to its enemies (or non-friends, at least). It is suggested that everyone participates in this process voluntarily (in anticipation of trading roles as exploiter and exploited now and then, one must suppose) but this is demonstrably false by virtue of the fact that no right to opt out is admitted.

(Thoroughness requires at least a mention of the perennial argument made to the feeble-minded that the government is itself the proper or most competent arbiter of what is in the best interest of every individual, whether any given individual is wise enough to agree or not, but I'll not insult the reader's intelligence by dwelling further on this transparently self-serving and absurd nonsense...)

***

Were Americans actually trapped on a wheel of mild or bitter enslavement as the fortunes of their personal political factions waxed and waned per the mythology outlined above (or its like), we would have been sorely betrayed by our ancestors. Having had the chance of the ages to establish a new order of society based on the self-evident propositions that all men are created equal; are endowed by their Creator with certain unalienable Rights, among which are Life, Liberty, and the Pursuit of Happiness; and that lawful and righteous governments are instituted in order to secure these Rights, rather than to violate them in service to the interests of the dominant political faction by turns; those ancestors would have blown it.

Instead, our forefathers would have saddled us with the slow-motion catastrophe known as "a democracy", as is corruptly suggested by those who speak in the name of the government. Happily, they did no such thing.

In fact, our revolutionary ancestors-- an assemblage of political scientists, historians, and courageous, self-sacrificing persons of integrity the like of which the world has never known before or since-- recognized democracy for the perpetual war of all-against-all that it is:

> *"[D]emocracies have ever been spectacles of turbulence and contention; have ever been found incompatible with personal security, or the rights of property; and have, in general, been as short in their lives as they have been violent in their deaths."*
> -James Madison
>
> *"Remember, democracy never lasts long. It soon wastes, exhausts, and murders itself. There never was a democracy yet that did not commit suicide."*
> -John Adams
>
> *"A democracy is a volcano which conceals the fiery materials of its own destruction. These will produce an eruption and carry desolation in their way. The known*

> *propensity of a democracy is to licentiousness which the ambitious call, and ignorant believe to be liberty."*
> -Fisher Ames

> *"We have seen the tumult of democracy terminate . . . as [it has] everywhere terminated, in despotism. . . . Democracy! savage and wild. Thou who wouldst bring down the virtuous and wise to thy level of folly and guilt."*
> -Gouverneur Morris

> *"[T]he experience of all former ages had shown that of all human governments, democracy was the most unstable, fluctuating and short-lived."*
> -John Quincy Adams

> *"A simple democracy . . . is one of the greatest of evils."*
> -Benjamin Rush

> *"In democracy . . . there are commonly tumults and disorders. . . . Therefore a pure democracy is generally a very bad government. It is often the most tyrannical government on earth."*
> -Noah Webster

> *"Pure democracy cannot subsist long nor be carried far into the departments of state, it is very subject to caprice and the madness of popular rage."*
> -John Witherspoon

What our Founding Fathers DID erect is a political and governmental structure in which *"None of the above"* is enshrined as the pre-eminent principle informing the whole of their Constitutional creation, and in no regard more forcefully and comprehensively than in preserving the control of individual Americans over the disposition of their own persons and property. The simple, tragic reality is that this magnificent and virtuous instrument by which this structure is established has been under relentless assault since the very moment it was adopted.

It should surprise no one that this is so. After all, the Constitution is the mortal enemy of every rent-seeking, power-grabbing, self-aggrandizing despotic institution and tradition by which human history has been plagued since the first charlatan met the first fool. Everyone who seeks to take his ease and enrich himself by the political means of exercising power over others, rather than by the more strenuous economic means of productivity and voluntary exchange, has an abiding interest in convincing his fellows that the Constitution says and means what it actually does not. Libraries-worth of "interpretations" have been churned out by these enemies of liberty in endless efforts to distort the meaning of this simple 7,478 word instrument from its true character.

Unfortunately, even many friends of liberty have come to misunderstand the true character of the Constitution. They are prone to look at the state of America as it has come to be and conclude that the Constitution was a flawed instrument at best, if not an deliberately subversive one. This cynical view is perhaps best expressed by Lysander Spooner's 1867 complaint about the corrupt excesses of the Lincoln administration, in which Spooner observes that the Constitution *"...has either authorized such a government as we have had, or has been powerless to prevent it."*

The first part of Spooner's dark declaration is mere bitterness. He was well aware that Lincoln had to go so far as to threaten to imprison the Chief Justice of the Supreme Court in order to practice the outrages against the Constitution his policies required. It can hardly be said that such policies were "authorized" by the Constitution, and Spooner couldn't have really meant this facile accusation to be taken for other than rhetoric.

On the other hand, there can be little doubt that Spooner sincerely meant what he said about the Constitution having proven powerless to prevent its own subversion., and in saying so, Spooner is entirely correct. He is also entirely missing the substance of his own observation, as do all those who echo his words today.

The simple fact is, the Constitution IS powerless to prevent its own subversion. It has no armies, no militia, no will of its own. As has been famously remarked recently, it's *"Just a g*******d piece of paper!"*

The fact is, the Constitution cannot, and does not, enforce Itself.

That falls to us.

***

Happily, the means of enforcing the Constitution were provided for by its authors. Thus, when we rise to exercise those means and assert and defend our rights, we stand in obvious and explicit harmony with both the spirit and the letter of the Constitution. By virtue of the same provisions, those who oppose us just as clearly and explicitly stand against the Constitution and the rule of law.

The provisions made by the Framers include having withheld from the government they designed any powers to inhibit free speech, both political and testimonial; or to prevent the citizenry from assembling for any reason (and particularly for the reason of discussing the offenses of those wielding power, and what must be done about them). Eventually, any attempts to exercise such powers were explicitly prohibited under the Bill of Rights.

The Framer's further withheld (and, eventually, explicitly prohibited) federal power to invade anyone's privacy in an effort to uncover pretexts for claims, charges or trials; or to dictate the outcome of trials which might come to pass by legitimate means.

It is by virtue of these provisions that abusive behavior by the federal government against Americans is formally anticipated, and declared unlawful.

Most significantly, the Framers carefully withheld from the government they designed (and, in fact, explicitly prohibited from the very beginning) any power to compel Americans to subsidize those wielding the power of the federal government, other than through the politically accountable, deliberately difficult and restraint-inducing mechanism of an apportioned tax laid on-- and remitted by-- the governments of the States.

It is by virtue of this last provision alone that the Framers ensured that Americans could not be individually or collectively ruined by an rogue and oppressive government even while exercising the other means provided; or simply be forced, under the pretence of a lawful process, to finance their oppressors. As John Marshall, first chief justice of the United States Supreme Court once observed, "The power to tax is the power to destroy." The framers of the United States Constitution did not grant to the dangerous servant they carefully created and reluctantly adopted the unlimited power to destroy its creators; nor did they rely upon the mere and obviously insufficient fact that federal office-holders are elected, and can be replaced:

> *"No Capitation, or other direct, Tax shall be laid, unless in Proportion to the Census or Enumeration herein before directed to be taken."* United States Constitution, Article 1, Section 9

It is by virtue of this last provision alone that Americans are not, in fact, slaves to their government, with little more control over the disposition of their labor and property than the chance to choose new masters every few years.

However, all of these provisions mean nothing, and offer nothing, unless Americans, one by one, stand and act.

The Constitution is NOT *"Just a g*******d piece of paper!"*, but it IS powerless to prevent such a government as we have had, by itself.

I intend to support, defend, and enforce the Constitution-- which means <u>the rule of law</u>-- using every means available.

How about you?

Stand With The Founders And Retake Control The Disposition Of Your Own Wealth

In 1787, upon emerging from the constitutional convention which formed the basis for our federal government, Ben Franklin was approached by a woman outside the hall.

"Mr. Franklin," she asked "What kind of government have you given us?"

"A Republic, madam," Franklin replied, "If you can keep it..."

Individual Virtue Is The Most Powerful Weapon (Against A Corrupt State)

EVER WONDER WHAT LIES BEHIND the studious institutional enmity toward moral consciousness we see all around us in America (and elsewhere) today? It is an institutional recognition that the greatest stumbling-block to the core ambition of the unbridled state (the unhindered exercise of power on behalf of its clients) is the stature of individual morality as a popular value. This is because while all the mundane costs of compliance with the state can be manipulated in the state's favor, the moral cost of compliance with illegitimate state behavior cannot be. The only tool the state has in that regard is the undermining of morality in general.

I will offer taxation as a convenient model: It is easy to see that merely by manipulating the rate of any given tax, the state can make the cost of resistance-- either resistance as a matter of political opposition, or even as legal resistance to the misapplication of the tax-- greater than the cost of compliance, if the only considerations are out-of-pocket expenses and expenditures of effort. If these were the only considerations, and everything else about it remained the same, would anyone invest much in opposition to, for example, an actual aggregated net "income" tax burden of, say, 5%? Or 10%? Even when the tax was being misapplied in defiance of the law, resistance wouldn't be worth it. Indeed, at the right rate, even the trouble of saving receipts and calculating deductions wouldn't be worth bothering with.

However, when the cost of compliance with any policy or demand involves the violation of moral principles, the calculation is quite different. In that case, a moral person will find no price of resistance too high.

CONTINUING WITH THE "INCOME" TAX EXAMPLE: When compliance with the state's ambition requires false testimony about ones own earnings and/or payments made to others, and/or cooperation with, or acquiescence to, the illegitimate use of force against others, a moral individual simply cannot comply, regardless of the cost of refusal, and regardless of how inexpensive any other cost of compliance is made to be. The two positions-- respect for, and embrace of, morality; and cooperation with, and participation in, institutionalized immorality-- simply cannot co-exist. A moral person will choose the course illuminated by the instruction, *"Render unto Caesar that which is Caesar's, and unto God that which is God's"*, understanding that while Caesar is entitled to look after his legitimate interests, he is entitled to the cooperation of others in doing so only insofar as that cooperation is compatible with God's requirement's.

Thus, the subversion of morality is necessary to the state's purpose, and is cunningly and relentlessly practiced. This subversion is often highly specialized, as in this "income" tax-related example excerpted from 'Why It Matters' in CtC:

> *Effectively presented as an involuntary requirement, the scheme corrupts our fundamental*

principle of equal treatment under the law with a progressive structure under which some citizens are able to force a benefit for themselves out of the pockets of their neighbors. This callous design, intended to maximize the protective political support for the scheme by invoking Shaw's principle that, "A government which robs Peter to pay Paul can always depend on the support of Paul", engenders institutional endorsement of the proposition that a form of slavery is a fundamental element of social justice. (Where the tax lawfully applies, of course-- as an expected cost of voluntarily enjoying the benefit of federal privilege-- unequal treatment is no more unfair than is having to pay more for good seats at the show).

This is a particularly noxious perversion, in that under this "justice" a heavier burden is extracted from some Americans precisely because they have already made a greater contribution to the common weal than others. After all, one earns one's unprivileged receipts solely by serving the interests of one's neighbors.

Furthermore, contrary to the many false intellections marshaled to support this aspect of the scheme, the more such receipts that one's good service brings in, the less demand one places on, and the less benefit one has from the community resources-- making the progressive structure of the tax even more obscene. The reality is that a successful wealth-producer has typically been more adamant and persistent than others in defying and surmounting the public infrastructure and its typically sclerotic defense of the status quo. (The exception is those who have used government to their advantage; their gains, of course, are the lawful objects of the "income" tax as properly applied).

> *As to public services, the well-to-do place far less demand on such expenses than others-- they draw no public welfare, they are privately insured, they live where the local services are equitably paid for out of (typically) high local tax rates. In other words, they pay their own way. The vigorous efforts of many in positions of authority and respect to seduce Americans into accepting the standing of these truths on their heads, in order to ensure that the gravy-train of professional fees, bureaucratic power, and re-election will continue, is a national scandal. That these efforts have largely been successful is a national shame.*

Similar efforts are focused upon many other areas in which the ambitions of the state and its clients are hindered or inconvenienced by an upright citizenry insistent on lawful, limited government. Paralleling such targeted efforts is a general pressure against morality, in service to the understanding that once any corrupt practice is excused, forgiven, or rationalized, the rot will soon spread.

John Adams once observed that, *"Public virtue cannot exist in a nation without private, and public virtue is the only foundation of republics"*, and he and the other Founders wisely equipped us with a fundamental law which is fully supportive of our private virtue. Enjoying the benefits of that virtuous fundamental law simply depends on the firm embrace of that same private virtue by each of us-- one by one.

A Few Words About The Second Amendment

"A nation of sheep will beget a government of wolves."
-Edward R. Murrow

"A well-regulated militia being necessary to the security of a free State, the right of the people to keep and bear arms shall not be infringed."
-United States Constitution

Let's begin with the plain and straightforward intent of those who wrote and adopted the amendment, and then some observations by a few other specialists:

> *"The strongest reason for the people to retain the right to keep and bear arms is, as a last resort, to protect themselves against tyranny in Government."*
> -Thomas Jefferson

> *"The Constitution shall never be construed... to prevent the people of the United States who are peaceable citizens from keeping their own arms."*
> -Samuel Adams

"Americans have the right and advantage of being armed—unlike the citizens of other countries whose governments are afraid to trust the people with arms."
-James Madison

"God grants liberty only to those who love it, and are always ready to guard and defend it."
-Daniel Webster

"[The right to keep and bear arms] may be considered as the true palladium of liberty .... The right of self defence is the first law of nature: in most governments it has been the study of rulers to confine this right within the narrowest limits possible. Wherever standing armies are kept up, and the right of the people to keep and bear arms is, under any colour or pretext whatsoever, prohibited, liberty, if not already annihilated, is on the brink of destruction. In England, the people have been disarmed, generally, under the specious pretext of preserving the game: a never failing lure to bring over the landed aristocracy to support any measure, under that mask, though calculated for very different purposes. True it is, their bill of rights seems at first view to counteract this policy: but the right of bearing arms is confined to protestants, and the words suitable to their condition and degree, have been interpreted to authorize the prohibition of keeping a gun or other engine for the destruction of game, to any farmer, or inferior tradesman, or other person not qualified to kill game. So that not one man in five hundred can keep a gun in his house without being subject to a penalty.

"The congress of the United States possesses no power to regulate, or interfere with the domestic concerns, or police of any state: it belongs not to them to establish any rules respecting the rights of property; nor will the constitution permit any prohibition of arms to the people;..."
-Saint George Tucker, close friend of Thomas Jefferson and Justice of the Virginia Supreme Court, in his edition of 'Blackstone's Commentaries On The Law' (1803)

"The next amendment is: 'A well regulated militia being necessary to the security of a free state, the right of the people to keep and bear arms shall not be infringed.'

"The importance of this article will scarcely be doubted by any persons, who have duly reflected upon the subject. The militia is the natural defence of a free country against sudden foreign invasions, domestic insurrections, and domestic usurpations of power by rulers. It is against sound policy for a free people to keep up large military establishments and standing armies in time of peace, both from the enormous expenses, with which they are attended, and the facile means, which they afford to ambitious and unprincipled rulers, to subvert the government, or trample upon the rights of the people. The right of the citizens to keep and bear arms has justly been considered, as the palladium of the liberties of a republic; since it offers a strong moral check against the usurpation and arbitrary power of rulers [meaning that they are on notice that bad behavior will be punished -PH]; and will generally, even if these are successful in the first instance, enable the people to resist and triumph over them."
-United States Supreme Court Justice Joseph Story, in '<u>Commentaries On The Constitution Of The United States</u>' (1833)

"The [second] amendment, like most other provisions in the Constitution, has a history. It was adopted with some modification and enlargement from the English Bill of Rights of 1688, where it stood as a protest against arbitrary action of the overturned dynasty in disarming the people, and as a pledge of the new rulers that this tyrannical action should cease. The right declared was meant to be a strong moral check against the usurpation and arbitrary power of rulers, and as a necessary and efficient means of regaining rights when temporarily overturned by usurpation."

"The Right is General. -- It may be supposed from the phraseology of this provision that the right to keep and

bear arms was only guaranteed to the militia; but this would be an interpretation not warranted by the intent. The militia, as has been elsewhere explained, consists of those persons who, under the law, are liable to the performance of military duty, and are officered and enrolled for service when called upon. But the law may make provision for the enrollment of all who are fit to perform military duty, or of a small number only, or it may wholly omit to make any provision at all; and if the right were limited to those enrolled, the purpose of this guaranty might be defeated altogether by the action or neglect to act of the government it was meant to hold in check. The meaning of the provision, undoubtedly is, that the people, from whom the militia must be taken, shall have the right to keep and bear arms, and they need no permission or regulation of law for the purpose, but this enables the government to have a well regulated militia; for to bear arms implies something more than the mere keeping; it implies the learning to handle and use them in a way that makes those who keep them ready for their efficient use; in other words, it implies the right to meet for voluntary discipline in arms, observing in doing so the laws of public order."
-Thomas Cooley, Justice of The Michigan Supreme Court, in 'Principles Of Constitutional Law' (1880)

The prospect of tyranny may not grab the headlines the way vivid stories of gun crime routinely do. But few saw the Third Reich coming until it was too late. The Second Amendment is a doomsday provision, one designed for those exceptionally rare circumstances where all other rights have failed — where the government refuses to stand for reelection and silences those who protest; where courts have lost the courage to oppose, or can find no one to enforce their decrees. However improbable these contingencies may seem today, facing them unprepared is a mistake a free people get to make only once.
-Federal appellate Judge Alex Kozinski in the 2003 case of Silveira vs. Lockyer.

***

Now let's analyze the amendment (and arguments intended to eviscerate it) logically:

As plain and straightforward as the Second Amendment is, and despite the helpful expressions of the incontrovertible authorities quoted above, strenuous efforts are made by its enemies to evade the Amendment's purposes and provisions. These efforts focus, in practice, on distorting the meaning of two elements of the wording of the Amendment: the terms "militia" and "well regulated". A few observations about these terms are therefore appropriate here, and should suffice to deal with these corrupt efforts.

The more overtly targeted of the two terms is "militia". The efforts against it involve attempting to morph the general understanding of the word "militia" into meaning nothing more than "National Guard" (or its functional equivalent), as though a military organization of, and subordinate to, a state government provides against the need to put down a federal government gone awry-- a purpose of the Second Amendment which its enemies realize is still vaguely understood by the American people as a whole.

At the very same time, of course, those who argue the "militia means National Guard" notion also contend that the state governments are generally subordinate to the federal government, and particularly maintain that any state government that deployed military power against the federal government would be acting unconstitutionally (or improperly under some other label); and indeed, what other position could the federal government itself take, rightly or wrongly, under such circumstances? Thus, the "militia means National Guard" notion is plainly a deliberate intellectual ploy intended to bleed energy from general comprehension of the true meaning of the Second Amendment. (The recent federal acts claiming presidential authority to commandeer the National Guard, such as in the 'John Warner Defense Authorization Act of 2007', dramatically emphasize this point.)

This ploy also seeks to exploit general ignorance of the legal nature of the several states themselves-- a subject rarely addressed in the American dialogue. Doing real justice to the subject is beyond the needs of this discussion; it will suffice to observe that the state governments themselves are no more than constructs erected at, and for, the convenience of the individual sovereign people residing within the borders of each, and against which the people's authority to act militarily is self-evidently incapable of lawful compromise. That is, we the people have an absolute right to alter, abolish, or put down by force if necessary any and all government.

Thus, while the Second Amendment may be properly viewed as providing-- in part-- for the exercise of state military power against the federal government, it invokes, and partakes of, the same sovereign authority of the people to act in like manner against their state governments. As such, the militia cannot be an organ of the state government or, if the term "militia" were held to mean such an organ, an unnamed and still more fundamental and inherently superior military liberty-- incapable of lawful compromise or oversight by any governmental authority, and obviously including the right of the people to keep and bear arms-- is necessarily implied.

In fact, the term "militia", properly understood, has two Constitutional meanings, depending on context. One of those meanings is the body of Americans not part of the federal armed forces, but of "military age" and capacity, and available for deployment by the federal government in times of need as an auxiliary force. Specific federal Constitutional provisions are made in regard to this form of militia.

For example, in Article 1, Section 8, Congress is given authority to provide for organizing, arming and disciplining the Militia. Plainly, if "militia" in the Second Amendment meant nothing more than is comprehended by this first definition, the

Amendment itself would be entirely superfluous. (See 'Gun Control And The Federal Government' in 'Upholding the Law And Other Observations' for an in-depth discussion of this point, and of the relevant body of judicial doctrine-- including the uniquely aberrant Miller decision.)

The other meaning of the term, and the one obviously used in the Second Amendment, is simply, "the whole people"-- by which is necessarily meant "the people" as discrete individuals, of course. Groups don't have rights, so the right recognized by the amendment must be an individual right.

***

In addition to attempting to foster and exploit general confusion about the term "militia", those who fear and seek to evade the Second Amendment rely upon a broad and deeply-entrenched misunderstanding of the term "regulate". A very brief discussion will serve to correct this misunderstanding and clarify the use of the phrase "well regulated" in the amendment:

We in our heavily bureaucratized modern America tend to think of the word "regulate" as meaning "to issue and enforce governmental rules about something". However, this is neither the general definition nor the historic usage of this term.

> ***REGU'LATE***, *v.t.*
>
> 1. *To adjust by rule, method or established mode; as, to regulate weights and measures; to regulate the assize of bread; to regulate our moral conduct by the laws of God and of society; to regulate our manners by the customary forms.*
> 2. *To put in good order; as, to regulate the disordered state of a nation or its finances.*
> 3. *To subject to rules or restrictions; as, to regulate trade; to regulate diet.*
>
> Webster's Dictionary Of The English Language, 1828 Edition

> ***reg·u·late***, *v.t.*
>
> 1. *to control or direct by a rule, principle, method, etc.*

2. *to adjust to some standard or requirement, as for amount, degree, etc.*
3. *to adjust so as to ensure accuracy of operation.*
4. *to put in good order.*

Random House College Dictionary, Revised Edition (1975)

As can be readily seen by the definitions given above--one from close to the time of the adoption of the Second Amendment, and one from our own time, the general meaning of "regulate" is "to put or maintain in good working order", in accordance with a rule, principle or established mode. The synonym of "regulate"-- "regularize"-- illuminates this meaning: *"To bring into conformity with rules or principles or usage."*

This is precisely the meaning of "a well regulated militia" in the Second Amendment: *"the whole people, equipped and in good order for the exercise and enforcement of their sovereignty, by right and in conformity with the principles under which their servant governments have been created"* To put it another way, the means by which the militia referred to in the Second Amendment is "well regulated" is by prohibiting the government from infringing upon the right of the people to keep and bear arms.

***

P. S. We still have the ballot (it would appear), and that's the proper place to rest our faith, for now. But the prudent man looks around and looks ahead, with open eyes and a jealous regard for his liberties. In fact, it is just that jealous regard, and the preparation it inspires, that generally spares a free people the turmoil for which the Second Amendment is provided. Call it an expressions of the "peace through strength" principle.

"Political power grows out of the barrel of a gun."
-Mao Zedong

NOTE: To learn how the United States Supreme Court has, with near perfect consistency, upheld every word and sentiment expressed above, and the simple legal sleight-of-hand by which Congress has beguiled the ignorant into believing otherwise in regard to all federal gun laws, see *'Gun Control And The Federal Government'* in my book 'Upholding the Law and Other Observations'.

***

By the way, authority over the power of direct (involuntary) taxation is also denied the federal government, in an acknowledgement of individual sovereignty from the same vein as that from which the Second Amendment springs. Just as the government created by the Constitution is expressly prohibited from any effort or initiative to disarm the people, or, implicitly, to compel them to use their arms in its service, it is prohibited from seizing their property, or compelling them to relinquish property against their will.

And no surprise, of course. Is it conceivable that the same Framers who pointedly ensured that the citizenry retained the means to shoot their rogue governors would have stuck at ensuring the power of the citizenry to simply withhold money from those same governors? Or is it conceivable that the same Framers who provided the Second Amendment would simultaneously allow, to the very government against which that Amendment stands, the power to forcibly take from the people the means by which they put food in their stomachs, or bullets in their guns? The questions answer themselves.

"Those who hammer their guns into plows will plow for those who do not."
(These words are often attributed to Thomas Jefferson. That attribution may or may not be accurate, but there is no doubt that Jefferson would agree with the observation.)

Put Up, Or Shut Up-- And Hang It Up
(An Educational Rant)

"Give me a child for ten years and I'll give you a communist for life."
-V. I. Lenin

You know what? I don't ever again want to hear a complaint from anyone about what goes on in government schools. Read the label, people-- THEY'RE GOVERNMENT SCHOOLS!!! They exist to serve the government's purposes, not yours. If you are bothered by what their owners and/or operators do with them, or require of you to enjoy their services, PUT YOUR KIDS IN YOUR OWN (HOME) SCHOOLS! Then you can make the rules.

If you're not willing to go to that little bit of trouble (which is really no trouble at all, but instead is both easy and the most rewarding thing you'll ever do in your life), then please confine your complaints to your local school board meetings. Stop cluttering up cyberspace.

In fact, why even bother complaining? That it will do no good at all is so well-established as to have become a cliché.

After all, when you've handed your kids over to the government schools, you've already given up all oversight authority. At that point, while in concert with enough of your neighbors you could theoretically call the shots, individually, your preferences are just annoying invitations for some version of the old, "Gee, Mr. Smith, you're the only parent who's ever expressed a concern about that..." brush-off and shut-down. The only personal authority you have and can exercise extends no further than your willingness to pull your kid out of the school and see to his education yourself. This prospect doesn't worry the government schoolmasters too much...

If you show signs of reaching your distant limit, the school will buy some fancy marching band uniforms to remind you that YOU can't provide that kind of important scholastic equipment or experience. Or it will change the names of everything in its math textbooks so that the homework your kids ask for help with suggests that you no longer understand the subject well enough to teach it yourself.

If it appears necessary, the government school industry will even go so far as to invent some "critical issue" in the upbringing or education of children that allegedly can only be addressed in an institutional setting (e.g. "socialization"), and rely on you to buy it due to the fact that you were never taught anything about the history of government schools when YOU were abandoned to them by YOUR parents. Consequently, you don't know that they are less than 100 years old in most parts of America, during which time academic performance, as well as civic virtue, has been steadily declining-- in light of which the school's claim to indispensability is revealed as a cynical, laughable fraud.

Or the government school and its many clients-- both those making a living off it and those using it as day-care subsidized by their neighbors-- will deploy some other cheap gimmick, and you will subside. You always have.

The fact is, if you're the typical American parent, you're a proven performer. You've long-since demonstrated that you're just a sucker who is easily seduced into handing control over your own future (as well as that of your kids) to the competitor and exploiter of you both.

What it comes down to is your inability to understand that the state is not your partner, but your competitor. Not your competitor in a cordial debate over the best methods by which your interests can be served, but your focused competitor in a deadly-serious contest over who will rule you, and who will control and benefit from your resources.

In particular, the state (by which we always mean "those who control the state apparatus") wants to exercise control over your labor and your wealth, as well as your physical (military) power (both to exploit it for its own purposes, and to prevent you from using that power to defend yourself against the state's predations). The absolute key to victory in every aspect of this broad and generations-old contest is the perspective with which your future fellow citizens and successors in the battle (your children, and those of your neighbors) will be equipped when it is their turn to stand up, or stand down.

For instance, through careful study of 'Cracking the Code- The Fascinating Truth About Taxation In America', many of you reading these words have learned how to secure immediate control over the bulk of your wealth, thanks to the existing structure of Constitutional and statutory law. You have acted accordingly, and achieved freedom in this oh-so-important area for the first time in your lives.

But even Constitutions can be changed, if the perceptions of enough people come under the sway of those who would see this done. How long will your new understanding avail you, and your freedom be preserved, if more and more of your neighbors are conditioned to mindless dependency upon-- and subservience to-- the state whose ambitions your knowledge thwarts?

Legal structures are never anything more than practices by which a majority agree to abide. At bottom, the only concrete thing that ever stands between any one person and slavery of one kind or another at the hands of those possessed of superior force or better organization under any regime of social organization-- be it a dictatorship, a Constitutionally-limited republic, or even raw anarchy-- is the willingness of one's fellows to stand up on one's behalf. Thus, the question of YOUR freedom ultimately hinges on how many of your fellows become trained and habituated to view the state as their benevolent and righteous master-- or mystic, ever-present, force-of-nature parent-figure in whose unquestioned authority they themselves have a stake-- and how many do not.

The simple, raw truth is, every kid in a government school is a future agent or supporter of the state (and an ignorant lout, as well-- it is not possible to be successfully taught that the expansionist state is a net good while receiving any kind of decent education in other respects, such as in history, economics, political science, etc.).

On the other hand, every kid raised outside those conditioning centers will be your ally in defending the individual liberty to which each human being is self-evidently entitled and naturally predisposed.

The bottom line is thus simple and straightforward: Complaining about the government schools is an exercise in futility. If you want to secure your own liberty into the future, you've got to forget about talking, and start walking.

A Brief Discussion Of What "Income" In The Income Tax Law Means, And Why

First, one must remember that the Constitution provides that:

> *"No capitation, or other direct, Tax shall be laid, unless in Proportion to the Census or Enumeration herein before directed to be taken."*
> United States Constitution, Article 1, Section 9

Then, one must understand that the 16th Amendment brought nothing under the taxing power that had not been taxable as "income" before:

> *"The provisions of the Sixteenth Amendment conferred no new power of taxation . . ."*
> United States Supreme Court, Stanton v. Baltic Mining Co., 240 U.S. 103 (1916)

> *"The Sixteenth Amendment, although referred to in argument, has no real bearing and may be put out of view. As pointed out in recent decisions, it does not extend the taxing power to new or excepted subjects..."*
> United States Supreme Court, Peck v. Lowe, 247 U.S. 165 (1918)

> *"The legislative history merely shows... ...that the sole purpose of the Sixteenth Amendment was to remove the apportionment requirement for whichever incomes were otherwise taxable. 45 Cong. Rec. 2245-2246 (1910); id., at 2539; see also Brushaber v. Union Pacific R. Co., 240 U.S. 1, 17 -18 (1916)."*
> United States Supreme Court, South Carolina v. Baker, 485 U.S. 505 (1988)

And, it has to be understood that the income tax has ALWAYS been an excise tax-- that is, an indirect tax:

> *"I hereby certify that the following is a true and faithful statement of the gains, profits, or income of _____ _____, of the _____ of _____, in the county of _____, and State of _____, whether derived from any kind of property, rents, interest, dividends, salary, or from any profession, trade, employment, or vocation, or from any other source whatever, from the 1st day of January to the 31st day of December, 1862, both days inclusive, and subject to an income tax under the excise laws of the United States:"*
> (from the first income tax return form);

> *"The income tax is, therefore, not a tax on income* [earnings] *as such. It is an excise tax with respect to certain activities and privileges which is measured by reference to the income which they produce. The income is not the subject of the tax: it is the basis for determining the amount of tax."*
> F. Morse Hubbard, Treasury Department legislative draftsman. House Congressional Record, March 27, 1943, page 2580;

> *"...in Springer v. U. S., 102 U.S. 586 , it was held that a tax upon gains, profits, and income was an excise or duty, and not a direct tax, within the meaning of the constitution, and that its imposition was not, therefore, unconstitutional."*
> United States Supreme Court, Pollock v. Farmer's Loan & Trust, 158 U.S. 601, 1895;

"...taxation on income was in its nature an excise entitled to be enforced as such,"
United States Supreme Court, Brushaber v. Union Pacific R. Co., 240 U.S. 1 (1916), quoting and reiterating language used in its ruling in Pollock v. Farmer's Loan and Trust as part of the passage below, to which I have added a few bracketed explanatory notes to help the reader get through Chief Justice White's lengthy sentences:

"...the conclusion reached in the Pollock Case did not in any degree involve holding that income taxes generically and necessarily came within the class of direct taxes on property, but, on the contrary, recognized the fact that taxation on income was in its nature an excise entitled to be enforced as such unless and until it was concluded that to enforce it would amount to accomplishing the result which the requirement as to apportionment of direct taxation was adopted to prevent [that is, allowing the federal government to lay taxes directly on the citizenry]*, in which case the duty would arise to disregard form*

[that is, any pretense by which it is made to *appear* that the tax is being confined to its proper limits when it is not-- such as calling it an "income" tax but creatively construing the meaning of "income" so as to reach things not appropriate to an excise tax, or the use of some pretense, scheme or construction by which non-specialized revenue or activities are made to appear otherwise so as to be deemed subject to the tax] *and consider substance alone* [that is, what the tax is actually falling upon as a practical reality, as in a structuring of the tax so as to actually make it function as a capitation or other direct tax regardless of name or form-- which was precisely the practical reality perceived by the Pollock court in regard to the 1894 act]*, and hence subject the tax to the regulation as to apportionment which otherwise as an excise would not apply to it. Nothing could serve to make this clearer than to recall that in the Pollock Case, in so far as the law taxed incomes from other classes of property than real estate and invested personal property, that is,*

> *income from* [federally-licensed and civil-service-- see the discussion of "privilege" and "non-privileged" below, and www.losthorizons.com/appendix.htm#professions] *'professions, trades, employments, or vocations', its validity was recognized; indeed, it was expressly declared that no dispute was made upon that subject, and attention was called to the fact that taxes on such income had been sustained as excise taxes in the past."*

(Regarding the Pollock case and the 16th Amendment: The Pollock court said that a tax on dividends (and other property-ownership-related receipts) was NOT an "income" tax, legally, but actually a "property" tax, which thus had to be apportioned, because of the intimate relationship of the receipts with the underlying property from which they are derived. All the 16th Amendment did was to sever that "derivation relationship", allowing those receipts to be taxed by the "income" excise along with everything else which was, and always had been, taxable thereby.

Remember, the "income" tax was conceived and instituted during the Lincoln administration, 51 years before the 16th Amendment. It was then administered and collected for more than a decade, before being temporarily suspended in 1873. That is, the "income" tax operated for some 11 years in the latter part of the 19th century-- surviving Supreme Court scrutiny in the case of Springer v. United States, 102 U.S. 586 (1880) and other cases-- WITHOUT apportionment, and WITHOUT the benefit of a "16th Amendment". Clearly, such an amendment was not needed, and did not serve, to make a tax on "income" Constitutional. Such a tax had always been Constitutional, because it has never been, and still is not, a capitation or other direct tax-- due to the limited meaning of "income" within the context of the tax. Again, the 16th Amendment did nothing but undo the Pollock court's doctrine, which had sheltered "income" derived from property from the tax.)

Continuing with the Brushaber ruling:

> *"We are of opinion, however, that the confusion is not inherent, but rather arises from the conclusion that the 16th Amendment provides for a hitherto unknown power of taxation; that is, a power to levy an income tax which, although direct, should not be subject to the regulation of apportionment applicable to all other direct taxes. And the far-reaching effect of this erroneous assumption will be made clear by generalizing the many contentions advanced in argument to support it..."*
>
> ...
>
> *"But it clearly results that the proposition and the contentions under it, if acceded to, would cause one provision of the Constitution to destroy another; that is, they would result in bringing the provisions of the Amendment exempting a direct tax from apportionment into irreconcilable conflict with the general requirement that all direct taxes be apportioned."*

...which was nicely summarized by Howard M. Zaritsky, Legislative Attorney, American Law Division of the Library of Congress, in Report No. 80-19A, entitled "Some Constitutional Questions Regarding The Federal Income Tax Laws", page CRS-5 (1979):

> *"The Supreme Court, in a decision written by Chief Justice White [the Brushaber ruling], first noted that the Sixteenth Amendment did not authorize any new type of tax, nor did it repeal or revoke the tax clauses of Article I of the Constitution, quoted above. Direct taxes were, notwithstanding the advent of the Sixteenth Amendment, still subject to the rule of apportionment and indirect taxes were still subject to the rule of uniformity."*

So, we can forget the 16th entirely (for purposes of general consideration of the tax), and we must remember excise...

> *"So the* [16th] *amendment made it possible to bring investment income within the scope of the general*

income-tax law, but did not change the character of the tax. It is still fundamentally an excise or duty with respect to the privilege of carrying on any activity or owning any property which produces income."
F. Morse Hubbard, Treasury Department legislative draftsman. House Congressional Record, March 27, 1943, page 2580;

"The terms "excise tax" and "privilege tax" are synonymous. The two are often used interchangeably."
American Airways v. Wallace 57 F.2d 877, 880 (Dist. Ct., M.D. Tenn., 1937);

...the requirement to pay such [excise] *taxes involves the exercise of privilege."*
United States Supreme Court, Flint vs. Stone Tracy Co. 220 U.S. 107 (1911);

...privilege...

"PRIVILEGE: A particular benefit or advantage enjoyed by a person, company, or class beyond the common advantages of others citizens. An exceptional or extraordinary power of exemption. A particular right, advantage, exemption, power, franchise, or immunity held by a person or class, not generally possessed by others."
Black's Law Dictionary, 6th Ed.;

...and what DOESN'T qualify as privilege:

"The right to follow any of the common occupations of life is an inalienable right...
It has been well said that 'the property which every man has in his own labor, as it is the original foundation of all other property, so it is the most sacred and inviolable. The patrimony of the poor man lies in the strength and dexterity of his own hands, and to hinder his employing this strength and dexterity in what manner he thinks proper, without injury to his neighbor, is a plain violation of this most sacred property'."

United States Supreme Court, Butcher's Union Co. v. Crescent City Co., 111 U.S. 746 (1883);

"Included in the right of personal liberty and the right of private property- partaking of the nature of each- is the right to make contracts for the acquisition of property. Chief among such contracts is that of personal employment, by which labor and other services are exchanged for money or other forms of property"
United States Supreme Court, Coppage v. Kansas, 236 U.S. 1 (1915);

...the essence of all of which is underscored here:

'Direct taxes bear immediately upon persons, upon the possession and enjoyments of rights; indirect taxes are levied upon the happening of an event or an exchange.'
United States Supreme Court, Knowlton v. Moore, 178 U.S. 41 (1900), quoting the long-standing official French definitions as helpfully illustrative of the distinctions drawn in the United States Constitution.

In pointing out that a tax on the exercise of a right is a direct tax, these definitions also express the fact that only the exercise of a privilege could qualify as an indirect-taxable event, exchange, or other activity (and thus be applied without apportionment). The fact that the event, etc. might be identical in every other respect to one occurring without the involvement of privilege is immaterial.

For instance, working, and being paid for doing so, is every person's right, and therefore not an indirect-taxable activity. On the other hand, working for, and being paid by, the federal government is a privilege (obviously, no one has an unalienable right to a federal job...), and IS indirect-taxable, even though the work done might otherwise be the same in each case. The same is true of investing and receiving dividends, or of any other kind of economic or remunerative activities.

To summarize what we have seen so far:

Only Activities Involving The Exercise Of Privilege Can Qualify As The "Income" Taxed Under The Non-Apportioned "Income Tax"

> (By the way,
> *"And where not otherwise distinctly expressed or manifestly incompatible with the intent thereof, the word "person", as used in this title, shall be construed to mean and include a partnership, association, company, or corporation, as well as a natural person."*
> Revised Statutes, Title XXXV, Internal Revenue, section 3140.

So, the law does not distinguish between a business and an individual person, neither specifically within the internal revenue statutory structure, nor in general. The right to contract AS a worker is the same as the right to contract WITH a worker--whether as a property owner hiring a plumber, or as a sole proprietor, partnership, corporation etc. hiring workers. Indeed, under the law generally, a business which has any independent legal status-- that is, status of its own, apart from that of the natural persons who own it-- is considered to BE a "person" in every commercially- and contractually-related respect.)

***

Now, Let's Look At The Subject From Another Angle

> Start out by remembering once again that,
> *"No capitation, or other direct, Tax shall be laid, unless in Proportion to the Census or Enumeration herein before directed to be taken."*
> United States Constitution, Article 1, Section 9;

...and then examining what 'capitation' means:

"The taxes which, it is intended, should fall indifferently upon every different species of revenue, are capitation taxes,"... "Capitation taxes, if it is attempted to proportion them to the fortune or revenue of each contributor, become altogether arbitrary. The state of a man's fortune varies from day to day, and without an inquisition more intolerable than any tax, and renewed at least once every year, can only be guessed at."..."Capitation taxes, so far as they are levied upon the lower ranks of people, are direct taxes upon the wages of labour, and are attended with all the inconveniences of such taxes."..." In the capitation which has been levied in France without any interruption since the beginning of the present century, the highest orders of people are rated according to their rank by an invariable tariff; the lower orders of people, according to what is supposed to be their fortune, by an assessment which varies from year to year."
Adam Smith, The Wealth of Nations, Book V, CH. II, Art. IV (which can be found in its entirety on the CtC Companion CD). (Bear in mind that Smith is using the common word 'wages', not the custom-defined legal term "wages" found in the modern revenue laws.)

"In the different poll-taxes which took place in England during the reign of William III the contributors were, the greater part of them, assessed according to the degree of their rank; as dukes, marquisses, earls, viscounts, barons, esquires, gentlemen, the eldest and youngest sons of peers, etc.

...

Several of those who in the first poll-tax were rated according to their supposed fortune were afterwards rated according to their rank. Serjeants, attorneys, and proctors at law, who in the first poll-tax were assessed at three shillings in the pound of their supposed income, were afterwards assessed as gentlemen. In the assessment of a tax which was not very heavy, a considerable degree of inequality had been found less insupportable than any degree of uncertainty."
Ibid.

> ('Income' is also used in its everyday meaning in this excerpt-- that is, as 'earnings'. Smith pre-dated the evolution of specialized revenue-law-terms such as "wages" and "income" by more than a century.)

(I'm sure everyone noticed that a poll tax sometimes took the form of an assessment of *"three shillings in the pound of [someone's] supposed income (earnings)"*. As such taxes *are* of the class of *"capitation[s] or other direct taxe[s]"*, Smith's observation here nicely supplements the language in his more general definition of capitations by which it is made clear that Article 1, Section 9 of the Constitution prohibits any tax claiming some part of *"every species of revenue"* (except by means of apportionment); and that, therefore, the "specie of revenue" addressed by our "income" tax is, of necessity, a distinct one-- that is, one amenable exclusively to an indirect form of taxation, meaning a privilege-based excise.)

> *"...Albert Gallatin* [Pennsylvania congressman, United States Senator and Representative, United States Minister to England and France, respectively, and the longest serving Secretary of the Treasury in American History -PH], *in his Sketch of the Finances of the United States, published in November, 1796, said: 'The most generally received opinion, however, is that, by direct taxes in the constitution, those are meant which are raised on the capital or revenue of the people;...' He then quotes from Smith's Wealth of Nations, and continues: 'The remarkable coincidence of the clause of the constitution with this passage in using the word 'capitation' as a generic expression, including the different species of direct taxes-- an acceptation of the word peculiar, it is believed, to Dr. Smith-- leaves little doubt that the framers of the one had the other in view at the time, and that they, as well as he, by direct taxes, meant those paid directly from the falling immediately on the revenue;..."* United States Supreme Court, Pollock v. Farmer's Loan & Trust, 157 U.S. 429 (1895)

To summarize what we've just learned:

A Tax On Revenue, Particularly As Either A Fixed Or Percentage-Calculated Levy On Earnings, Is A Capitation.

So,

since

- The "income" taxable under the non-apportioned "income tax" **must** be something that can be taxed as, and only as, an excise (a tax on the proceeds of the exercise of a privilege);

and

- The "income" being taxed **cannot** be something such that a tax upon it would constitute a capitation (a tax on general, unprivileged receipts or earnings);

...even without looking at a word of the income tax law itself, we can see that the "income" upon which it lays a tax doesn't include unprivileged earnings, receipts, pay, or profits-- because it cannot.

> *"It is elementary law that every statute is to be read in the light of the constitution. However broad and general its language, it cannot be interpreted as extending beyond those matters which it was within the constitutional power of the legislature to reach."* McCullough v. Com. of Virginia, 172 U.S. 102 (1898)

Thus, it is no surprise to find that when we DO look at the words of the law, we find that they entirely conform to this limitation. For instance, look at the definitional structures of two key reporting-related terms in the law, the application of one or the other of which underlies nearly all presumptions of income tax liability:

Sec. 3401. - Definitions
a) Wages
For purposes of this chapter, the term "wages" means all remuneration (other than fees paid to a public official) for services performed by an employee for his employer,
...
c) Employee
For purposes of this chapter, the term "employee" includes an officer, employee, or elected official of the United States, a State, or any political subdivision thereof, or the District of Columbia, or any agency or instrumentality of any one or more of the foregoing. The term "employee" also includes an officer of a corporation* [That is to say, a "United States Corporation", defined in Sec. 207 of the Public Salary Tax Act as, *"a corporate agency or instrumentality, is one (a) a majority of the stock of which is owned by or on behalf of the United States, or (b) the power to appoint or select a majority of the board of directors of which is exercisable by or on behalf of the United States..."* However, we are instructed by the IRS in Pub. 15A that even U.S. corporation officers are only to be considered "employees" if they are paid as a consequence of their positions.]

("FICA" provisions are similarly defined, but in a more complex fashion, which would require an unreasonable amount of space to include here. See CtC for details.)

and:

Sec. 7701. - Definitions
(a) When used in this title, where not otherwise distinctly expressed or manifestly incompatible with the intent thereof -
Trade or business
The term "trade or business" includes the performance of the functions of a public office

(Narrower versions of this definition, specifying only certain public offices, are deployed in regard to certain aspects of the tax, such as that involving "self-employment income". See CtC and The Digital Appendix for more on this.)

Clearly, the law's own words confine its application within the limits that our discussion above has identified. (Close study of ALL of the law reveals that it NEVER seeks to escape these limits, even though much of its language, when excerpted and seen out of-- or in ignorance of-- the broad context of the law, can appear otherwise-- a fact that is widely and shamefully exploited by the beneficiaries of misunderstanding. See 'Cracking the Code- The Fascinating Truth About Taxation In America' for that close study, a more comprehensive specification of what qualifies as "income", and everything else most Americans need to know about the "income" tax.)

A Few Thoughts On A Recent Tax Court Dialogue

A CtC-educated American in Tax Court recently trying to get a ruling to remand a "determination" (for pre-CtC years) back to the Appeals Office for lack of having had a face to face hearing was asked to describe his work arrangement. He made a reply and things moved on, but afterwards decided that he wasn't really happy with his answer. He also concluded, on reflection, that this question and answer seemed to be given much significance by the judge and the "Respondent" (IRS attorney), and thus sent me an email asking what I would have said in the same situation.

I agree that this question is significant-- indeed, the very fact that it is asked at all is significant. After all, if "everything that comes in" in exchange for delivering labor by way of ANY "work arrangement" is inherently a measure of an applicable tax, the particulars of the "work arrangement" are immaterial, especially since my correspondent had already testified that he had not been paid "wages", while at the same time acknowledging the receipt of payment and that he was a permanent (that is, non-contractor) member of the paying entity's workforce. The question, then, can only be in hopes of eliciting a self-contradiction from the careless (the utility of which hinges on the fact that "everything that comes in" in exchange for delivering labor by way of ANY work arrangement is NOT inherently a measure of the tax, but "what comes in" from "work arrangements" of a certain distinguished character is).

I know that this question has been asked in a number of dialogues between CtC-educated Americans and agency personnel, sometimes in Tax Court or collections hearings and sometimes in simple phone conversations, so I thought it worthwhile to post my response to this inquiry in case others are interested as well: If I were asked to describe a non-federally-connected "work arrangement", I would likely reply with something along the line of, *"An entirely private agreement to trade my personally-owned skills, time and effort for some of the other party's supply of negotiable I.O.U.'s."*

My correspondent also reports that at another point in this hearing (right after being asked whether he had received "wages"), he was asked to explain the withheld amounts being claimed as refunds on his return. This inquiry ended when the gentleman simply pointed out that the total reported on line 64 of his return (and carried forward as indicated for the rest of the return) was the combined total of all federal withholdings (nominal "income tax withheld" plus "Social Security tax withheld" and "Medicare tax withheld").

Interestingly, the inquisitor didn't move on to the previously typical follow-up of, *"AHA! If you didn't receive "wages", Mr. Tax-Defier, then how is it that you had amounts withheld?!"* Frankly, I wouldn't be surprised if this triumphantly-issued challenge is being discouraged lately, since it emphasizes the linkage between pay distinguishable as "wages" and the propriety of "withholding"-- inviting the response of, *"Are you thereby admitting that if my pay DOESN'T qualify as "wages", then nothing should be, nor should have been, withheld from it?"*

In any event, the challenge wasn't issued this time, but has been often enough in the past under these same general circumstances that I'll take this occasion to share the response I'd be inclined to make should the opportunity arise:

"Surely no one here would dispute that one can have a trading relationship with someone who simply misunderstands or mischaracterizes the relationship, or something about it (or about themselves), or who misunderstands the nature and limitations of the "income tax", and who, for one or more of these or other reasons (none of which it is my responsibility to explain), misapplies certain "withholding" protocols to the victim?!

Obviously, "information return" preparers are capable of making mistakes-- it would be ludicrous to suggest otherwise. These mistakes could be small or they could be large; and they could be of any and all varieties.

Obviously, among those mistakes could be the mischaracterization (and treatment) of payments made to the victim of the mistake as "wages" when they are not.

Indeed, the law anticipates just such mistakes, as is expressed in numerous ways throughout the tax-related-statutory and regulatory structure. There's even a specific statutory provision for a victim to bring civil suit against someone guilty of making exactly this mistake**...*

What a stupid question, Mr. "Respondent"!

Haven't you ever actually read the law?"

*See 'About 1040s And Claiming Refunds' in CtC
**See pp. 141-143 of CtC)

A "Wage" By Any Other Name Is Taxed The Same...

It's come to my attention recently that some folks are confused by the casual use of terms like "salary" by tax agency-types in a context in which these folks expect to see the term "wages" used instead. The problem lies in mistaking the *label* for the *determinant* of the legal character of any given receipts.

The reality is that it is the legal character of the activity producing the receipts that matters, not what the receipts are called (nor what the activity is called, for that matter); and, in fact, "wages" is properly understood as a label for a *class of receipts* rather than a *type of receipt*. It is the class of all remuneration paid to those meeting the IRC chapter 24 custom-definition of "employee" for purposes of general withholding under that chapter, or, for the purposes of FICA "income" taxes in chapter 21, the class of all remuneration paid in respect of "employment" as that term is custom-defined therein.

The following excerpt from the Treasury Department regulations posted in the Federal Register edition of Tuesday, September 7, 1943, upon the revival of "withholding" by way of the 'Current Tax Payment Act of 1943', illustrates this reality. Explaining the class "wages" for purposes of the general chapter

24 withholding provisions, the regulations make clear that the label under which qualifying remuneration is paid is immaterial:

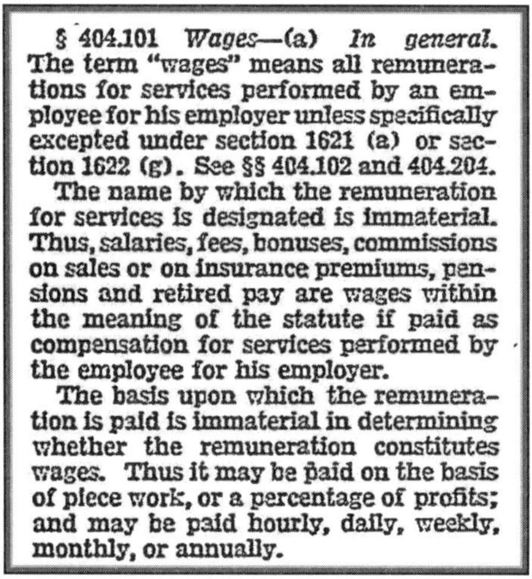
§ 404.101 *Wages*—(a) *In general.* The term "wages" means all remunerations for services performed by an employee for his employer unless specifically excepted under section 1621 (a) or section 1622 (g). See §§ 404.102 and 404.204.

The name by which the remuneration for services is designated is immaterial. Thus, salaries, fees, bonuses, commissions on sales or on insurance premiums, pensions and retired pay are wages within the meaning of the statute if paid as compensation for services performed by the employee for his employer.

The basis upon which the remuneration is paid is immaterial in determining whether the remuneration constitutes wages. Thus it may be paid on the basis of piece work, or a percentage of profits; and may be paid hourly, daily, weekly, monthly, or annually.

***

By the way, the language above may seem confusing at first glance, in light of the exception within 3401(a) (the definition of "wages", which was originally codified in the 1943 version of the "IRC of 1939" as § 1621) presented as "(other than fees paid to a public official)":

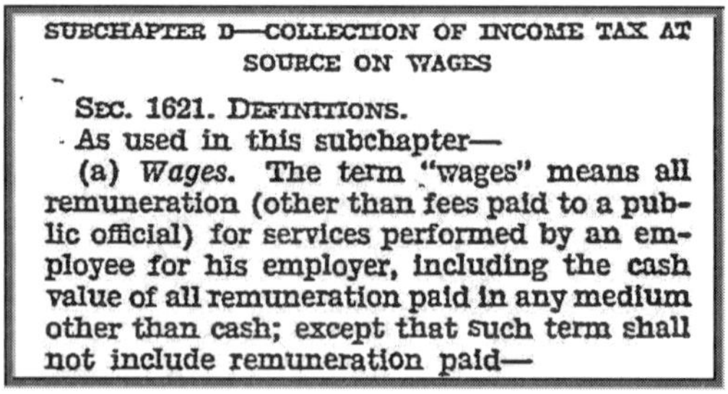
SUBCHAPTER D—COLLECTION OF INCOME TAX AT SOURCE ON WAGES

SEC. 1621. DEFINITIONS.

As used in this subchapter—

(a) *Wages.* The term "wages" means all remuneration (other than fees paid to a public official) for services performed by an employee for his employer, including the cash value of all remuneration paid in any medium other than cash; except that such term shall not include remuneration paid—

However, there is no actual inconsistency. The "fees" that count as "wages" are payments made to, and for the remunerative benefit of, the "service-provider" himself. In other words, they are compensatory payments which simply happen to be going under the label of "fees". Those that are excluded are fees being collected by the "service-provider" on behalf of the office he or she is administering. Such fees may be collected in connection with the rendering of a service, but they are not received by the "employee" as personal compensation.

For instance, a clerk handling a passport application will collect a fee which is imposed to cover the labor costs of processing the application, but that fee is paid to the United States Treasury, not to the worker. See the following additional excerpt from the Federal Register on this subject, and note the exclusion of "compensation" in the rule:

> § 404.102 *Exclusions from wages*—(a) *Fees paid to a public official.* Authorized fees paid to public officials, such as notaries public, clerks of courts, sheriffs, etc., for services rendered in the performance of their official duties are excepted from the definition of the term "wages" and hence are not subject to withholding. However, salaries paid such officials by the Government, or government agency or instrumentality are subject to withholding.

(See pages 51 and 52 of CtC for some related material, and the chapter 'Withholding The Truth' for the entire body of information on the subject of "wages" and the provisions of Subtitle C.)

Forms in which "income" (the use of federal property, privilege or prerogative, measured by the resulting gain) can be realized:	**Forms in which non-"income" (earnings/receipts NOT resulting from the use of federal property, privilege or prerogative) can be realized:**
• Compensation for services, including fees, commissions, fringe benefits, and similar items;	• Compensation for services, including fees, commissions, fringe benefits, and similar items;

• Receipts derived from business; • Gains derived from dealings in property; • Interest; • Rents; • Royalties; • Dividends; • Alimony and separate maintenance payments; • Annuities; • Gains from life insurance and endowment contracts; • Pensions; • Gains from discharge of indebtedness; • Distributive share of partnership gross receipts; • Receipts in respect of a decedent; and • Receipts from an interest in an estate or trust; • ...plus any other form in which such a gain can come into the control of a recipient for his separate use and disposal (although not every such gain may actually be taxed).	• Receipts derived from business; • Gains derived from dealings in property; • Interest; • Rents; • Royalties; • Dividends; • Alimony and separate maintenance payments; • Annuities; • Gains from life insurance and endowment contracts; • Pensions; • Gains from discharge of indebtedness; • Distributive share of partnership gross receipts; • Receipts in respect of a decedent; and • Receipts from an interest in an estate or trust; • ...plus any other form in which such a gain can come into the control of a recipient for his separate use and disposal.

It's Past Time To Stand Up, And Getting Later Every Minute

"It is not the function of our Government to keep the citizen from falling into error; it is the function of the citizen to keep the Government from falling into error."
-Justice Robert H. Jackson

Essayist and retired president and CEO of the Pennsylvania Manufacturers' Association Jim Panyard recently reported that:

> *"As of June 2009, 155 million people were laboring in the shrinking private sector of the American Empire with a per capita income of $39,751 and a per household income of $50,740.*
>
> *In addition to supporting themselves and their dependents on those earnings, they were also supporting:*
>
> - *22.5 million government employees at the federal, state and local levels. The average pay of those on the federal government payroll is $75,419 this year, according to Econwatch. The story is much the same at the state and local levels. In Pennsylvania, for example, the average state employee has a pay package of*

about $68,000 per year, while the state's household income is $48,576. (As an aside, there are only about 20 million jobs in the nation's manufacturing and construction sectors, combined.)

- *39 million welfare recipients*

- *46.5 million Social Security recipients, a number projected to rise to about 72 million in the next 20 years.*

- *14.7 million Americans drawing unemployment benefits, with that number expected to rise consistently in the foreseeable future.*

The productive sector workers are also paying for everything the Leviathan State does, such as wars, roads, Imperial adventures, private stadiums, bailouts, counterfeiting, ad infinitum. They also pick up the soaring tabs for 47 million Medicaid and 42 million Medicare recipients."

Panyard goes on to ask the question,
"How can 155 million productive workers support themselves, nearly 100 million nonproductive others and a seemingly endless list of government endeavors?"

Darn good question...

The simple and obvious answer is, "They can't." The simple follow-up observation is, "They don't have to keep trying to do so, either, nor should they."

It is almost impossible to conceive of a shorter road to catastrophe for any society than its being successfully conditioned to tolerate the riding of some on the backs of others under any protocol other than 100% voluntarism-- by which I mean voluntarism on an individual level, whereby the individual "mount" is free to say "No more" to the "mounted", and individually shuck off the load. Anything else is serfdom of the productive, and results in the inevitable collapse of the society overall as the unproductive ranks swell. The dynamic is simple: Each additional increment of burden on the productive causes more from that group to fall off the edge into beneficiary status (as a welfare recipient of some kind), thus increasing the burden on the remainder yet further, which causes more to fall off... You see how this goes.

(In 1990, my brother and I created the board game 'Lose', which modeled this dynamic. Each player struggles to be the last one standing while supporting the ever-increasing welfare load of bankrupt players who have succumbed to the bleeding inflicted upon them by routine demands of the state and the regulatory and tax burdens imposed on them by other players' manipulation of the political process during the course of the game. See a short news blurb on 'Lose' at www.losthorizons.com/Newsletter/LoseNews.wmv.)

Happily, our Founding Fathers anticipated precisely this dynamic, which their close study of history had demonstrated to them time and again. That's why they equipped the people with individual control over their individual wealth, prohibiting capitations and other direct taxes except by the mechanism of apportionment , which are therefore very difficult to successfully abuse, due to the political accountability and competing interests of the state governments which that mechanism invokes. (See 'Cracking the Code- The Fascinating Truth About Taxation In America'.)

The whole point of that provision, aside from its necessity as a matter of respect for individual rights, is to serve as a governor on the political system, starving it of fuel when its excesses grow inconvenient (or at least protecting the wise from the expenses of the foolish). As even so ardent a statist as Alexander Hamilton pointed out in Federalist #21:

> *"Imposts, excises, and, in general, all duties upon articles of consumption, may be compared to a fluid, which will, in time, find its level with the means of paying them. The amount to be contributed by each citizen will in a degree be at his own option, and can be regulated by an attention to his resources."*

However, that prescient provision isn't self-actuating, of course. Its protection requires each individual that would enjoy it to have enough brains and gumption to stand up and say, "The rest of you do what you wish-- it's a free country. But you can pay for your universal health care, and the golden parachutes you want to give away, and the missiles you want to unload against unoffending foreigners, and your "Second Deputy Under Secretaries for Natural Resources and Environment", and your Bridges to Nowhere and all the rest of your demented excesses and corruptions yourself. For my part, no more."

Hard as it sometimes is to step out of the crowd like this, there is no other way, and morality and self-respect allow no alternative, anyway. As Thomas Jefferson said, *"In matters of style, swim with the current. In matters of principle, STAND LIKE A ROCK."*

Taking charge of who disposes of your property IS a matter of principle, and not just of pragmatism. For one thing, to relinquish such control is to effectively embrace the principle that the collective (or whoever claims to represent the collective) has acquired the right to control the disposal of your property in your stead. This is just as definitively true whether you say it in so many words, or simply abandon efforts to enforce your own rights. "I can quit anytime" may be technically true, but until you DO quit, the cigarettes are running your show.

There is also the matter of YOU being morally responsible for the consequences of the disposal of your property. If the product of your labor is being used to facilitate or finance violations of the Constitution with your passive acquiescence, then like it or not, you are participating in what inevitably amounts to a violation of the rights of someone else.

This is not to say that the "pragmatic" consideration is anything to laugh off, either, of course. In addition to the simple practical importance of keeping your own property in order to be able to look after yourself and your family, the things that others will do with it are not confined to mere wastefulness, graft and corruption.

Anyone old enough to be reading these words is able to recite a litany of offenses steadily committed against the rule of law by those who have been allowed to get into the habit of disposing of other people's property for their own purposes. Each such offense brings us closer to the time when the rule of law is entirely abandoned by a population increasingly conditioned to the exercise of arbitrary power, which will then participate without a glimmer of conscience or consciousness in the binding down of themselves and their neighbors at the bidding of a then entirely unbound state.

Here's a harbinger of the sort of thing that lies ahead for a complacent or intimidated America:

> DAILY EXPRESS (UK), August 4, 2009: *The Children's Secretary set out £400million plans to put 20,000 problem families under 24-hour CCTV super-vision in their own homes.*
> *They will be monitored to ensure that children attend school, go to bed on time and eat proper meals.*
> *Private security guards will also be sent round to carry out home checks, while parents will be given help to combat drug and alcohol addiction.*
> *Around 2,000 families have gone through these Family Intervention Projects so far.*
> *But ministers want to target 20,000 more in the next two years, with each costing between £5,000 and £20,000 – a potential total bill of £400million.*

One doesn't have to look into the question of what constitutes a "problem family" for the British government, because it doesn't matter. Whatever it may be, this program--currently in operation in an increasingly degenerate socialist cesspool to which the United States regularly looks for social policy inspirations-- is enough to make any sensible person's skin crawl even if the standard is a habit of feeding the kiddies heroin for breakfast.

Does anyone out of diapers doubt that whatever they may be now, the qualifications for "interventions" under this program will constantly expand? If such a program should be implemented here, it would doubtless begin as some kind of "sentencing alternative" in cases everyone agrees involve the dregs of society with whom no one sympathizes, and therefore will seem threatening to no one else. Kind of like "sex offender registration". But like the RICO laws we all were told were created just to deal with the Mafia, this is not where such a program would stop.

Indeed, the Department of Homeland Security recently offered us all a list of what IT presently considers to be American "problem people", which basically consisted of everyone who doesn't already love Big Brother... That's ominous enough by itself, of course, but think about this: do you prefer to keep your kids out of government schools? Do you criticize the state (or its clients) in front of them at your dinner table? Even if the justification for such a program of intervention ostensibly remained "protection of the children" I think you might find that sooner or later you'll also qualify as a "problem family" to somebody.

The essay by Jim Panyard with which I began these comments goes on to expressions of despair, based on Panyard's belief that America has already crossed the point of no return. While I grant that we are dangerously far down the road, I disagree with Panyard's conclusion, for two reasons.

First, as individuals, we are never past the point of redemption. We are free moral actors, and can and must do the right thing whenever we become aware of it, whether it offers practical benefit or not.

Secondly, this great country is blessed with a foundational structure of law and tradition in which we can always find support for what is right, and repudiation of what is not. That is, our unique American heritage of liberty, individual rights and limited government properly established solely for the preservation of those rights-- and the logic and historical evidence by which that heritage was chosen for us by our forefathers, is-- and always will be-- on the side of the good guys, and can be invoked on their behalf. The bad guys, on the other hand, must ever resort to a fragile tissue of lies in support of their agenda.

Still, the hour is late. The time to stand up and put your foot down is now.

"Cowardice asks the question - is it safe?
Expediency asks the question - is it politic?
Vanity asks the question - is it popular?
But conscience asks the question - is it right? And there comes a time when one must take a position that is neither safe, nor politic, nor popular; but one must take it because it is right."
-Dr. Martin Luther King, Jr.

If The State's Lips Are Moving, It's Lying

"Of course the people don't want war. But after all, it's the leaders of the country who determine the policy, and it's always a simple matter to drag the people along whether it's a democracy, a fascist dictatorship, or a parliament, or a communist dictatorship. That is easy. All you have to do is tell them they are being attacked, and denounce the pacifists for lack of patriotism, and exposing the country to greater danger."
-- Herman Goering at the Nuremberg trials

The April 25th/May 2nd, 2008 edition of the Lost Horizons newsletter had occasion to note the anniversary of the May 7, 1915 sinking of the British ship Lusitania with the loss of 128 American lives, and the use of this tragedy as a propaganda tool in overcoming American resistance to participation in the then-ongoing World War I. By coincidence, that same edition covered this anniversary, as well:

> *"April 25, 1898- The United States declares war on Spain, using the pretext of the mysterious sinking of the USS Maine in a Cuban harbor. The war resulted in U.S. claims of ownership of the Philippines, Guam, and Puerto Rico, and a more limited sovereignty over Cuba."*

In fact, over the course of 2008 we have had occasion to note the "Gulf of Tonkin Incident", the contrivance used to justify the Mexican-American war, the Nazi regime's attack on Germany's Gliewitz Radio Station staged in order to serve as the pretext for its invasion of Poland, and several other famous "false-flag" operations as well, the most significant of which (in terms of immediacy, anyway) is that of "9/11", of course.

All of these scams share common characteristics. Among these are that each was deployed in order to engineer the consent (or passive acceptance) of the citizenry to some ambition of the state which was inherently adverse to the citizens' interests; and each was effectuated and sustained by a massive, systematic cacophony of disinformation from all government organs, and all others who perceived their interests as aligned with, or dependent upon, the government. That is, each of these scams, by which a state ambition adverse to the people was accomplished, relied upon a relentless drumbeat of lies by agents of the state and their fellow travelers.

The lying about each subterfuge committed by the state against the people is typically perpetual, of course. Those directly responsible for any one of these crimes hardly want their culpability revealed during their own lifetimes-- crimes of the sort involved here typically result in the needless deaths of thousands, if not millions. Furthermore, even when those responsible for any given offense hand over the reins of the state to their successors and pass from the scene, the inheritors of the state apparatus have an abiding interest in sustaining the lies, so as to allow them to successfully pull off the same sort of scam, at the expense of an unschooled, and thus unsuspecting citizenry, whenever it might suit their own ambitions.

Usually this program works like a charm: A loud, relentless drumbeat of lies surrounding the immediate "incident", all off the same "sound bite" memo; the mobilization of resources and commitment of policy on a rush basis, before any sober and independent evaluation or investigation of the pretext can be conducted; the maintenance of the campaign of lies and denigration of dissenting or suspicious voices long enough for the purpose of the subterfuge to become a fait accompli, and the public to be distracted by ongoing, new issues and concerns; and then a more desultory (but still careful and deliberate) incorporation of the lie-- often customized at this point to account for the more egregious and inescapable evidence to the contrary unearthed by voices of opposition over the intervening years-- into the official historical record and government school curricula.

In most cases, the nature of the original subterfuge and its effects are such that the passage of time serves the purposes of this program, making the truth more obscure, or at least, harder to prove and less likely to excite interest. Witnesses passing on; physical evidence being destroyed or scattered; dialogue on the matter coming to be increasingly cluttered with speculations and disinformation; and the state's endless, ubiquitous and generic "I-am-the-people's-friendly-servant" propaganda campaign, along with reluctance of second-stage victims (those of the mobilization in "response" to the false-flag "incident") to face the fact that their personal tragedies were due to their own unquestioning embrace of a lie and the contrary interests of those invested in, or benefiting from, the new status quo all conspire to bury the truth beyond conclusive disinterment.

Sometimes, however, we are blessed with a glitch in the program...

Over the holiday season just past, such a glitch manifested, concerning the Lusitania affair with which this discussion began. To round out the story of that ill-fated ship and its use by the Wilson administration to drag a previously opposed America into war in Europe, let me explain that German intelligence had determined that the Lusitania would be carrying munitions from America to Great Britain-- one of the belligerents that had declared war on Germany in the then-ongoing World War I. As EyewitnessToHistory.com recounts:

> *"The British Admiralty had secretly subsidized her construction and she was built to Admiralty specifications with the understanding that at the outbreak of war the ship would be consigned to government service. As war clouds gathered in 1913, the Lusitania quietly entered dry dock in Liverpool and was fitted for war service. This included the installation of ammunition magazines and gun mounts on her decks. The mounts, concealed under the teak deck, were ready for the addition of the guns when needed.*
>
> *"On May 1, 1915, the ship departed New York City bound for Liverpool. Unknown to her passengers but probably no secret to the Germans, almost all her hidden cargo consisted of munitions and contraband destined for the British war effort."*

It was for this reason that Germany considered the ship a legitimate target of attack (as was an accepted principle under the rules of war), and had taken pains to warn Americans to stay off the ship:

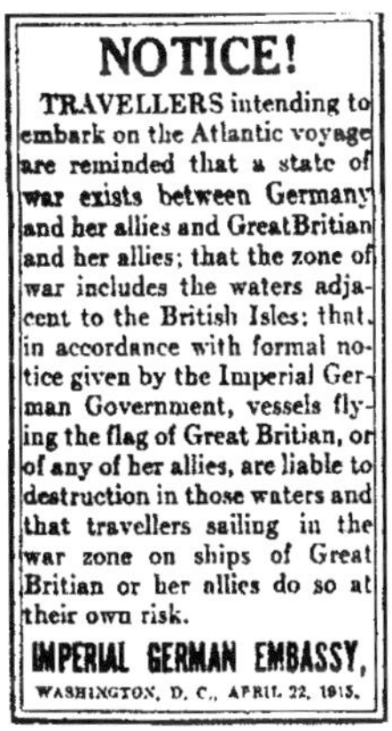

NOTICE!

TRAVELLERS intending to embark on the Atlantic voyage are reminded that a state of war exists between Germany and her allies and GreatBritian and her allies; that the zone of war includes the waters adjacent to the British Isles; that, in accordance with formal notice given by the Imperial German Government, vessels flying the flag of Great Britian, or of any of her allies, are liable to destruction in those waters and that travellers sailing in the war zone on ships of Great Britian or her allies do so at their own risk.

IMPERIAL GERMAN EMBASSY,
WASHINGTON, D. C., APRIL 22, 1915.

This notice was placed in newspapers prior to the May 1, 1915 sailing of the Lusitania, in some cases appearing alongside ads for that very voyage. The British and the Wilson administration, however, publicly discounted the warnings as merely intended to discourage peaceful trade, withheld from public knowledge the fact that the Lusitania was, in fact carrying munitions bound for the British military, and thus acted to ensure that Americans WOULD be on the ship when it set sail.

After the sinking of the ship on May 7, both the Wilson administration and the British government denied that the Lusitania had been outfitted as a British naval auxiliary and was carrying munitions (the admission of which would have undermined the affair's utility as a tool in fomenting enthusiasm for American entry into the war in Europe). Wilson actually wrote a note of protest to Germany following the sinking, expressing these denials (and prompting his own Secretary of State, William Jennings Bryant, to resign in protest):

> *"Your Excellency's note, in discussing the loss of American lives resulting from the sinking of the steamship Lusitania, adverts at some length to certain information which the Imperial German Government has received with regard to the character and outfit of that vessel, and your Excellency expresses the fear that this information may not have been brought to the attention of the Government of the United States.*
>
> *It is stated in the note that the Lusitania was undoubtedly equipped with masked guns, supplied with trained gunners and special ammunition, transporting troops from Canada, carrying a cargo not permitted under the laws of the United States to a vessel also carrying passengers, and serving, in virtual effect, as an auxiliary to the naval forces of Great Britain.*
>
> *Fortunately these are matters concerning which the Government of the United States is in a position to give the Imperial German Government official information. Of the facts alleged in your Excellency's note, if true, the Government of the United States would have been bound to take official cognizance in performing its recognized duty as a neutral power and in enforcing its national laws.*
>
> *It was its duty to see to it that the Lusitania was not armed for offensive action, that she was not*

> *serving as a transport, that she did not carry a cargo prohibited by the statutes of the United States, and that, if in fact she was a naval vessel of Great Britain, she should not receive clearance as a merchantman; and it performed that duty and enforced its statutes with scrupulous vigilance through its regularly constituted officials.*
>
> *It is able, therefore, to assure the Imperial German Government that it has been misinformed. If the Imperial German Government should deem itself to be in possession of convincing evidence that the officials of the Government of the United States did not perform these duties with thoroughness, the Government of the United States sincerely hopes that it will submit that evidence for consideration."*

In concert with official denials of this sort, the sinking of the Lusitania and related loss of American lives was subsequently treated as an illegitimate provocation by the Wilson administration in order to sway American public opinion toward entry into the war against Germany.

These efforts DID ultimately help persuade Congress to declare war on Germany-- resulting in direct American casualties totaling more than 320,000, and many other adverse consequences that reverberated throughout the rest of the twentieth century and into the present.

This is all old news, of course-- long out of the American consciousness. What controversy did exist over the Lusitania and its cargo, and the exploitation (if not connivance, or contrivance) of the tragedy for use as a propaganda tool to further the ambitions of a nearly hundred-year-past political faction has been supplanted by all the ploys of the same sort that have followed. But in 2008 this hoary and mostly-forgotten object lesson in the systemic mendacity of the state re-surfaced, when a salvage team began bringing up from the wreck of the Lusitania the first batch of munitions located in the sunken ship's cargo holds: more than 4,000,000 rounds of British military ammunition.

Take this serendipitous reminder, and the lesson it teaches, to heart: When the federal state ventures beyond guarding the borders against invasion and seeing that you have judicial remedy for physical aggressions against your person or property, it is no longer your servant or your friend. On the contrary, at that point, the state is your competitor and your enemy. At that point its words, and those of its sycophants, agents and beneficiaries, should be taken as a matter of course to be lies, as any fair reading of the historical record proves them always to have been.

"There is no safety for honest men but by believing all possible evil of evil men."
– Edmund Burke

A Tax Tip Potpourri

73 Am Jur 2d § 146 Operation of legislative definitions, generally
Research References
West's Key Number Digest, Statutes 223.1

The lawmaking body's own construction of its language, by means of definitions of the term employed, should be followed in the interpretation of the act or section to which it relates and is intended to apply.[1] By the same token, the courts should not enlarge statutory definitions so as to include a situation or a condition which it might be assumed the legislature would have covered by an enlarged definition if its existence had been contemplated.[2] A statutory definition supersedes the common-law,[3] colloquial,[4] commonly accepted, dictionary or judicial definition.[5] In this regard, where statute itself contains a definition of a word used therein, the definition controls, however contrary to the ordinary meaning of the word it may be,[6] and the term may not be given the meaning in which it is employed in another statute, although the two may be in pari material.[7] Where the legislature has defined words which are employed in a statute, its definitions are binding on the courts since the legislature has the right to give such signification as it deems proper to any word or phrase used by the statute, irrespective of the relationship of the definition to other terms.[8] Furthermore, where a word that already has a definite, fixed, and unambiguous meaning is redefined in a statute, the definition must be taken literally by the courts.[9]

[1]Curle v. Superior Court, 24 Cal. 4th 1057, 103 Cal. Rptr. 2d 751, 16 P.3d 166 (2001); State v. Olsen, 618 N.WE.2d 346 (Iowa 2000); Ohio Civil Rights Commission v. Parklawn Manner, Inc., 41 Ohio St. 2d 47, 70 Ohio Op. 2d 148, 322 N.E.2d 642 (1975); Devers v. Scranton City, 308 Pa. 13, 161 A. 540, 85 A.L.R. 692 (1932).

[2]Lenox Realty Co. v. Hackett, 122 Conn. 143, 187 A. 895, 107 A.L.R. 1306 (1936); Robertson v. Western Baptist Hosp., 267 S.W.2d 395 (Ky. 1954).

[3]Rayonier, Inc. v. Polson, 400 F.2d 909 (9th cir. 1968); 1137 18th Street Associates, Ltd. Partnership v. District of Columbia, 769 A.2d 155 (D.C. 2001).

[4]Western Union Telegraph Co. v. Lenroot, 323 U.S. 490, 65 S. Ct. 335, 89 L. Ed. 414 (1945).

[5]Stenberg v. Carhart, 530 U.S. 914, 120 S. Ct. 2597, 147 L. Ed. 2d 743 (2000); Driscoll v. General Nutrition Corp., 252 Conn. 215, 752 A.2d 1p069 (2000); Erlandson v. Genesee County Employees' Retirement Com'n, 337 Mich. 195, 59 N.W.2d 389 (1953); Appeal of Clayton-Marcus Co., Inc., 286 N.C. 215, 210 S.E.2d 199 (1974); Minnix v. State, 1955 OK CR 37, 282 P.2d 772 (Okla. Crim. App. 1955).

[6]Appeal of Clayton-Marcus Co., Inc., 286 N.C. 215, 210 S.E.2d 199 (1974).
The general Assembly's own construction of its language as provided by definitions, controls in the application of a statute, and such definition will be given great weight against any claim that application of the statutory definition defeats the general purpose of the statute. Ohio Civil Rights Commission v. Parklawn Manner, Inc., 41 Ohio St. 2d 47, 70 Ohio Op. 2d 148, 322 N.E.2d 642 (1975).

[7]Davison v. F. W. Woolworth Co., 186 Ga. 663, 198 S.E. 738, 118 A.L.R. 1363 (1938).

[8]People v. Dugan, 91 Misc. 2d 239, 397 N.Y.S.2d 878 (County Ct. 1977).

[9]Young v. O'Keefe, 246 Iowa 1182, 69 N.W.2d 534 (1955); State v. Standard Oil Co., 61 Or. 438, 123 P. 40 (1912).

***

A Checklist For A New Warrior

- Have I read CtC, thoroughly and carefully?

- Do I understand that if I use anyone else's services in helping me do paperwork, I have to be the one to determine and specify what, if any, of what I have received during the relevant period qualifies as "income" (after which any H & R Block on-the-job-trainee can do all the rest)?

- Am I keeping in mind core definitional issues, such as that where "State" is defined without mention of "the several states" or "the 50 states", that definition doesn't include Ohio, Michigan, etc.? That "domestic corporation" means "a corporation of the "United States""? That "U.S. person" doesn't mean "American"...?

- Do I understand that labels and locations can be deceiving, and are subordinate to the actual specifications in the statutes? For instance, do I understand that even though they are listed separately on a W-2 and 4852, amounts withheld under the labels "Social Security and Medicare taxes" are really just specially-named parts of what is called "federal income tax withheld" on a 1040, being merely what has been withheld as deposits against the possibility that I had "income" in the form of "wages" which not only qualify as the "wages" of an "employee" (as defined in 26 USC 3401(c) et seq.) subject to the normal tax, but ALSO qualify as "wages" from "employment" (as defined in 26 USC 3121(b) et seq.) and thus are subject to the FICA surtax as well?

- Do I understand that unless I have my filing comprehensively witnessed (as discussed in CtC), there is a possibility that a tax agency might pretend that it never received my mailed return?

- Do I understand that <u>anything</u> I attach to (or include with) my return <u>will be deemed to contain my own testimony</u>-- even if that's not what I actually intend (if, for instance, I attach or include a W-2, everything on it will be deemed to be being affirmed by me as true-- even if that content was produced by someone else, and even if it contradicts what appears on my other documents, such as the 1040 and/or 4852, and thereby renders my filing "frivolous" under the provisions of 26 USC 6702(a)(1)(B) and (a)(2)(A))?

- Do I understand also that anything concerning me alleged by others over a jurat, such as the allegations on W-2s, 1099s, and other "information returns", will stand as presumptively true-- even if wildly wrong-- unless formally rebutted with accurate testimony in a fashion cognizable by the relevant government agency or actor?

- Do I understand that I've got nothing to argue about, or explain, or defend or justify as part of my filing, or afterward? That I don't have to convince anyone that I'm right, I just have to speak the truth and demand that the "system" <u>obey the law</u>-- the details of which I also don't have to explain to anyone?

- Do I understand that if I have acted on misunderstanding in the past, such as filing "Schiff" "zero returns", or not filing, despite allegations being made about me by others on "information returns", and so forth, tax agency responses to this past behavior may already be in process (or have been waiting to begin), and may manifest itself coincidentally with (or shortly after) my educated filings, either by chance or in a deliberate attempt to use nominally appropriate responses to the past practices to make it appear as though the educated filings have prompted those responses?

- Do I also understand that "collections activities" concerning years in which I have acted on misunderstandings will almost certainly be being conducted by a tax agent who will not be aware (or who can plausibly deny being aware, anyway) that educated filings have been made for those years unless he or she has personally received copies of those filings?

- Do I understand that even with no more basis than their simple desire to live at my expense, those whose wealth and power have come from exploiting widespread ignorance about the tax and the law might try to frighten me into reversing myself? That even though the odds are very much that I won't, it's possible I may have to put up with anything from a single challenge to my resolve to a series of scary-looking "notices" and "letters"-- all carefully-designed to look significant while just as carefully-designed to not be-- over a period of months before the law-defiers give up and behave in accordance with the law?

- Do I understand that any governmental action outside, or subversive of, the bounds of the Constitution is inherently unlawful and despotic? That in acting on what I have learned about the tax, I am standing up on behalf of the Rule of Law, as intended-- indeed, relied upon-- by those patriots whose brilliance, integrity, blood and sacrifice established this great country? That I am rising to enforce and sustain the fundamental law in the only way it can be enforced and sustained-- by each man and woman, one by one?

Do I understand?

Yes?

Then I'm ready.

***

The Power of Analogy

There may be good reasons why logic, a subject that was "core curriculum" in the ancient republics, throughout the Renaissance, in the schooling of our Founders and in that of our own grandparents, for that matter, isn't taught to most Americans today. Those good reasons escape me, but maybe they exist...

In any event, one of the tools of logical analysis is the analogy. It is a cognitive tool designed to help people reason through complex language, and to overcome the natural human tendency to assume what is necessary to reconcile what is read and heard with what one already imagines that material to mean.

The use of analogy in this sense involves replacing assumption-freighted elements with substitutes not so burdened, while retaining the active dynamics relevant to the language being parsed. This process allows what is really being said in the original language to stand clear of the fog generated by presumptions as to its meaning which had been harbored prior to its critical examination.

Here's an example:

In the federal "income" tax laws we find specifications regarding the reporting of "wages" paid to those defined as "employees" and/or as "in employment" (in two different protocols). Looking at the former (which defines "wages" as the remuneration for services performed by an "employee"), we find that the relevant definition of "employee" lists particular varieties of workers, but uses the term "includes" in its construction, as follows:

> *(c) Employee*
> *For purposes of this chapter, the term "employee" includes an officer, employee, or elected official of the United States, a State, or any political subdivision thereof, or the District of Columbia, or any agency or instrumentality of any one or more of the foregoing. The term "employee" also includes an officer of a corporation.*

Because long habit developed over the years prior to examination of this language has trained the analyst to imagine that "employee", whether as defined in tax law or otherwise, always means, "anyone who works for anyone else in a long-term, subordinate position" (or the like), the analyst assumes that whatever is necessary to make the language of the definition above mean just that-- anyone who works for anyone else-- is present in this language, and reads it in just that way. But now let us apply the power of analogy.

Recognizing that the list of workers in the statute above IS, in fact, a discrete list, let's replace the familiar elements with others which are identically discrete, but simply amount to a different such list:

> *(c) Employee*
> *For purposes of this chapter, the term "employee" includes a secretary, file clerk or janitor of the Microsoft Corporation, or any subsidiary thereof. The term "employee" also includes a software engineer.*

Now we can easily see that to imagine that the actual statutory definition of "employee" should be read as embracing "anyone who works for anyone else" is just as ridiculous as imagining that "employee", if defined as "including a secretary, file clerk or janitor of the Microsoft Corporation, or any subsidiary thereof, and also including a software engineer", should be read as meaning "anyone who works for anyone else". Obviously, NO ONE would do the latter, and just as obviously (now that we have applied the analogy), NO ONE SHOULD DO THE FORMER.

(By the way, the custom rule of construction for "includes" at 26 USC 7701(c) doesn't diminish the clarifying power of this analogy. Applying that provision-- explained by the Treasury Department as, *"Meaning of Terms: The terms "includes and including" do not exclude things not enumerated which are in the same general class"* -- to, *"For purposes of this chapter, the term "employee" includes a secretary, file clerk or janitor of the Microsoft Corporation, or any subsidiary thereof. The term "employee" also includes a software engineer,"* clearly doesn't make ""employee" mean "anyone who works for anyone else""...

Furthermore, it's obvious that if that provision-- or any other aspect of the statutory structure-- were somehow intended to be read as making the "employee" before the "includes..." mean "anyone who works for anyone else", there would be no point in listing the Microsoft folks at all. The same would be true in regard to the listing of officers, employees and other members of the *federal* workforce that is found in the actual statutory language.)

So, why don't the government schools teach logic...?

Anyway, here's the 'tip' part of this 'Tax Tip': Analogy is a flexible cognitive tool. As Wikipedia puts it, *"Analogy plays a significant role in problem solving, decision making, perception, memory, creativity, emotion, explanation and communication." " It has been argued that analogy is "the core of cognition" (Hofstadter in Gentner et al. 2001)".* It is immensely useful in communicating clarity of understanding to those befuddled by the fog of the "ignorance tax" beneficiaries. Learn how to use it, and do so.

***

Regarding "Frivolous Returns" And The Burden Of Proof

Over the years, we have occasionally seen a CtC-educated filer treated to notices-- such as LTR 3176s, for instance-- that appear intended to be understood as suggesting that a failure to adopt the testimony of an "information return" on a filed 1040 amounts to a legal defect in that return, such as to cause it to meet the statutory provisions of 26 USC 6702 ("frivolous return"). These notices don't actually say this, of course (perhaps because simply failing to adopt the testimony of another in no way renders the return defective in this way). Nonetheless, it is clear that the notices are intended to be misunderstood. A few words about two statutes which are often overlooked-- despite being explicitly cited in this regard on pp. 183 and 184 of CtC-- should help clarify the matter.

In any controversy (real or contrived) in which the allegations made on an "information return" (W-2, 1099, K-1 etc.) are, or are purported to be, involved, and a filing controverting them has been made, the burden of proof as to the correctness of those allegations automatically and as a matter of statute falls on the government (even without regard to the statutory obligations on the government to simply receive the testimony on the 1040). This is true in any hearing, any litigation, or any other legal proceeding (including proceedings in Tax Court), whether the proceeding concerns the "information return" allegations directly, or indirectly hinges upon them, as would be the case if a return were actually being disregarded due to a failure to adopt those allegations (or a "deficiency" were being calculated based on the admission of the "information return" allegations while the countervailing testimony on a filed 1040 was being disregarded).

> *26 USC § 7491. - Burden of proof*
> *(a) Burden shifts where taxpayer produces credible evidence*
> *(1) General rule*
> *If, in any court proceeding, a taxpayer introduces credible evidence* with respect to any factual issue relevant to ascertaining the liability of the taxpayer for any tax imposed by subtitle A or B, the Secretary shall have the burden of proof with respect to such issue.*

and

> *26 USC § 6201 -Assessment authority*
> *(d) Required reasonable verification of information returns*
> *In any court proceeding, if a taxpayer asserts a reasonable dispute* with respect to any item of income reported on an information return filed with the Secretary under subpart B or C of part III of subchapter A of chapter 61 by a third party and the taxpayer has fully cooperated with the Secretary (including providing, within a reasonable period of time, access to and inspection of all witnesses, information, and documents within the control of the taxpayer as reasonably requested by the Secretary), the Secretary shall have the burden of producing reasonable and probative information concerning such deficiency in addition to such information return.*
> ("Subpart B or C of part III of subchapter A of chapter 61" refers to the statutory authorities for W-2s, 1099s, and other "information returns".)

*An allegation on an "information return" is "reasonably disputed" merely by a sworn rebuttal, each being of the same legal stature-- Joe's affidavit v. Sam's affidavit. For a Tax Court discussion of the meaning of "credible evidence" cited in 26 USC § 7491, see www.losthorizons.com/tax/TCCase.htm.

The Eighth Circuit Court of Appeals explained this latter provision concisely in Mason v. Barnhart, 406 F.3d 962 (8th Cir. 2005):

> *"Receipt of a Form 1099 does not conclusively establish that the recipient has reportable income. If a recipient of a Form 1099 has a reasonable dispute with the amount reported on a Form 1099, the Code places the burden on the Secretary of the Treasury to produce reasonable and probative information, in addition to the Form 1099, before payments reported on a Form 1099 are attributed to the recipient. See I.R.C. § 6201(d)."*

(Keep in mind that the "amount reported" means "the amount paid in the course of the payer's "trade or business"" in the case of a 1099, or "the amount of "wages" as defined at 3401(a) and/or 3121(a) reported" in the case of a W-2. It is only those things that are to be reported on these forms in the first place, so what must be substantiated under 6201(d) is not the accuracy of the report in regard to "the amount of dollars paid", but is the accuracy of the report in regard to "the amount of dollars paid that meet the statutory specifications for reporting with these forms".)

Plainly, the legitimacy of any suggestion that a return is defective ("frivolous") due to not having incorporated the allegations on an "information return" would rest on the validity of those allegations; and, per the statutes above, when a return has been filed disputing those allegations, the burden of proof regarding their validity falls on the government. Thus, since a return obviously cannot be deemed "frivolous" for failing to incorporate invalid allegations, and the allegations, once controverted, are <u>presumptively invalid</u> unless and until the government carries its burden of proof, a return CANNOT be deemed "frivolous" for failing to incorporate "information return" allegations until that issue has been litigated and the government has carried its burden. Any suggestion that a return has been so deemed prior to such litigation is inherently vaporous, even without any other considerations.

Furthermore, never forget that "frivolous penalties" themselves must by assessed as taxes:

> *26 USC § 6671. Rules for application of assessable penalties*
> *(a) Penalty assessed as tax*
> *The penalties and liabilities provided by this subchapter* [which includes section 6702 -PH] ***shall be paid upon notice and demand*** *by the Secretary, and* ***shall be assessed and collected in the same manner as taxes.*** *Except as otherwise provided, any reference in this title to "tax" imposed by this title shall be deemed also to refer to the penalties and liabilities provided by this subchapter.*
>
> *"Tax liability is a condition precedent to the demand. Merely demanding payment, even repeatedly, does not cause liability. For the condition precedent of liability to be met, there must be a lawful assessment, either a voluntary one by the taxpayer or one procedurally proper by the IRS. Because this country's income tax system is based on voluntary self-assessment, rather than distraint, Flora v. United States, 362 U.S. 145, 176, 80 S.Ct. 630, 646-47, 4 L.Ed.2d 623 (1960), the Service may assess the tax only in certain circumstances and in conformity with proper procedures."* Bothke v. Terry, 713 F. 2d 1405, at 1414 (1983).

In the event that "notice and demand" for a "frivolous" penalty ever actually IS issued (and by this I mean a notice of assessment, not some computer-generated, scary "LTR"), and it is contested, there must BE a "proceeding"-- just as is inescapably implied by the statutory language discussed above. Nobody gets to impose a penalty (that is, actually take somebody's stuff-- not merely threaten, "charge" "assert" or otherwise meaninglessly suggest the "imposition" of a penalty) on anybody else in this country-- in the face of a challenge-- without judicial process. In such a proceeding, the burden of proof as regards the penalty is also on the government:

> *26 USC § 7491(c):*
> *(c) Penalties*
> *Notwithstanding any other provision of this title, the Secretary shall have the burden of production in any court proceeding with respect to the liability of any individual for any penalty, addition to tax, or additional amount imposed by this title.*

Consider the following: Unless there is some kind of contract or other arrangement with these people giving them authority to "penalize" someone, what could really be being said when a "penalty" is alleged? How could it be anything more than, "We allege that you owe us money"? Imagine that you had sent me some paperwork-- perhaps an invoice (or a claim for the return of money owed to you by someone else who had sent it to me by mistake). In reply, I send you a letter suggesting that what you sent was defective according to some standard of mine, and saying, "I've charged you a penalty of $5,000. Send me a check." Or, "I've determined that you owe me a penalty of $500." (Or, moving into more general allegations, "I've changed your account. You owe me $XXX.") What would you do? Send me the money? Quake in fear? I don't think so. I think you'd write back saying something like, "I think you're crazy. But if you don't think so, sue me, and bear your burden of proof."

***

The Legislative Intent Behind 26 USC § 6702

> *"Section 6702 of the Code was enacted by the Tax Equity and Fiscal Responsibility Act of 1982, P.L. 97-248, 96 Stat. 324. According to the Senate Report, S.*

Rep. No. 97-494, Vol. 1, 97th Cong., 2d. Sess. 277 (1982), the penalty is intended to attack a variety of tax protest activities including: (1) irregular forms 1040 not in processible form because of altered or incorrect descriptions of line items or other provisions; (2) references to spurious constitutional arguments instead of required completion of a tax form; (3) forms on which there is incomplete information to calculate tax liability; (4) presentation of information which is clearly inconsistent, such as the listing of only a few dependents by a person who claims 99 exemptions; (5) "gold standard " or "war tax" deductions; and (6) deliberate use of incorrect tax tables."

"Virtually all of the authority for treating a signed Form 1040 as a nullity relies upon the fact that the taxpayer refused to provide any information pertaining to his or her income, or provided de minimis income information and accompanied the purported return with tax protestor type arguments." IRS Office of Chief Counsel Memorandum 200107035:

"[T]he Ninth Circuit Court of Appeals held in United States v. Long, 618 F.2d 74 (9th Cir. 1980), that a return containing zeros on most of the lines and signed by the taxpayer without modifications, additions, or deletions to the attestation statement [such as to render the affirmation as to what is reported on the return in doubt] would be sufficient to calculate tax liability, and, therefore, constitute a valid return." RS Office of Chief Counsel Memorandum 200114033:

"[T]he legislative history of § 6702... ...indicates that the frivolous return penalty was meant to apply to returns "in which many or all of the line items are not filled in except for reference to spurious constitutional objections." S.Rep. No. 494, 97th Cong., 2d Sess. 278, reprinted in 1982 U.S.Code Cong. & Ad.News 781, 1024." Leogrande v. U.S. 811 F.2d 147 C.A.2 (N.Y.) (1987)

> *"We therefore hold that the honesty and genuineness of the filer's attempt to satisfy the tax laws should be determined from the face of the form itself... The filer's subjective intent is irrelevant."* Colson v. United States, 446 F.3d 836 (8th Cir. 2000)

I recently heard from a Warrior who had sought an "abatement" of a "frivolous" penalty about which he had received a "threat letter". The IRS turned him down (unsurprisingly, since not only is the "abatement" protocol inappropriate for such purposes anyway, it's hard to imagine how a fiction could be "abated"...), but in doing so underscored the specific, limited application of the "frivolous return" penalty as illuminated above. Here is the letter:

Internal Revenue Service
Department of the Treasury
1973 North Rulon White Blvd.
Ogden, UT 84404-0040

Date: August 19, 2009

Mail Stop:4452
Person to Contact: Ms. Weaver
Employee Number: 0469245382
Telephone Number:
1-866-899-9083
Extension: 8471
Hours: 7:00 AM - 2:30 PM
Mountain Time
Monday - Thursday
Taxpayer Identification Number:

Tax Year(s): 2005

Dear Mr.

Thank you for your correspondence dated received March 10, 2009

The information you submitted does not establish reasonable cause or show due diligence.

There are no statutory provisions for abatement of the Civil Penalty for reasonable cause; therefore, we must deny your request for abatement of the Civil Penalty.

The intent of the Civil Penalty is to discontinue the flow of returns, amended returns, and documents that purport to be returns, and contain altered line items, and/or claim clearly unallowable deductions or credits based on a frivolous position. It is the responsibility of the taxpayer to ensure that all returns are correctly filed and paid timely.

If you have any questions about this matter please contact the person whose name, telephone number and contact hours are shown above.

Please accept our apology for the delay in responding to you.

Thank you for your cooperation.

Sincerely,

Ms. Weaver
Tax Technician
Examination Branch

Disregarding the typical agency incoherence with which "Ms. Weaver" first declares that the applicant's information "does not establish reasonable cause or show due diligence", and then proceeds to acknowledge that there's no provision for abatement of even *actual* "frivolous penalties" for "reasonable cause" anyway..., "Ms. Weaver's" "special letter" goes on to declare the purpose of the "[not so] civil penalty" remains just what the congressional records and other authorities cited above have consistently said: the penalizing of filings which purport to be returns but are distinguished from proper returns by containing altered line items and/or improper deductions or credits based on a "frivolous position" (which must be declared on the form itself, per the Congressional record and relevant jurisprudence previously cited).

Thank you, Ms. Weaver!

***

A Few Words From The Horse's Mouth On "SFRs"

> **Agency Comments**
>
> We requested comments on a draft of this letter from the Commissioner of Internal Revenue or his designee. On February 9, 2000, we received comments from responsible IRS officials in the Examination and Customer Service Divisions. Although the Examination Division said it had no comments, Customer Service Division officials commented on the phrase "Substitute for Return." They asked us to emphasize that even though the program is commonly referred to as the SFR program, no actual tax return is prepared. Instead, these officials noted that IRS prepares a document that substitutes for the return and that proposes an assessment, which is posted to the taxpayer's account and is subject to the collection process. We added a footnote to the letter to explain this and revised references in the draft to clarify this point.

(From a February 17, 2000 GAO response to an inquiry about the SFR program by Senator Daniel Moynihan.)

Your Papers, Please...

I recently became aware of a brash new governmental attempt to evade the law: USA passport applications now include a request for a Social Security number. The request suggests, on its face, that the furnishing of a number is required. However, those behind this little scheme include language proposing a legal rationale for the request on the application form itself-- conscious, no doubt, that it would be illegal to pose such a request as though it is an unambiguous requirement when it really isn't. The presence of the rationale serves to alert the wary that they are simply being invited to accept its reasoning, rather than being commanded to do so. A brief analysis reveals that rationale to be an amusingly bold and creative version of the old "lifting yourself off the ground by standing in a bucket and tugging mightily on its handle" routine.

Here's how the scam works: First, the application (which seeks to justify this 'demand' by laying out its reasoning) cites 26 USC 6039E, which provides that,

> *a) General rule*
> *Notwithstanding any other provision of law, any*

individual who—

(1) applies for a United States passport (or a renewal thereof), or

(2) applies to be lawfully accorded the privilege of residing permanently in the United States as an immigrant in accordance with the immigration laws,

shall include with any such application a statement which includes the information described in subsection (b).

(b) Information to be provided

Information required under subsection (a) shall include—

(1) the taxpayer's TIN (if any),

(2) in the case of a passport applicant, any foreign country in which such individual is residing,

(3) in the case of an individual seeking permanent residence, information with respect to whether such individual is required to file a return of the tax imposed by chapter 1 for such individual's most recent 3 taxable years, and

(4) such other information as the Secretary may prescribe. [No such prescriptions exist at the time of this writing]

From this it can be seen that while *"in the case of a passport applicant,"* nothing more than the identification of any foreign country in which the applicant is residing is required, in the case of a "taxpayer"-- perhaps when applying for *either* a passport or permanent residence in the United States, depending on how this statute is construed-- a "TIN" (if any) is demanded. OK, fair enough. Those who are "taxpayers" (anyone "subject to any internal revenue law"-- 26 USC 7701(a)(14)) must furnish a number-- all the rest of us just have to identify any foreign country in which we might be living.

However, this liberty-friendly distinction doesn't suit the interests of the ambitious state. So, the bureaucrats behind the passport application invite us to take a mind-numbing trip through the looking-glass world. Toward this end, they next cite 31 USC 7701, and trot out a little tiny portion of its language by which we are reminded (with context omitted) that those who "do business" with the federal government are, therefore, "taxpayers", and must furnish a TIN to the agency with whom they do that business. Then they close the circle by announcing that, *because an applicant for a passport pays a processing fee to the Department of State, he or she could be 'considered' (their word) to be "doing business" with a federal agency-- and therefore to be "taxpayers" and required (under a possible construction of 26 USC 6039E) to furnish a TIN (in the form of a Social Security number)!* You'd think that it would be easier just to reform 6039E to say directly that anyone applying for a passport has to furnish a TIN, wouldn't you? Well, no, actually. At least, not by virtue of THIS "argument".

Needless to say, the actual provisions in the law related to "doing business with the government" under which any requirements to furnish an ID number arise address only those involved in a profitable relationship with the government, who thus incur a related tax liability in regard to which the government has a legitimate interest in identifying the recipient. 31 USC 7701 is no exception:

> *(b) The head of an agency administering an included Federal loan program shall require a person applying for a loan under the program to provide that person's taxpayer identifying number.*
>
> *(c)*
>
> > *(1) The head of each Federal agency shall require each person doing business with that agency to furnish to that agency such person's taxpayer identifying number.*
> >
> > *(2) For purposes of this subsection, a person shall be considered to be doing business with a Federal agency if the person is—*
> >
> > > *(A) a lender or servicer in a Federal guaranteed or insured loan program administered by the agency;*
> > >
> > > *(B) an applicant for, or recipient of, a Federal license, permit, right-of-way, grant, or benefit*

> *payment administered by the agency or insurance administered by the agency;*
> *(C) a contractor of the agency;*
> *(D) assessed a fine, fee, royalty or penalty by the agency; and*
> *(E) in a relationship with the agency that may give rise to a receivable due to that agency, such as a partner of a borrower in or a guarantor of a Federal direct or insured loan administered by the agency.*

Obviously, this section of law has nothing to do with a passport application, or its associated fee; and the imaginative legal construct in which it is deployed does not add up to a legitimate governmental authority to demand Social Security numbers from all passport applicants. Still, though this is mere filthy and corrupt tyranny on the march, you've got to admire the creativity being put to work in this inspired 'Orwellian' effort to track the movements of Americans, to secure from them potentially debilitating legal declarations, and to train them to the idea that the law is elastic, and means whatever the government wants it to mean at any given time.

A Few Observations About Money

Literary Lesson On Monetary Truths

I took C. S. Lewis's classic, 'Out Of The Silent Planet' along for a re-read during my recent vacation. Upon being reminded of the fact that the villains in the story were motivated by the discovery that the alien world they had found possessed gold in plentiful and relatively unguarded supply, I found myself reflecting on how, despite the hype and contrivances of its creators and beneficiaries, the utterly fictional and fraudulent "value" ascribed to fiat currency never really fools anyone outside its own artificial context.

Can you imagine anyone in the circumstance of Lewis's venal explorers being similarly excited by finding a cache of some alien state's paper money? Or even any paper money other than the one currently being accepted in the market in which they wish to trade? Had these two come across a room full of, say, 1980's Nicaraguan Cordobas, or 1920's German Reichsmarks, they would have closed the door and moved on without a second thought or glance back. Had they exhibited any excitement at such a find, not one of Lewis's readers would have bought it.

More to the immediate point for American readers (and others in the world induced to accept Federal Reserve notes), had Lewis's villains come across a room full of revolutionary American "Continentals", or United States "greenbacks", they would have been similarly uninterested in what would be useful as nothing more than kindling or wallpaper. Even if they had found a great cache of present-day paper "dollars", they would have had to ask each other, "Are these still worth anything?"

Lewis, like all authors of similar tales, knew the transcendent truth about such matters. We need to keep that truth in mind ourselves.

Your Cash Ain't Nothin' But Trash, But Gold Is Always As Good As... Well, Gold

During a recent conversation with a friend, I became aware that the systematic and deliberate disparagement of real money (gold) routinely conducted in an effort to foster tolerance of the state's paper version has left many Americans without a clear understanding of the immutability of the value of gold. Here is what needs to be clearly comprehended in this regard: Gold NEVER loses its value, <u>even if its paper "dollar" price declines!</u>

If you buy an ounce of gold for, say, 900 paper "dollars", and later can get only 450 paper "dollars" for that ounce, this is NOT because the gold has lost value [purchasing power]. It is because the paper "dollars" have increased in value. That is, the purchasing power of the 900 paper "dollars" traded for the gold ounce in the first place is now achieved with only 450 such "dollars". The value of the gold has not changed at all.

YOU CANNOT LOSE VALUE FROM AN INVESTMENT IN GOLD, NO MATTER WHAT HAPPENS TO ITS PAPER "DOLLAR" PRICE.

When it takes 900 paper "dollars" to buy an ounce of gold, it is because at that point 900 paper "dollars" can buy 'x' goods and services, the same purchasing power as the ounce of gold. If the price of the gold ounce declines to 450 paper "dollars", it reflects the fact that the paper "dollars" have now increased in value to the point at which 450 such "dollars" can now buy the same 'x' that required 900 at the earlier time. The gold ounce can still do the same.

The purchasing power of the gold hasn't changed, but the purchasing power of the paper has, so the 450 paper "dollars" for which the gold can be traded now have the same purchasing power that was possessed by the original 900. Whatever the number of paper "dollars" for which the gold trades AT ANY TIME, they will still represent the same purchasing power in your pocket as whatever was the number with which you bought the gold in the first place.

Of course, the paper "dollars" are virtually certain to NOT regain their relative value, and, even if subject to temporary fluctuations, certainly will not do so over the course of even a relatively brief passage of time.

For instance, while the ounce of gold your grandfather acquired in 1900 will still buy today what it would then (more, actually, due to the effect of productivity gains, all of which adhere to hard money, the paper "dollar" gramps also set aside that year now needs the help of 113.13 of its fellows to buy what it once could handle by itself (as of 2006, using an "unskilled labor rate" computation-- the comparison best insulated from improper productivity and quality-improvement skewing of such calculations, in my view).

THE BOTTOM LINE IS SIMPLE: HOLDING PAPER "DOLLARS" IS A FOOL'S GAME, WHILE HOLDING GOLD IS FOOLPROOF.

(Needless to say, more gold goes into circulation periodically, as it is discovered and mined. However, unlike paper trash, the production of gold-- or silver-- is invariably a consequence of a corresponding expenditure of capital and labor. Thus, every ounce introduced into circulation acquires and represents the inherent value of that expenditure, as well as being itself a durable-- indeed, near permanent-- capital asset added to the economy at the same time, making such increases in supply non-inflationary.)

A German of the 1920s burning hyper-inflated Reichsmarks (the "federal reserve notes" of that time and place) to heat her home.

Thomas Paine on Paper Money

"I remember a German farmer expressing as much in a few words as the whole subject requires; *"money is money, and paper is paper."*

"All the invention of man cannot make them otherwise. The alchemist may cease his labors, and the hunter after the philosopher's stone go to rest, if paper can be metamorphosed into gold and silver, or made to answer the same purpose in all cases.

"Gold and silver are the emissions of nature: paper is the emission of art. The value of gold and silver is ascertained by the quantity which nature has made in the earth. We cannot make that quantity more or less than it is, and therefore the value being dependent upon the quantity, depends not on man. Man has no share in making gold or silver; all that his labors and ingenuity can accomplish is, to collect it from the mine, refine it for use and give it an impression, or stamp it into coin.

"Its being stamped into coin adds considerably to its convenience but nothing to its value. It has then no more value than it had before. Its value is not in the impression but in itself. Take away the impression and still the same value remains. Alter it as you will, or expose it to any misfortune that can happen, still the value is not diminished. It has a capacity to resist the accidents that destroy other things. It has, therefore, all the requisite qualities that money can have, and is a fit material to make money of — and nothing which has not all those properties can be fit for the purpose of money.

"Paper, considered as a material whereof to make money, has none of the requisite qualities in it. It is too plentiful, and too easily come at. It can be had anywhere, and for a trifle.

"There are two ways in which I shall consider paper.

"The only proper use for paper, in the room of money, is to write promissory notes and obligations of payment in specie upon. A piece of paper, thus written and signed, is worth the sum it is given for, if the person who gives it is able to pay it, because in this case, the law will oblige him. But if he is worth nothing, the paper note is worth nothing. The value, therefore, of such a note, is not in the note itself, for that is but paper and promise, but in the man who is obliged to redeem it with gold or silver.

"Paper, circulating in this manner, and for this purpose, continually points to the place and person where, and of whom, the money is to be had, and at last finds its home; and, as it were, unlocks its master's chest and pays the bearer.

"But when an assembly undertakes to issue paper *as* money, the whole system of safety and certainty is overturned, and property set afloat. Paper notes given and taken between individuals as a promise of payment is one thing, but paper issued by an assembly *as* money is another thing. It is like putting an apparition in the place of a man; it vanishes with looking at it, and nothing remains but the air.

"Money, when considered as the fruit of many years' industry, as the reward of labor, sweat and toil, as the widow's dowry and children's portion, and as the means of procuring the necessaries and alleviating the afflictions of life, and making old age a scene of rest, has something in it sacred that is not to be sported with, or trusted to the airy bubble of paper currency.

"By what power or authority an assembly undertakes to make paper money, is difficult to say. It derives none from the Constitution, for that is silent on the subject. It is one of those things which the people have not delegated, and which, were they at any time assembled together, they would not delegate. It is, therefore, an assumption of power which an assembly is not warranted in, and which may, one day or other, be the means of bringing some of them to punishment.

"I shall enumerate some of the evils of paper money and conclude with offering means for preventing them.

"One of the evils of paper money is that it turns the whole country into stock jobbers. The precariousness of its value and the uncertainty of its fate continually operate, night and day, to produce this destructive effect. Having no real value in itself it depends for support upon accident, caprice, and party; and as it is the interest of some to depreciate and of others to raise its value, there is a continual invention going on that destroys the morals of the country.

"It was horrid to see, and hurtful to recollect, how loose the principles of justice were left, by means of the paper emissions during the war. The experience then had should be a warning to any assembly how they venture to open such a dangerous door again.

"As to the romantic, if not hypocritical, tale that a virtuous people need no gold and silver, and that paper will do as well, it requires no other contradiction than the experience we have seen. Though some well-meaning people may be inclined to view it in this light, it is certain that the sharper always talks this language.

"There are a set of men who go about making purchases upon credit, and buying estates they have not wherewithal to pay for; and having done this, their next step is to fill the newspapers with paragraphs of the scarcity of money and the necessity of a paper emission, then to have a legal tender under the pretense of supporting its credit, and when out, to depreciate it as fast as they can, get a deal of it for a little price, and cheat their creditors; and this is the concise history of paper money schemes.

"But why, since the universal customs of the world has established money as the most convenient medium of traffic and commerce, should paper be set up in preference to gold and silver? The productions of nature are surely as innocent as those of art; and in the case of money, are abundantly, if not infinitely, more so. The love of gold and silver may produce covetousness, but covetousness, when not connected with dishonesty, is not properly a vice. It is frugality run to an extreme. But the evils of paper money have no end. Its uncertain and fluctuating value is continually awakening or creating new schemes of deceit. Every principle of justice is put to the rack, and the bond of society dissolved. The suppression, therefore, of paper money might very properly have been put into the act for preventing vice and immorality.

"The pretense for paper money has been that there was not a sufficiency of gold and silver. This, so far from being a reason for paper emissions, is a reason against them.

"As gold and silver are not the productions of North America, they are, therefore, articles of importation; and if we set up a paper manufactory of money, it amounts, as far as it is able, to prevent the importation of hard money, or to send it out again as fast it comes in; and by following this practice we shall continually banish the specie, till we have none left, and be continuously complaining of the grievance instead of remedying the cause.

"Considering gold and silver as articles of importation, there will in time, unless we prevent it by paper emissions, be as much in the country as the occasions of it require, for the same reasons there are as much of other imported articles. But as every yard of cloth manufactured in the country occasions a yard the less to be imported, so it is by money, with this difference, that in the one case we manufacture the thing itself and in the other we do not. We have cloth for cloth, but we have only paper dollars for silver ones.

"As to the assumed authority of any assembly in making paper money, or paper of any kind, a legal tender, or in other language, a compulsive payment, it is a most presumptuous attempt at arbitrary power. There can be no such power in a republican government: the people have no freedom — and property no security — where this practice can be acted: and the committee who shall bring in a report for this purpose, or the member who moves for it, and he who seconds it merits impeachment, and sooner or later may expect it.

"Of all the various sorts of base coin, paper money is the basest. It has the least intrinsic value of anything that can be put in the place of gold and silver. A hobnail or a piece of wampum far exceeds it. And there would be more propriety in making those articles a legal tender than to make paper so.

"It was the issuing base coin, and establishing it as a tender, that was one of the principal means of finally overthrowing the power of the Stuart family in Ireland. The article is worth reciting as it bears such a resemblance to the process practiced in paper money.

> *Brass and copper of the basest kind, old cannon; broken bells, household utensils were assiduously collected; and from every pound weight of such vile materials, valued at four pence, pieces were coined and circulated to the amount of five pounds normal value. By the first proclamation they were made current in all payments to and from the King and the subjects of the realm, except in duties on the importation of foreign goods, money left in trust, or due by mortgage, bills or bonds; and James promised that when the money should be decried, he would receive it in all payments, or make full satisfaction in gold and silver. The nominal value was afterwards raised by subsequent proclamations, the original restrictions removed, and this base money was ordered to be received in all kinds of payments As brass and copper grew scarce, it was made of still viler materials, of tin and pewter, and old debts of one thousand pounds were discharged by pieces of vile metal amounting to thirty shillings in intrinsic value.* (Leland's *History of Ireland*, vol. iv. p. 265.)

Had King James thought of paper, he needed not to have been at the trouble or expense of collecting brass and copper, broken bells, and household utensils.

"The laws of a country ought to be the standard of equity, and calculated to impress on the minds of the people the moral as well as the legal obligations of reciprocal justice. But tender laws, of any kind, operate to destroy morality, and to dissolve, by the pretense of law, what ought to be the principle of law to support, reciprocal justice between man and man —

and the punishment of a member who should move for such a law ought to be *death.*

"When the recommendation of Congress, in the year 1780, for repealing the tender laws was before the Assembly of Pennsylvania, on casting up the votes, for and against bringing in a bill to repeal those laws, the numbers were equal, and the casting vote rested on the speaker, Colonel Bayard.

""I give my vote," said he, "for the repeal, from a consciousness of justice; the tender laws operate to establish iniquity by law." But when the bill was brought in, the House rejected it, and the tender laws continued to be the means of fraud.

"If anything had or could have a value equal to gold and silver, it would require no tender law; and if it had not that value it ought not to have such a law; and, therefore, all tender laws are tyrannical and unjust and calculated to support fraud and oppression.

"Most of the advocates for tender laws are those who have debts to discharge, and who take refuge in such a law, to violate their contracts and cheat their creditors. But as no law can warrant the doing an unlawful act, therefore the proper mode of proceeding, should any such laws be enacted in future, will be to impeach and execute the members who moved for and seconded such a bill; and put the debtor and the creditor in the same situation they were in, with respect to each other, before such a law was passed.

"Men ought to be made to tremble at the idea of such a bare-faced act of injustice. It is in vain to talk of restoring credit, or complain that money cannot be borrowed at legal interest; until every idea of tender laws is totally and publicly reprobated and extirpated from among us.

"As to paper money, in any light it can be viewed, it is at best a bubble. Considered as property, it is inconsistent to suppose that the breath of an assembly, whose authority expires with the year, can give to paper the value and duration of gold. They cannot even engage that the next assembly shall receive it in taxes. And by the precedent (for authority there is none), that one assembly makes paper money, another may do the same, until confidence and credit are totally expelled, and all the evils of depreciation acted over again. The amount, therefore, of paper money is this, that it is the illegitimate offspring of assemblies, and when their year expires, they leave a vagrant on the hands of the public....

"Paper money is like dram-drinking, it relieves for a moment by deceitful sensation, but gradually diminishes the natural heat, and leaves the body worse than it found it. Were not this the case, and could money be made of paper at pleasure, every sovereign in Europe would be as rich as he pleased. But the truth is, that it is a bubble and the attempt vanity. Nature has provided the proper materials for money: gold and silver, and any attempt of ours to rival her is ridiculous...."

"It is well enough that people of the nation do not understand our [Federal Reserve] banking and monetary system, for if they did, I believe there would be a revolution before tomorrow morning."

-Henry Ford

Why Capitations Are Strictly Limited Under The Federal Constitution

Capitations, as the term is meant in the United States Constitution, are taxes on economic activity indiscriminately--that is, without special qualifications which distinguish activities that are taxable from those that are not, and which render those that are taxable as being of a voluntary nature. There were two chief reasons for the prohibition on capitations (other than through the mechanism of apportionment). The first is that the Founders didn't want the federal government to be in control of its own supply of revenue, other than through a very politically-accountable mechanism (and not at all by way of extractions directly from the people, as though it were a ruler and they mere subjects).

The second reason capitations are Constitutionally prohibited is that it is the nature of such taxes to transfer power wholesale to the government which is permitted to impose them. This is because when a government is authorized to tax all economic activity per its own discretion, it can then dispense tax benefits and tax punishments according to its own purposes-- manipulating private behavior otherwise outside of its authorized reach, and to a great degree evading any explicit boundaries laid upon its powers. The United States Supreme Court nicely expresses one aspect of this concern in its ruling in Bailey v. Drexel Furniture Co., 259 U.S. 20 (1922):

> *"[A]ll that Congress would need to do, hereafter, in seeking to take over to its control any one of the great number of subjects of public interest, jurisdiction of which the states have never parted with, and which are reserved to them by the Tenth Amendment, would be to enact a detailed measure of complete regulation of the subject and enforce it by a so-called tax upon departures from it. To give such magic to the word 'tax' would be to break down all constitutional limitation of the powers of Congress and completely wipe out the sovereignty of the states".*

Thus, such authority has never been granted. Unfortunately, the pretense of such authority has been so relentlessly asserted, and ignorance of the truth has become so widespread, that a de facto capitation authority IS exercised by the federal government and many co-conspirator state governments as well. The consequence of this corruption of morality and understanding has proven to be precisely what the Founders so rightly feared.

For instance, churches across this country-- once bastions of liberty, and rightfully proud of their independence of the secular authorities-- now cower before Leviathan, obediently silent in matters of politics lest they lose favored tax status, when the fact is that few of them are inherently subject to the tax in the first place! Ignorant of the law, the leaders of most American churches <u>make</u> themselves subject. At the same time, they invoke special exemptions, the protection of which becomes a gag they stuff into their own mouths, much to the government's satisfaction. The same is true of business-owners across the country, who make many decisions about their private businesses in response to tax policy to which they are not, in fact, subject at all (or would not be, if they were to learn the truth about the tax and the law, and act accordingly).

Indeed, as any conscious observer recognizes, the federal government now exercises vast influence in service to its own aggrandizement and the benefits of its clients, and has made itself a golden goose of power and pelf for control of which factions wage constant battle across an American legal and political landscape now lying largely in ruins as a consequence. I urge everyone to do what they can to spread the truth about the tax-- especially to their church leaders-- and help restore the restraints upon Leviathan for which the Founders so wisely provided.

The Insidious Encroachment Of The Collectivist Paradigm

The other day, I came across a news story in which what was once the merely descriptive phrase "first responders" made an appearance as a title. My hackles rose.

The use of the phrase "first responders" to describe emergency response workers has always been a bit awkward at best. For one thing, "first responders" necessarily implies "second responders", and so forth. One can only think of such expressions of cultural pathology as the "Crisis Counseling" industry, and the various and ever-increasing ranks of self-important, oxygen-stealing federal, state and local busybody bureaucracies, as next in line in the implicit hierarchy of place in this unhealthy pyramid of assumed interest and authority.

More importantly, the treatment of emergency workers as "first-responders" serves to push the REAL first responders-- the live, grown-up (or even not grown-up) autonomous human beings directly affected by the event-- into a subordinate, almost object-like role in the affair. Thanks to the adoption of these labels and the perspective they imply, the actual interested parties-- the ONLY actual interested parties in any legal or moral sense-- are relegated to the status of helpless, powerless victims-- mere wards of the state. By the same process, of course, those we've put on retainer to assist us when called upon are encouraged to deviate from their proper, "What can I do to help you?" role to an unnatural and unhealthy, "Keep quiet and do what you're told! We're in charge, here!" position.

The reality, of course, is that the various governmental emergency workers are only *the state's* "first responders", and when they are characterized as such without qualification, the label is an invitation to the rest of us to perceive ourselves as cogs in a great collectivist machine.

Cogs in the state's machine are looked after by the state for its own purposes, not ours. The fact that looking after us in the manner and to the degree which the state finds fitting may benefit some of us some of the time does not diminish this reality in any way. It is simply an expression of a political reality. We must be kept happy (or, at least, not severely discontented) or we will cause trouble; furthermore, our discontent (or sufficiently overt neglect) would undermine the fiction by which the state justifies its efforts to control so much of our wealth and authority, which control is, in turn, the means by which the state's operators and clients profit from its existence. Providing benefits to us is merely a means. Control is the end.

In short, when we allow (or worse, adopt) the use of the collectivist fiction's labels, we discipline our own habits of thought into self-destructive modes. When we use labels implying ourselves to be helpless victims needing rescue and protection by the state, and relegate ourselves to the role of mere subordinate beneficiaries of that succor, rather than the purchasers and masters of such emergency response efforts, we soon come to think of ourselves in that way, and encourage, if not pressure, others to do the same. The imposition of status as no more than a member of the hive is only a short step away once we have become habituated to thinking of ourselves that way, or when enough of our fellows have adopted such roles as to make independence highly difficult, if not impossible.

Does it seem like I'm picking at nits? Perhaps, but I don't think so. Words have great power, and those used as labels are often selected in service to an agenda. (Think of the label, "enhanced interrogation", for instance...) Furthermore, vague terms-- like "First Responders"-- tend to be picked for service to agendas of manipulation, rather than the honest and straightforward variety.

I don't like vagueness OR manipulation, and I don't like life in the hive. I'll stick with the honorable and more accurate labels of "cop" and "firefighter".

Non-Filing Only Benefits The IRS (Almost As Much As Filing Inaccurately)

Among the most pernicious, and persistent, bits of nonsense hindering many Americans otherwise ready and willing to stand and act on behalf of the rule of law in regard to the "income" tax is the notion that executing a tax return has inherently adverse legal effects. In fact, nearly the exact opposite is clearly and demonstrably true-- FAILING to execute a return (of one flavor or another, depending on circumstances) has inherently adverse legal consequences.

This is because the vast majority of Americans are made the subject of one or more "information returns" (W-2, 1099s, K-1s, etc.) each year, alleging that taxable-activity-related payments were made to those Americans. Indeed, pretty nearly EVERY work- or investment-related payment made to almost EVERY American during the course of EVERY year will be alleged to be connected with the exercise of a federal privilege (and thus to be taxable) by means of one of these instruments-- including payments which are NOT so related, and thus are NOT taxable.

Creating these information returns in connection with

every payment, and leaving the correction of those which are erroneous to the payee at the end of the year, has become the default procedure of most American businesses, thanks to a relentless tax agency campaign to encourage just such behavior, conducted over the decades. (Although this campaign includes strenuous efforts to conceal the legal import of information returns from those who create them, everyone is technically responsible for knowing such things.)

Obviously, any allegations on an information return-- as to both an amount paid, and its legal character-- are either correct, or incorrect. If the allegations are correct, it can only be because several other things are true, including that the American being testified about on the information return has voluntarily exercised a taxable privilege, and thereby voluntarily subjected himself or herself to the requirements of the relevant internal revenue laws. Submitting tax returns acknowledging such payments (and paying the resulting tax, of course) are among those requirements (which, arising as they do from a voluntary agreement, need not be published in the federal register, or conform to certain OMB provisions, etc.).

However, if those allegations are INCORRECT, a failure to answer them-- by introducing correcting testimony-- is to let them stand as the established facts-- *and thus to accept the same legal obligations that would arise if they WERE true*-- which include the requirements to file appropriate returns as noted above (and to pay the tax for which one is, by those unchallenged allegations, considered made liable). The law provides a means for introducing correcting testimony: **The filing of an accurate and proper tax return.** Thus, whether the allegations of others made on information returns are correct or incorrect, nothing but harm can result from a refusal to respond with a tax return.

So why would anyone refuse to file one?

The only reason I know of is that, decades ago, the idea arose in certain circles that the mere act of signing a tax return-- without regard to what is attested-to thereon-- performs a magical transformation of the signer into an entity whose every receipt is theoretically taxable. (The transformation must be imagined to be retroactive, by the way, as a return deals with events which have already transpired.) This notion, which is harbored even by those who will acknowledge that no language actually exists declaring such a thing to be true, draws primarily from two key misunderstandings of the law for its sustenance.

First, being ignorant of the "information return" mechanism in connection with which the use of a tax return for rebuttal arises, and therefore imagining the form's only use to be the acknowledgment of "income", those suffering from this notion conclude that to use the form is to invariably and necessarily assert (admit) that one is among those who MUST complete such a form-- that is, one who must acknowledge the receipt of "income"-- even when this is not true.

Intertwined with this assumption by those who view a tax return as a diabolical instrument-- and reflected by their disinterest in the actual content of the testimony submitted by way of the form-- is a belief that receipts acquire "income" taxable status because of who receives them (or, in variations on this misunderstanding, where the recipient is when receiving them, or the recipient's citizenship). In reality, neither of these notions is true in the least respect-- receipts which are "income" taxable are so <u>only</u> because of the activity in connection with which they are received. (For instance, that part of the president of the United State's earnings which is taxable is not so because he's president, or where he lives or works, etc., but because it is paid to him as a result of his activity as president. *"...the term gross income includes... ...in the case of the President of the United States... ...the compensation received as such."* If the president were to take a night job at a 7-Eleven just down Pennsylvania Avenue from the White House, his earnings from THAT job would NOT be taxable, even though he remained president and continued to be paid taxable compensation as such.) Further, nothing on a typical tax return automatically indicates or establishes the citizenship of the filer.

A complete forensic analysis of this "diabolical instrument" notion makes for a fascinating study, but it is beyond the scope of the current observation. It is sufficient to establish that this fear of signing a return is misconceived, and, more, extremely counter-productive. Earlier, I used the term "pernicious", and this is why: Whatever may be the individual motives of those who promote and embrace this fear, the fact is **the only interest served by a failure to file a tax return in the face of erroneous allegations of "income" paid is that of the government--** which is thus left free to treat the allegations on every information return as established facts; to calculate and demand taxes due as a consequence; and to consider itself on solid legal ground while doing both.

Simply put, there is nothing that can be done by an American about whom an erroneous information return has been created that is more contrary to his or her interests than not filing in response-- other than signing an erroneous return as well, and converting the presumptive evidence of the information return into established facts in the eyes of the law.

(I'll take advantage of this moment to briefly address another myth hindering those who wish to testify truthfully, but are discouraged in the face of complicated fears: Nothing anyone signs, or has signed, has the legal effect of making one's receipts "income", and thus taxable, when they otherwise are not; or of functionally compromising or contradicting the testimony ultimately appearing on a return. This includes W-4s, Social Security number applications, "employer identification number" applications, etc..

Each such signature may give color to presumptions about subsequent earnings, but nothing more than presumptions-- all of which are definitively resolved by the timely execution of an annual return. The only exceptions would be other instruments executed within the context of the revenue laws, explicitly declaring one's receipts to represent "income"-- either directly, or by declaring them to be "wages", or consequent to "trade or business" activity, etc.; and even such exceptions would do no more than create a conflict to the extent that they were out of harmony with the testimony on a subsequent return.)

Regarding The Limits Of The Law

"Rightful liberty is unobstructed action according to our will within limits drawn around us by the equal rights of others. I do not add 'within the limits of the law', because law is often but the tyrant's will, and always so when it violates the rights of the individual."

-Thomas Jefferson

***

"Verizon Communications -- the nation's second largest telecom company -- has admitted it turned over the private telephone records of its customers to the government 94,000 times since 2005. Verizon made the admission in a letter to Congressional Democrats. The Washington Post reports that in about 700 of the cases, Verizon turned over records even when federal investigators did not have a court order. AT&T and Qwest also responded to inquires from Congress but declined to say how often they handed over customer records. All three companies refused to answer most questions about their involvement in the government's domestic surveillance program." (10/16/07 democracynow.org)

AS EVERYONE READING THIS IS PROBABLY AWARE, the Washington crowd recently undertook the pretense of retroactively immunizing certain telecoms from legal liability for promiscuously cooperating with the Bush administration in committing countless Fourth Amendment felonies of the sort described above. This follows previous, similar pretenses at immunizing the executive department officials themselves for these and other egregious crimes, including systematic commission of assault, kidnapping, torture and a variety of war crimes, many of which are of so serious a nature as to bear death as the statutory penalty for violations thereof.

It will be noted that I say "pretenses"-- rather than "legislation" or "enactments"-- despite the fact that these pretenses have been ritualistically introduced, "considered", and voted on by both houses of Congress, and then subsequently signed by the President (with or without "statements"...). The reason I do so is simple: Neither Congress, nor any other branch (or combination of branches) of government in America has the least authority to actually enact laws accomplishing what is pretended to be accomplished by these rituals. In short, these rituals have NOT produced valid legislation-- they have produced mere fictions which we the people are invited to swallow as part of the Kool-Aid being passed out for years now by those who hate liberty and the rule of law.

The sordid reality is that the Washington political "Establishment" is a just a common perp which has taken stock of the carnage in its wake during a lull in its criminal frenzy. Looking about, it has noticed that blood is everywhere-- too much to clean up and conceal, and way more than it is willing to risk being made to pay for like a man. Time for a slight adjustment in the paradigm...

FOR A WHILE the perp attempted to rely on the easier lawyerly escape hatch of arguing that it didn't do what it clearly had done, or, in the alternative, did what it clearly had done but in "good faith" that doing it was proper and legal. It trotted out "legal opinions" it had conveniently issued to itself interpreting the prohibitions it had transgressed so as to permit the transgressions. This line of defense is reflected in both George Bush and Barack Obama's series of absurd declarations that those operating under their command "don't do torture"-- meaning, not as THEY define the term. It all depends on what the meaning of "is" is, remember?

However, the "redefining terms" dog hasn't been proving to be much of a hunter. Maybe the lies involved are just too small. (Speaking of which, have you noticed how much recent presidents have taken to channeling Eddie Haskell? Clinton did a fair job, but never quite managed Haskell's look of wide-eyed innocence when mouthing his lies. Bush had it cold after a few years of work to lose an early smirk; by his second term, you would swear that he actually believed what he was saying! Obama takes the prize, though-- he's actually advanced the role, and plays an Eddie Haskell who's all grown-up and so cock-sure as to be beyond redemption. What a talent!)

In any event, recent administrations (and complicit members of other parts of the political class) have long been constructing a backup for such mundane defensive tactics: The grand project of redefining the federal government itself. This is the project by which the whole concept that the executive and other elements of the "empowered" class are subject to any limitations whatsoever is done away with in practice, accompanied by the studied retention of a few bits of familiar Constitutional window-dressing in order to provide a psychic framework upon which the masses can hang illusions that things are being done in a "proper and lawful manner".

This grand project might well be called the *"Living Constitution"* project, although in recent years I've preferred to think of it as the *"It's just a g*******d piece of paper!"* project. A clunkier but more informative sobriquet might well be the *"Training Americans to abandon self-government and lose the ability to read and understand their own laws"* project.

The *"It's just a g*******d piece of paper!"* project is elaborate and often subtle in its implementation, but a general sense of its character can be illustrated by a quick sketch of one of the ways by which the project is being advanced. For example, "civics", as relevantly taught in the government schools to which the vast majority of America kids are committed, has become little more than a few lessons in the mechanics by which a bill becomes a law. Virtually no attention whatever is paid to the fact that American governments are strictly limited in their powers, such that while it may be true that any bill must go through certain steps on its way to enactment, only bills consistent with the limits can actually achieve standing as laws-of-the-land, while those not so consistent may well go through the motions, but even after doing so are nothing more than *"g*******d pieces of paper!"* (so to speak...).

The desired effect, of course, is to leave well-trained Americans with the sense that as long as pretty much ANY bill has gone through the ritualistic motions involved in becoming a law, the legitimacy of its actual content and consequence is not their business. All that matters at that point is having a functional understanding of what new positive acts are expected under the new decree, or what previously unhindered behavior will now result in punishment. If any malcontents DO happen to object to the decree, a judge or two will weigh in with a pronouncement, and that's that.

This cognitive reflex, once implanted in schoolkids, is then reinforced constantly by endlessly broadcast declarations from cooperative old-media talking-heads and self-serving beneficiaries, such as that, *"The Military Commissions Act authorizes the administration to..."*, or *"The USA PATRIOT ACT has gutted the Fourth Amendment and authorized warrantless wiretapping..."*, etc.-- every one of which invites us to imagine that something no one in government possesses the actual authority to do has, in fact, been done. Often enough, such declarations, when made by members of the media, are accompanied by soothing secondary disclaimers to the effect that, *"Civil libertarians plan to file suit..."*, or, *"Privacy experts challenge the Constitutionality..."*, but these secondary expressions don't make up for the FAILURE to say, in the first place, *"Congress purported to authorize the administration to _____ today, but guess what, folks! When we pulled out OUR copy of the Constitution, we discovered that Congress simply doesn't have the power to do that! Details at 6."*

ANYWAY, it was the grand project that was turned-to again in service of the telecom conspirators through the "retroactive immunity" pretense. I'll do here the job the media (at least the old media) didn't and won't be doing: Congress doesn't have the authority to retroactively immunize anyone from anything. Section 9 of Article 1 of the US Constitution specifically proscribes any ex post facto legislation: *"No Bill of Attainder or ex post facto Law shall be passed."* It didn't and wouldn't matter whether Congress went through the specified legislative rituals. Anything purporting to shield a malefactor from liability for its actions against someone else-- be that malefactor a telecom, an NSA geek, a CIA goon, George W. Bush or Barack Obama-- is null and void, even if those who currently fancy themselves to be "the deciders" intend to act otherwise for as long as they retain control of the institutional means by which the law is enforced.

The fact is, they're not "the deciders". We are, and we made our call long ago.

Remember that next time Katie Couric or Rush Limbaugh tells you what Congress did today. (And think about it again when you next find yourself wondering why it is that the old media and the political establishment were so hell-bent on thwarting Ron Paul's campaign...)

"... whenever the Legislators endeavour to take away, and destroy the Property of the People, or to reduce them to Slavery under Arbitrary Power, they put themselves into a state of War with the People, who are thereupon absolved from any farther Obedience ... [Power then] devolves to the People, who have a Right to resume their original Liberty, and, by the Establishment of a new Legislative (such as they shall think fit) provide for their own Safety and Security, which is the end for which they are in Society."

–John Locke

Regarding The Use Of Government-Printed Forms (Such As 1040s)

For most Americans, the question of whether anyone can be *required* to file a 1040 is entirely irrelevant. Indeed, it is worse-- it is a harmful distraction from understanding and addressing the reality of the "income" tax scheme. For most Americans, the real "file-or-not-file" question is, *"Do I file a return for my own good (voluntarily), or do I not file and instead accept liability for a tax I don't really owe, and kiss a whole lot of money, power and integrity good-bye?"*

This is so because the reason you (anyone) are presumed to be, and are legally treated as, liable for the tax, is that somebody has said that you engaged in a taxable activity (conventionally expressed by saying you "received income"). Period. That is the case regardless of whether you really did engage in a taxable activity, because it is only by way of such an assertion-- either made by someone who paid you, by you yourself, or by some contrivance of circumstantial evidence presented by a bureaucrat or a prosecutor-- that "the system" which enforces such liabilities can be made legally aware of the possibility that you might owe a tax.

If that assertion stands unanswered, "the system" which enforces the associated liabilities IS ENTITLED TO ENFORCE THEM, AND WILL DO SO. Look at it this way. When someone says you did something which, if true, would mean that you owe a debt, and you stand mute, you're going to be held to owe the debt. Judgment goes to the alleged creditor by default. What part of this is hard to understand?

Filing a proper, truthful and accurate return is the means provided by law for the definitive affirmation, or correction, of allegations about having engaged in an "income" taxable activity.

> *"And be it further enacted,...that any party, in his or her own behalf,...shall be permitted to declare, under oath or affirmation, the form and manner of which shall be prescribed by the Commissioner of Internal Revenue,... ...the amount of his or her annual income,... liable to be assessed,... and the same so declared shall be received as the sum upon which duties are to be assessed and collected."* Revenue Act of 1862, Sec. 93

> Senator Clark: *"Of course, you withhold not only from taxpayers but nontaxpayers."*
> Mr. Hardy: *"Yes."*
> ...
> Senator Danaher: *"I have only one other thought on that point. In the event of withholding from the owner of stock and no taxes due ultimately, where does he get his refund?"*
> Mr. Friedman: *"You're thinking of a corporation or an individual?"*
> Senator Danaher: *"I am talking about an individual."*
> Mr. Friedman: *"An individual will file an income tax return, and that income tax return will constitute an automatic claim for refund."*
> From a hearing before a subcommittee of the committee on finance, United States Senate, during the 77th Congress, Second Session on withholding provisions of the 1942 Revenue Act on August 21 and 22, 1942.

> *"Even if you do not otherwise have to file a return, you should file one to get a refund of any Federal income tax withheld."* From the instructions for the 2002 Form 1040
>
> *26 CFR § 301.6402-3 Special rules applicable to income tax.*
> *(a) In the case of a claim for credit or refund filed after June 30, 1976--*
> *(1) In general, in the case of an overpayment of income taxes, a claim for credit or refund of such overpayment shall be made on the appropriate income tax return.*
>
> *26 CFR § 301.6203-1 Method of assessment.*
> *... The amount of the assessment shall, in the case of tax shown on a return by the taxpayer, be the amount so shown,...*
> (... and even "$0.00" is an amount. By the way, those disturbed by the gratuitous use of the term "taxpayer" in this regulation should relax and read 'About 1040s And Claiming Refunds' in CtC.)

I said "the definitive affirmation, or correction,..." and that's exactly what I meant. Until a return is made, any presumptions favorable to any tax agency's desire to claim your money will be sustained. But once a return is made, that return rules, legally.

That said, let me clarify something for the benefit of those who have not actually read CtC, but have instead gotten what they imagine to be a sense of its lessons by way of the descriptions or explanations of others (which in some cases, at least, means from others who wish to discourage the reading of the book): What is taught about the law in CtC has nothing to do with any particular forms (or any particular formal procedures) as such. The discussion of certain treasury department forms in the book, such as 1040s, 4852s, etc., takes place not because these forms are integral to its message, but because the existence, nature and declared purposes of these forms help communicate that message.

CtC explains what is subject to the "income" tax, and why; how it is that much that is NOT subject to the tax is made to appear as though it were (and comes to be treated by the law as though it were); that there are, of necessity, remedies to the misapplication of the law; and why the whole subject is critically important. The part of the book that deals with remedies to the misapplication of the law discusses the basic principles of due process, and the inherent right of anyone being made the subject of a legal proceeding-- such as someone about whom tax-related allegations have being made-- to introduce his or her own testimony into the proceedings at a legally meaningful time and in a legally meaningful manner. The fact that the government itself produces and makes available instruments such as 1040s and 4852s by which this right can be readily exercised, and specifies the use of these instruments for this purpose, helps to make clear that this fundamental principle of law is fully integrated into the tax structure. That integration is not dependent on the existence of such forms, of course. One's rights remain fully intact, whether a ready means of exercising them has been helpfully provided by government or not.

Nor does the existence of forms like 4852s and 1040s limit or shape the right to testify. Such forms simply facilitate the exercise of that right. One's right to testify is not dependent on the use, or controlled by the format, of some prescribed or pre-printed form or another. If erroneous testimony has been made on a W-2, for instance, the victim of the offense could rebut that testimony on a napkin or a piece of birch-bark with just as much fundamental legal significance as doing so on a "Form 4852", as long as all pertinent assertions are meaningfully addressed. The same is true of the broader testimony typically submitted by way of a 1040. There are only a few "rules" about the validity of a tax return: That the instrument purports to be a return; that it contains sufficient information by which a tax liability can be calculated; that it represents an honest effort to abide by the tax laws; and that it be executed under penalties of perjury. These simple requirements can be met without the use of a "Form 1040":

> *"Anyway, as we held in Salberg, the obligation to file a tax return stems from 26 U.S.C. 7203, not from any agency's demand. The Paperwork Reduction Act does not repeal 7203. " "...7203 requires a "return" but does not define that word or require anyone to use Form 1040, or any "official" form at all. All that is required is a complete and candid report of income."*
>
> 7th Circuit Court Of Appeals, United States v. Partridge, (2007)

(Also, see the IRS Office of Chief Counsel Memorandum at www.losthorizons.com/tax/taximages/OCCO107035.pdf.)

However, the practical utility of testimony submitted on napkins or birch-bark is pretty obviously compromised, in the sense that any bureaucratic recipient of such testimony will be unable to handle it in the routine manner. Further, and more importantly, the chances of any home-made version of a testimonial form actually comprehending all the aspects of the law to which it is intended to relate are remote. If this IS accomplished, the home-made form will end up being identical in every significant respect to the form being spurned, making the effort a pointless exercise.

To summarize, then: No aspect of the provisions of law involved in rebutting, or otherwise responding to, "income" allegations discussed in CtC rely upon, or inherently relate to, forms such as 1040s, 4852s, etc.. But when such forms are prescribed and provided, obvious benefits accompany their informed, accurate and truthful deployment.

Can Anyone Be Required To Accept A Legal Infirmity In Order To Exercise A Right?

It should be clear without extended explanation that under no circumstances can the exercise of a right be the occasion of the diminishment, or impairment, of any other right. For purposes of this discussion, this means that the exercise of one's right to answer the testimony of others about one's receipts, and to assert one's claim for the recovery of property put into the hands of a government against the possibility of the arising of a tax liability during the relevant period, cannot result, in and of itself, in any legal infirmity:

> *"...a statute which imposes a tax upon an assumption of fact which the [presumed] taxpayer is forbidden to controvert is so arbitrary and unreasonable that it cannot stand under the Fourteenth Amendment."* United States Supreme Court, Heiner v. Donnan 285 U.S. 312 (1932)

> *"...irrebuttable presumptions have long been disfavored under the Due Process Clauses of the Fifth and Fourteenth Amendments."* United States Supreme Court, Vlandis v. Kline, 412 U.S. 441 (1973)

> *"A fundamental requirement of due process is "the opportunity to be heard." Grannis v. Ordean, 234 U.S. 385, 394 . It is an opportunity which must be granted at a meaningful time and in a meaningful manner."* United States Supreme Court, Armstrong v. Manzo, 380 U.S. 545 (1965)

The exchange of evidence by way of returns (information returns and 1040s, etc..) IS the "meaningful time and manner" involved in the "income" tax, so much so that penalties can be imposed on someone about whom an information return is created by someone else, should that person fail to file a response. Further, the testimony of that information return will be taken as true even when doing so significantly disadvantages its silent subject.

So, no burden or punishment, either civil or criminal, can attend the exercise of one's right to testify by way of a tax return, with the sole and indirect exception being that the testimony submitted, like all testimony, must be affirmed under oath. The statutory structure provided by Congress fully complies with this fundamental legal principle, ensuring that timely testimony to whatever is true, complete and correct to the best of the knowledge and belief of the filer invites no adverse consequences whatsoever.

Indeed, to attempt to burden, punish, prevent, discourage or even merely influence such testimony without direct personal knowledge of the matter being attested to, is criminalized-- as a misdemeanor at least, if not a felony. For instance:

> *Title 18 § 1512. Tampering with a witness, victim, or an informant*
> *(b) Whoever knowingly uses intimidation, threatens, or corruptly persuades another person, or attempts to do so, or engages in misleading conduct toward another person, with intent to—*
> *(1) influence, delay, or prevent the testimony of any person in an official proceeding;*
> *(2) cause or induce any person to—*
> *(A) withhold testimony, or withhold a record, document, or other object, from an official proceeding;*
> *shall be fined under this title or imprisoned not more than ten years, or both.*
> *(d) Whoever intentionally harasses another person and thereby hinders, delays, prevents, or dissuades any person from—*
> *(1) attending or testifying in an official proceeding;*
> *or attempts to do so, shall be fined under this title or imprisoned not more than one year, or both.*

(The filing of a tax return, particularly one which involves rebutting the testimony of another filer, is every bit an "official proceeding"-- but even if doubts were entertained in that regard, the testimony made on a return is unquestionably relevant to, and anticipatory of, more formal judicial contests of several varieties, and Congress has thoughtfully provided that,

> *(f) For the purposes of this section—*

> *(1) an official proceeding need not be pending or about to be instituted at the time of the offense;*)

I'll say it one more time: However much some may have convinced themselves to the contrary, no legitimate criminal or civil penalty, loss of rights or property, alienation of citizenship or other civil diminishment, obligatory assumption of contract, or infirmity of any other kind whatsoever is, or can be, attendant upon the making of an honest tax return as a response to an information return created by another or to claim the return of one's property; rather, the precise opposite is true-- one or more of these ill effects can result from FAILING to respond.

The above being true, is it possible that honest, good-faith use of a form prescribed by the Secretary of the Treasury for the making of a return can, secretly or otherwise, impose or establish a criminal or civil penalty, loss of rights, alienation of citizenship or other civil diminishment, obligatory assumption of contract, or infirmity of any other kind whatsoever? Obviously not.

Is A 1040 A "Tax Return For A U.S. Individual" Or A "U.S. Tax Return For An Individual"? Does It Matter?

I deliberately included the expression "good-faith" in the last paragraph because a portion of those to whom these words are addressed do their mental stumbling over the issue of WHICH form to use, even if they recognize their unencumbered right to make a return. These folks have been convinced to forego the exercise of their rights by the proposition that the form they use in that exercise imposes upon them the status or legal characteristics of some class of persons which is bureaucratically intended to use that form. That is, if there is a class of persons of unique or specialized legal status known as "U.S. Individuals", for instance, and one uses a form specified as being for the use of "U.S. Individuals", one thus adopts the status (and related infirmities, if any) of a "U.S. Individual".

However, even if a form bore an unambiguous specification as to those for whose use it is intended, it's not that easy to change one's legal status, and, in any case, the law does not favor complicated and irrational presumptions over the simple and obvious. If one were to use a form intended exclusively for the use of some group or class to which one did not actually belong, all it would presumptively mean is that *one had made a mistake*.

That the use of the wrong form is/was an inadvertent mistake would be self-evident if that use caused membership in a special group, attendant upon which is some legal infirmity to which the filer is not already subject. No one in their right mind would do such a thing, and one who did so, having self-evidently been ignorant of the legal import of their actions, would be relieved of the consequences of those actions. One cannot be bound by mere presumptions arising from a legal process undertaken in ignorance of the consequences. If the mistake was not thus self-evident (because no ill consequences are attendant upon the use of the form), it would be readily established by declaration, if necessary, although I have yet to see a single case in which anyone has ever been accused, or even notified, of "Using The Wrong Form" in the fashion or context being discussed here.

As noted in the subtitle above, the intended use of the "Form 1040 U.S. Individual Income Tax Return is certainly not unambiguously confined to "U.S. Individuals"-- which is not, in any case, a defined category of persons-- even if it being so would raise one's hackles. Looking at the specifications for its use relevant to most Americans:

> *§ 301.6402-3 Special rules applicable to income tax.*
> *(a) In the case of a claim for credit or refund filed after June 30, 1976—*

> *(1) In general, in the case of an overpayment of income taxes, a claim for credit or refund of such overpayment shall be made on the appropriate income tax return.*
> ...
> *(5) A properly executed individual, fiduciary, or corporation original income tax return or an amended return (on 1040X or 1120X if applicable) shall constitute a claim for refund or credit within the meaning of section 6402 and section 6511 for the amount of the overpayment disclosed by such return (or amended return)*
> ...
> *(e) In the case of a nonresident alien individual or foreign corporation, the appropriate income tax return on which the claim for refund or credit is made must contain the tax identification number of the taxpayer required pursuant to section 6109 and the entire amount of income of the taxpayer subject to tax, even if the tax liability for that income was fully satisfied at source through withholding under chapter 3 of the Internal Revenue Code (Code). ...*

(There IS an alternative version of the 1040, known as "Form 1040NR", which is particularly adapted to special provisions of the law regarding the taxation of "income" received under certain circumstances by "non-resident aliens". However, while the IRS instructions for "non-resident aliens" specify the use of that form in lieu of a standard 1040 when those special provisions are being exploited, or for non-resident aliens who are *"engaged in a trade or business in the United States, or have any other U.S. source income on which the tax was not fully paid by the amount withheld"*, the same instructions merely say that a return must be filed, without specification as to version, when a refund is being sought.)

Furthermore, the positions adopted by the IRS Office of Chief Counsel (OCC) regarding the content of a legitimate, valid 1040 (OCC memoranda about which have long been posted on this site for the benefit of anyone not too busy haring off after the latest "silver-bullet" distraction) make clear that a 1040 has no hidden agenda or effect. The OCC has admitted that any document merely purporting to be a "return", containing sufficient information by which a tax liability can be calculated, representing an honest effort to abide by the tax laws, and signed as an affidavit serves as a fully sufficient substitute for a 1040; by the same token a 1040 itself need have nothing more than these same characteristics to be a fully valid return, sufficient for all purposes for which the form is designed.

The OCC has also acknowledged that the addition of a declaration to a 1040 that signing the form is not to be taken as a waiver of any rights or an acceptance of any legal infirmity has no effect on the validity of the form. That is, a 1040 serves as a legitimate and fully functional tax return even when suspected secret agenda or hidden legal effects have been pre-emptively nullified.

Because there are none...

Only The Nominal "Profit" Portion Of "Income" Is Taxed, But That Doesn't Mean All Profit Is "Income"

Chinking Up Another Cognitive Crack

A little confusion has arisen in some quarters due to the nominally "profitable" characteristic of what qualifies as "taxable" under the "income" tax laws, and a certain casual use of the term 'profit' in some court cases and Congressional records.

Congress HAS provided that it will only tax what it deems to be the "profit" portion of the larger class of what qualifies as "gross income":

> *"... 'income', as used in the statute should be given a meaning so as not to include everything that comes in. The true function of the words 'gains' and 'profits' is to limit the meaning of the word 'income'."*
> United States Supreme Court, So. Pacific v. Lowe, 247 U.S. 330, (1918)

Indeed, it is that distinction that constitutes the substance of most of the tax-related litigation over the years. In such cases, the litigants don't dispute that any revenues involved are "income", but simply disagree over what portion of it is taxable based on either the idiosyncratic specifications in the statutes or the issue of what has actually been realized as bona fide "gains and profit".

The distinction is, of course, only nominal and highly arbitrary. For instance, all "income" received as "wages" over the statutory exemption amount is generally deemed to be "profit" in the context of the tax, and always has been. The exemption and percentages have changed over the years, but the general construction has not.

> *"The statute looks, with some exceptions, for subjects of taxation only to annual gains, profits, and income. Its general language is 'that there shall be levied, collected, and paid annually upon the gains, profits, and income of every person,' derived from certain specified sources, a tax of five per cent., and that this tax shall be 'assessed, collected, and paid upon the gains, profits, and income for the year ending the 31st of December next preceding the time for levying, collecting, and paying said tax.' This language has only one meaning, and that is that the assessment, collection, and payment prescribed are to be made upon the annual products or income of one's property or labor, or such gains or profits as may be realized from a business transaction begun and completed during the preceding year."*
> United States Supreme Court, Gray v. Darlington, 82 U.S. 63 (1872)

Nonetheless, this distinction helps illuminate the wording in the statutory definition of "gross income" as "gains, profits and income". To qualify, any given receipt must represent a profitable gain, as provided by statute , as well as being within the overall class of "income".

However, the distinction regarding 'profit' drawn within the context of the tax does not serve to draw profit which has NOT proceeded from the conduct of a taxable activity (and is thus already within the class of "income") into the ambit of the tax. (Merely realizing profit is not, itself, a taxable activity, even if it is realized as dividends or in some other "unearned" form.)

Unfortunately, overly casual use of the term "profit" in reference to what is taxed under the "income" tax, without the clarifying particulars, can mislead those unschooled in the true nature of the tax to the erroneous conclusion that any revenue which is greater than mere compensation, or represents a gain on an initial investment, qualifies as "income". Indeed, there has been an entire book written endeavoring to argue that the "income" tax applies to all "profit" of whatever provenance, based on this misunderstanding.

Not only is this plainly wrong, but it is "politically" disastrous, as well. Want to know how to alienate the entire business community from any interest in, and support for, the "tax honesty" movement? Encourage them to imagine that the law, even when properly understood and applied, holds all profit-- whether federally-connected or not-- to be inherently taxable...

At the same time, casual use of "profit" in this fashion will also lead the unschooled to the dangerous conclusion that anything anyone reasonably deems to not constitute 'profit' is thus untouched and untouchable by the tax, all other considerations and factors notwithstanding. Everyone should undertake to correct this error-- and those who promote it out of ignorance of the true nature of the tax-- whenever encountered.

> *"The 'Government' is an abstraction, and its possession of property largely constructive. Actual possession and custody of Government property nearly always are in someone who is not himself the Government but acts in its behalf and for its purposes. He may be an officer, an agent, or a contractor. His personal advantages from the relationship by way of salary, profit, or beneficial personal use of the property may be taxed..."*
> United States Supreme Court, United States v. County of Allegheny, 322 US 174 (1944)

(For more on this subject, see the second half of 'The Supreme Court And The Meaning Of "Income"' in CtC.)

"They hate our freedoms..."

...or so we have been endlessly told by George Bush, Dick Cheney, and their various fellow travelers in the think tanks, the munitions industry, Congress and the press. Good sound-bite line, certainly. Also demonstrable nonsense, of course. A brief contemplation of the fact that Switzerland, to pick one example, is not a target of this allegedly ideological hatred will make obvious that the mere enjoyment of freedom is not what enrages those who are enraged against the United States.

Certainly if "freedoms" were the casus belli, *someplace* other than America and its fellow-meddlers in Muslim lands would be the target of attacks by the same "extremists". For one thing, even a neocon organization like The Heritage Foundation acknowledges that several countries are more free than the USA; a more objective assessment has the USA even further down the list.

In fact, if "hatred of freedoms" is really the issue, America is not likely to be a target at all. Just as the United States somehow never gets around to actually attacking the really dangerous adversaries like China or Russia even when supposedly standing in firm *"bear any burden, pay any price"* opposition to evil regimes and instead chooses to pursue considerably softer targets in expressing this ideological commitment, any group actually motivated by a simple "hatred of freedoms" would be guided by the same considerations.

An ideologically-motivated group is one that intends to prevail, not accomplish its own utter destruction. Such a group would express its ire by choosing the nose of someone other than the most overwhelmingly dangerous adversary in human history to punch.

For instance, if the mere "possession of freedoms" by others was the burr under the Muslim extremist saddle, bombing the pot-smoking, prostitute-riddled, assisted-suicide practicing Netherlands would scratch that itch nicely, while making it personal to nothing more fearsome than the Dutch Army (which I presume they have, without ever having actually seen the two words together in the modern era...). Similarly, flying a plane or two into the unquestionably far more economically free-wheeling skyscrapers of Hong Kong or Singapore makes a great deal more sense than targeting the far less free New York, even without consideration of the fact that such an attack on (normally) heavily defended New York would be expected to fail...

And how does attacking the Pentagon fit into this *"They hate our freedoms"* assertion?

The fact is, any animosity harbored by Muslims against the United States has nothing to do with our possession or enjoyment of freedoms. The closest relationship between those two things that could be argued is that some Muslims hate the United States for what it has been able to promiscuously do in their backyards by virtue of the enormous wealth our possession and enjoyment of freedom has made possible (the transfer of which into the hands of the State as a preliminary to the conduct of these offensive little imperial adventures, has, ironically enough, been managed by a systematic erosion of American freedom...).

Anyway, my point here is not the real cause of animosity toward America, either as it was before the Bush administration and friends began the really serious trashing of the Muslim Middle East that's gone on over the last six years, or since then. I'll leave that to the very capable hands of Ron Paul, the CIA, various public officials not wedded to the neocon agenda, and anyone with more than an eighth-grade education.

What I want to observe here is that IF a hatred of our freedoms IS an explicit motivation for the declared enemies of America, as is claimed by the afore-mentioned loud voices, then any deliberate act or policy by which those freedoms are diminished constitutes the plain and unambiguous *"giving of aid and comfort to our enemies"*. Acts or policies which diminish our freedoms-- such as warrantless searches, the suspension of habeas corpus, the adoption of internal passports, the suppression of speech, efforts to enforce an unapportioned capitation, etc., etc.-- have always been unconstitutional, and have always been solely in the interests of those opposed to the principles of individual sovereignty that define America. But within the context of this war-mongering "they hate our freedoms" contrivance, it is <u>particularly</u> (and ironically) the case that any such act or policy undeniably and unambiguously constitutes TREASON.

***

"Necessity is the plea for every infringement of human freedom. It is the argument of tyrants; it is the creed of slaves."
-William Pitt

Needless to say, conducting assaults on our freedoms in the name of "necessity" or "security", or by way of clever or obscure legal arguments, changes the practical reality-- and thus the criminal character-- of the offense not one little bit. "I had to do it" is not a viable exculpatory argument for any kind of aggression against the American people (or anyone else), or against the Constitution itself. To say *"I had to gut (or ignore) the Fourth Amendment in order to protect us all from attack!"*, for example, is no different legally than saying *"I had to break into the Jones' house and tie them all up just in case they might decide to smuggle a criminal into the neighborhood!"* Put more plainly, what is being argued is, *"I had to seize and exercise a power over you illegally in order to protect you all from those who might illegally exercise power over you...!"*

Sorry, no.

And how faithless an expression! At its core this argument, in whatever variation it manifests itself (and only to the degree to which it might be imagined to be sincerely meant), is one of fundamental distrust of the principles of liberty and of the Constitution. The making of this argument, in whatever variation and whether in the context of war, or in service to any other State ambition hindered by the restraints of its charter, is an expression of profound disrespect for the instrument to which every federal and state office-holder in this country has sworn an oath of fealty!

Thus, even to the degree that this argument is sincerely meant, it is contemptibly faithless in both senses of the word. To the degree that it is mere mendacity, it is far worse. Either way, it must neither be tolerated nor forgiven.

This puts me in mind of another fatuous and irony-laden sound-bite often heard from the "they hate our freedoms" crew: *"If we don't fight the enemies of freedom over there, we'll have to fight them here!"*

Guess what...

On "Citizenship", Serving On Juries, Voting And The Fourteenth Amendment

I recently became aware that some in the "tax honesty" community are promoting behavior which is likely (if not guaranteed) to result in the actor being denied opportunities to serve on a jury. In fact, it appears that this is precisely what is intended by at least one such advocate, who advises his readers to reply to a jury summons with the submission of a letter in which elements of the affidavit of citizenship and residency included with the summons are challenged. As though it is something to be proud of, this fellow claims on his website that, *"To date, this jury letter has had a 100% success rate at stopping the jury summons process..."*

The reason given for this bizarre advocacy is to prevent a respondent to a jury summons from declaring himself to be a "citizen of the United States", which declaration is imagined to impose a legal infirmity. It is imagined that to make this declaration risks transforming oneself from a citizen of one of the several States into a "citizen of the federal government", which is perceived to be a lesser status-- indeed, little more than a serf, with no inherent, unalienable rights-- as though somehow the federal government has the power to strip people of their unalienable, inherent rights. The perspective on the meaning of "resident" is even more strained.

The language of the Fourteenth Amendment is, in large part, the inspiration for these delusions. The meaning and effect of that amendment (and the legality of its adoption, for that matter) is a subject upon which much could be written, and I do not intend to go into it here. (Nor will I discuss here the facts that the expression "citizen of the United States" predates the Fourteenth Amendment-- which wasn't "adopted" until 1868-- by 79 years; or that, absent a specification to the contrary or a clear contextual implication, the expression "The United States" as generally used means "The States United"*.) It will suffice for now to refer to the following words of the United States Supreme Court, reflecting the fact that when one or more of the several States cedes territory to the federal government by any means or for any purpose, it does not hand over the inhabitants of that territory as "federal (or "United States") citizen" slaves at the same time, the Fourteenth Amendment notwithstanding:

> *"And as the guaranty of a trial by jury, in the third article, implied a trial in that mode, and according to the settled rules of common law, the enumeration, in the sixth amendment, of the rights of the accused in criminal prosecutions, is to be taken as a declaration of what those rules were, and is to be referred to the anxiety of the people of the states to have in the supreme law of the land, and so far as the agencies of the general government were concerned, a full and distinct recognition of those rules, as involving the fundamental rights of life, liberty, and property.* ***This recognition was demanded and secured for the benefit of all the people of the United States, as well those permanently or temporarily residing in the District of Columbia as those residing or being in the several states. There is nothing in the history of the constitution, or of the original amendments, to justify the assertion that the***

> ***people of this District may be lawfully deprived of the benefit of any of the constitutional guaranties of life, liberty, and property;..."***
> United States Supreme Court, Callan v. Wilson, 127 U.S. 540 (1888) (Emphasis added)
>
> *"The congress of the United States, being empowered by the constitution 'to exercise exclusive legislation in all cases whatsoever' over the seat of the national government, has the entire control over the District of Columbia for every purpose of government,-national or local. It may exercise within the District all legislative powers that the legislature of a state might exercise within the state, and may vest and distribute the judicial authority in and among courts and magistrates, and regulate judicial proceedings before them, as it may think fit,* ***so long as it does not contravene any provision of the constitution of the United States.*** *Kendall v. U. S. (1838) 12 Pet. 524, 619; Mattingly v. District of Columbia (1878) 97 U.S. 687, 690; Gibbons v. District of Columbia (1886) 116 U.S. 404, 407, 6 S. Sup. Ct. 427."*
> United States Supreme Court, Capital Traction Co. v. Hof, 174 U.S. 1 (1899) (Emphasis added, and, for those who persist in misunderstanding or denying the point, the provisions of the Constitution which Congress cannot contravene even in DC include the prohibition against unapportioned direct taxes...)

(See your CtC Companion CD for both of these rulings in their entirety)

I will further present the following on the general nature and meaning of "citizen of the United States":

> *"Looking at the Constitution itself we find that it was ordained and established by 'the people of the United States, and then going further back, we find that these were the people of the several States that had before dissolved the political bands which connected them with Great Britain, and assumed a separate and equal station among the powers of the earth, and that had by Articles*

of Confederation and Perpetual Union, in which they took the name of 'the United States of America,' entered into a firm league of friendship with each other for their common defence, the security of their liberties and their mutual and general welfare, binding themselves to assist each other against all force offered to or attack made upon them, or any of them, on account of religion, sovereignty, trade, or any other pretence whatever._

Whoever, then, was one of the people of either of these States when the Constitution of the United States was adopted, became ipso facto a citizen-a member of the nation created by its adoption. He was one of the persons associating together to form the nation, and was, consequently, one of its original citizens. As to this there has never been a doubt. Disputes have arisen as to whether or not certain persons or certain classes of persons were part of the people at the time, but never as to their citizenship if they were.

...

The United States has no voters in the States of its own creation. The elective officers of the United States are all elected directly or indirectly by State voters. The members of the House of Representatives are to be chosen by the people of the States, and the electors in each State must have the qualifications requisite for electors of the most numerous branch of the State legislature. Senators are to be chosen by the legislatures of the States, and necessarily the members of the legislature required to make the choice are elected by the voters of the State. Each State must appoint in such manner, as the legislature thereof may direct, the electors to elect the President and Vice-President."

United States Supreme Court, Minor v. Happersett, 88 U.S. 162 (1874)

and that of residence:

"Now, the point that you are to decide, gentlemen, is this: Did the plaintiff, Gus. B. Ohle, at any time leave the state of Iowa for the purpose of taking up, actually

> *and in good faith, his residence and citizenship in Illinois? Now, I use the word 'residence,' meaning this: It would not be sufficient merely to show that he went and resided in the sense of living in Illinois. Residence is evidence of the citizenship. You are ultimately to find whether he became a citizen of Illinois. In deciding that question you have a right to consider what he did in the matter of residence; that is, where he actually lived; the place he occupied, what we ordinarily mean by the term living. ...*[That is] *that he had the intent at that time,-bona fide, actual intent,-of settling in Illinois."*
>
> The lower court jury instruction challenged and upheld in the United States Supreme Court in Chicago & NW RR Co. v. Ohle, 117 U.S. 123 (1886)

(Both of these rulings are well worth reading in their entirety. See www.losthorizons.com/CitizenshipCases.pdf.)

The citizenship and residency qualifications for being a juror are simply that one be an American citizen, and that one be resident in the judicial district deemed to have been appropriate for the trial which will be conducted. This is true in federal as well as state trials. As the U.S. District Court for the Southern District of Indiana helpfully puts it:

> *QUALIFICATIONS FOR FEDERAL JURY SERVICE*
>
> 1. *Must be a citizen of the United States of America, at least 18 years of age, who resided for a period of 1 year within the judicial district.*

The District Court for the Middle District of Florida puts it this way:

> *1) Must be a citizen of the United States of America, at least 18 years of age, who has resided for a period of 1 year within the judicial district;*

Some other districts express the same thing using only "United States citizen" or "citizen of the United States", because in the context of jury duty, they all mean the same thing. Just as they all mean the same thing in the context of voting in federal elections, by the way... (By the way, judicial districts, and residing therein, also have no nefarious, secret character. A judicial district is just an imaginary subdivision of the population to which a serving court is assigned, in what is intended to be an equitable distribution of resources.)

Oddball notions abound, of course, and many are harmless eccentricities. This one is not harmless. The power of the jury is the most significant check on the exercise of tyranny provided for by the Founders short of the power secured by the Second Amendment. The very idea that members of the "tax honesty" community-- arguably the most plugged-in, courageous and reliably principled Americans gracing this great country-- are being persuaded to withhold their wisdom and courage from the jury room where the fate of their neighbors is determined, and where judgment is rendered on the validity of every law which our servant government's seek to impose upon us all, is appalling! I call upon everyone to do everything possible to see to it that this nonsense goes no further than it already has. For more on this critically important issue, see 'The Power Of The Jury' in '<u>Upholding the Law And Other Observations</u>'

*But see, for instance the following from '<u>Bouvier's Dictionary of Law</u>', 6th edition, 1856:

> CITIZEN. 4. A citizen of the United States, residing in any state of the Union, is a citizen of that state. 6 Pet. 761 Paine, 594;1 Brock. 391; 1 Paige, 183 Metc. & Perk. Dig. h. t.; vide 3 Story's Const. '1687 Bouv. Inst. Index, b. t.; 2 Kent, Com. 258; 4 Johns. Ch. R. 430; Vatt. B. 1, c. Id, '212; Poth. Des Personnes, tit. 2, s. 1. Vide Body Politic; Inhabitant.
>
> UNITED STATES OF AMERICA. The name of this country. The United States, now thirty-one in number, are Alabama, Arkansas, Connecticut, Delaware, Florida, Georgia, Illinois, Indiana, Iowa, Kentucky, Louisiana, Maine, Maryland, Massachusetts, Michigan, Mississippi, Missouri, New Hampshire, New Jersey, New York North

> Carolina, Ohio, Pennsylvania, Rhode Island, South Carolina, Tennessee, Texas, Vermont, Virginia, Wisconsin, and California.

Also, see the words of the United States Supreme Court, after an exhaustive review of the subject in "United States v. Wong Kim Ark, 169 U.S. 649 (1898)":

> *"The real object of the Fourteenth Amendment of the Constitution, in qualifying the words, "All persons born in the United States" by the addition "and subject to the jurisdiction thereof," would appear to have been* [merely] *to exclude, by the fewest and fittest words (besides children of members of the Indian tribes, standing in a peculiar relation to the National Government, unknown to the common law), the two classes of cases -- children born of alien enemies in hostile occupation and children of diplomatic representatives of a foreign State -- both of which, as has already been shown, by the law of England and by our own law from the time of the first settlement of the English colonies in America, had been recognized exceptions to the fundamental rule of citizenship by birth within the country. Calvin's Case, 7 Rep. 1, 18b; Cockburn on Nationality, 7; Dicey Conflict of Laws, 177; Inglis v. Sailors' Snug Harbor, 3 Pet. 99, 155; 2 Kent Com. 39, 42."*

"Income" Doesn't Mean "Corporate Profit"

There is a long-standing misinterpretation of several Supreme Court case declarations which concludes that "income" means nothing more than 'corporate profit'. This conclusion arises from taking language from these rulings either out of context or incompletely, and from reading "only" where the word is actually not found. The key phrase misconstrued in service to this error is the line from Merchants Loan & Trust Co. v. Smietanka, 255 US 509, (1921):

> *"The word (income) must be given the same meaning in all of the income Tax Acts of Congress that was given to it in the Corporation Excise Tax Act of 1909, and what the meaning is has now become definitely settled by decisions of this court."*

Deriving from this language the meaning desired by the "income only means corporate profit" advocates is a truly gross disregard of its context, for just prior to making the above declaration, the court has listed the "definition" to which it refers:

> *"Income may be defined as a gain derived from capital, from labor, or from both combined, provided it be*

> *understood to include profit gained through sale or conversion of capital assets."*

Nothing in that definition is confined to corporate activity, and in fact, the context of this definition itself (which is quoted from Eisner v. Macomber, 252 U.S. 189, 207 (1921)) involves nothing but a question as to when receipts do and do not have the necessary character of 'gains'-- without regard as to the nature of the recipient. Indeed, in 'Merchants Loan' itself, the recipients involved were a woman and her four children (through a trustee)-- **not a corporation**.

Snippets of language from other cases are similarly misconstrued in service to this conceptual error. Prominent among these are the following cites from Flint vs. Stone Tracy Co. 220 U.S. 107 (1911):

> *"...when imposed in this manner it is a tax upon the doing of business, with the advantages which inhere in the peculiarities of corporate or joint stock organization of the character described. As the latter organizations share many benefits of corporate organization, it may be described generally as a tax upon the doing of business in a corporate capacity."*

and,

> *"The tax under consideration, as we have construed the statute, may be described as an excise upon the particular privilege of doing business in a corporate capacity, i. e., with the advantages which arise from corporate or quasi corporate organization; or, when applied to insurance companies, for doing the business of such companies. As was said in the Thomas Case, 192 U. S. supra, the requirement to pay such taxes involves the exercise of privileges, and the element of absolute and unavoidable demand is lacking. If business is not done in the manner described in the statute, no tax is payable."*

What is missed by those whose seize upon this language is that the issue here was not the definition of "income" generally, but only what "income" the Corporate Excise Tax Act specifically taxed-- which was that realized by corporations and a certain short list of other types of artificial entities. Certain other types of artificial entities were excluded from this list, which was the basis for the challenge which led to the language cited above.

The court rules that Congress is within its latitude in choosing to tax only "income" enjoyed by the listed recipients, and not others-- just as Congress is able to selectively impose a tariff on imports of a certain type, or from certain countries, and not others. Thus, the references in this language to corporate activity merely reiterate the distinctions drawn in the act itself.

As the Harvard Law Review observes in its 1910 publication "Federal Income Tax On Corporations":

> *"The new federal tax is expressed to be on corporations* doing business*, and is measured by the* net income *of such corporations. There are therefore three factors which determine whether the tax shall be levied,-- (1) existence as a corporation, (2) doing business, (3) the receipt of a certain income. Unless all of these three are present in a given case, no tax is levied; if they are all present, a tax is levied.*
>
> *Therefore according to the rules laid down above, this is a tax upon those several factors. The Tax can be avoided by ridding oneself of any one of these factors."*

"Income is only corporate profit" advocates, however, read an "only" into this language of the rulings where one does not exist. (The most substantial issue in Flint vs. Stone Tracy, by the way, was whether corporations chartered by union state governments could be subjected to the federal government's tax, even insofar as they enjoyed profits from federally-connected activities ["income"]. The court declares that they can, excepting only those engaged in activities of a strictly state governmental character-- and thus intimately related to, and partaking of, the sovereignty of the state.)

Another example of an oft-cited but misunderstood snippet is the following from Doyle v. Mitchell Bros. Co., 247 US 179 (1918):

> *"Whatever difficulty there may be about a precise and scientific definition of 'income,' it imports, as used here, something entirely distinct from principal or capital either as a subject of taxation or as a measure of the tax; conveying rather the idea of gain or increase arising from corporate activities."*

As in the errors observed above, this line is misconstrued due to a disregard of its context. Doyle v. Mitchell Bros. Co. is also a case arising under the 'Corporate Excise Act of 1909'. Consequently, the phrase *"corporate activities"* at the end of this quote could be replaced with, *"activities of the entities taxed under the act"* and convey precisely the same meaning as that of the language used. What the court is really and merely distinguishing in this phrase is "gain" as against "capital on hand". The following paragraph of the opinion makes this clear:

> *"Understanding the term in this natural and obvious sense, it cannot be said that a conversion of capital assets invariably produces income. If sold at less than cost, it produces rather loss or outgo. Nevertheless, in many if not in most cases there results a gain that properly may be accounted as a part of the 'gross income' received 'from all sources'; and by applying to this the authorized deductions we arrive at 'net income.' In order to determine whether there has been gain or loss, and the amount of the gain if any, we must withdraw from the gross proceeds an amount sufficient to restore the capital value that existed at the commencement of the period under consideration."*

***

The most egregious clash between plain reality and the advocacy of the "income only means corporate profit" argument can be seen by examining the "income" tax provisions reflected in Subtitle C of 26 USC. These provisions clearly declare themselves to be taxes on, or provisions involving, the same "income" taxed under Subtitle A; and many are just as clearly imposed exclusively upon, or related exclusively to, individual workers, rather than corporations. As an example, look at the surtax imposed under chapter 21 of Subtitle C:

> *"In addition to other taxes, there is hereby imposed on the income of every individual a tax equal to the following percentages of the wages (as defined in section 3121(a)) received by him with respect to employment (as defined in section 3121(b))"*

Similarly, withholding under chapter 24 in Subtitle C is nothing but a prepayment against the tax imposed under Subtitle A, which arises by virtue of, and is measured exclusively by, the receipt of the "wages" from which the withholding takes place:

> *Section 6401- Amounts treated as overpayments*
> *(b) Excessive credits*
> *(1) In general*
> *If the amount allowable as credits under subpart C of part IV of subchapter A of chapter 1 (relating to refundable credits) exceeds the tax imposed by subtitle A (reduced by the credits allowable under subparts A, B, D, and G of such part IV), the amount of such excess shall be considered an overpayment.*
> *(c) Rule where no tax liability*
> *An amount paid as tax shall not be considered not to constitute an overpayment solely by reason of the fact that there was no tax liability in respect of which such amount was paid.*
> *("Subpart C of part IV of subchapter A of chapter 1", to which 6401(b)(1) refers, is:*
> *Sec. 31 -Tax withheld on wages*
> *(a) Wage withholding for income tax purposes*
> *(1) In general*
> *The amount withheld as tax under chapter 24 shall be allowed to the recipient of the income as a credit against the tax imposed by this subtitle.)*

Even those provisions in Subtitle C that involve or relate to more (or other) than individual workers don't confine their application to corporations. Because all of this contradicts the "income only means corporate profit" premise, Subtitle C is either denied any place on the radar screen of those advocating this 'theory', or is wildly distorted by being imagined as dealing with a whole different class of tax known as "employment taxes" (conveniently assisted in this misconception by the tax-code-compiler's use of that phrase when the various "income" taxes applying to, and measured by, activity as a federally-connected worker were consolidated into Subtitle C).

A huge volume of subsidiary nonsense, such as that all Americans have been assigned corporate status at birth, has grown out of the original "corporate-profit-only" error. Still, the vigor and creativity behind them, and behind the original error as well, are heartening indicators of the depth and breadth of opposition to the mis-administered tax. I salute those who have had the courage to take this path, even while I hope that they expand the depth and breadth of the research that led them to it.

You Know You're In Denial If...

Denial has become practically a life-style choice for many Americans. Just as those interested in fitness and health choose active lives-- spending their time on the beach playing volleyball rather than sunbathing; taking the stairs instead of the elevator; etc., those interested in "not having to bother" choose to deny reality and reason-- spending their time watching football instead of reading non-government-controlled news; constantly adjusting their behavior and expectations to accommodate every new seizure of power and every new shucking-off of restraints ventured by those whose ambition and plan is to rule and exploit everyone else.

One of those quirky things about denial is that being in the state makes KNOWING that you're in the state difficult. Therefore, I offer the following randomly-selected tests you can use to overcome this narcotic-like impairment of objective judgment:

You know you're in denial if...

- ...you refuse to recognize that the better part of the entire existing "financial sector" could disappear tomorrow without causing anything but a momentary hiccup of inconvenience to the rest of us. Everyone owning stock in actual productive endeavors would still own their stock; everyone possessing surplus capital that can be invested in increasing production or productive capacity would still be able to loan it for these purposes; and new organizers of such capital and investments would appear immediately, just as happens in any case in which a market is otherwise under-served. Routine deposit account management would continue under the administration of receivers. The "bailout" is simply a swindle.

- ...you don't acknowledge that any organ of the press which a) is dependent on the good-will of the state for the preservation of its license, b) is doing well under the existing regime and thus has a practical interest in its preservation, and c) demonstrates that whatever it is doing is meeting with the approval of the political class by being granted regular access to members of that class, is nothing but a servant and a tool of the state, and will always put the interests of the state above yours. You may not understand how your interests are subverted by such an organ (the "cream" that rises to the top in this industry is made up of those best at concealing such things) but you're in denial if you don't take it on faith that they are. Eating at the table set by those tools of the state is a guarantee of malnourishment, if not outright poisoning.

- ...you're not facing the reality that children delivered into the hands of government schools will leave those schools conditioned to be incapable of understanding that there are no circumstances under which a government can lawfully suspend, ignore, "work around" or contradict provisions of the charter by which it is permitted to exist at all, not to mention to act in any fashion whatever; and that expressions like, "The Constitution is not a suicide pact" are idiotic sophistries capable of digestion only by government-school-conditioned victims like themselves. Such children will not only be reflexively accommodating of assaults on their liberty and interests, but will participate in implementing such measures against their fellows.

Likewise, you know you're in denial if...

- ...you don't understand that a state which gets away with commanding your resources at its discretion is neither your friend nor your servant, but is, instead, your competitor-- and ultimately, your master.

- ...you don't perceive that judges are not nominated and approved based on their predisposition to uphold the law against the perspectives and ambitions of their nominators, but rather are chosen based on their predisposition to creatively "interpret" and "construe" the law whenever possible to accommodate the perspectives and ambitions of their nominators; that laws which are vague enough to need "interpretation" and "construction" are inherently void; and that "interpretations" and "constructions" which expand or exceed the plain words of the law are inherently invalid.

- ...you don't recognize that the incumbents and leadership of the Democratic and Republican parties consist of those members who have been most successful under the current regime, and that those members act to preserve and expand that regime. Those seeking re-election are the same folks who gave us the "bailout", the PATRIOT Act, REAL ID, the Military Commissions Act and its suspension of habeas corpus, the FISA re-authorization and its retroactive immunization of illegal wiretapping pretense, the federally-funded militarization of our local police forces, secret prisons, torture and endless war.

- ...you don't notice that those seeking re-election, and those challengers approved by the Democratic and Republican leadership, are all monolithic supporters of the Federal Reserve and the imaginary money they insist you must use and accept even as they constantly bleed away its value to your great harm and their massive benefit. They are monolithic supporters of the careening empire. They are monolithic supporters of the governmental structure of which they intended to be a part. In short, they are tested tools and adherents of precisely the state apparatus that has steadily assaulted and eroded your well-being for decades. However, they are also accomplished actors well-coached to present themselves to you as being what you really want and what you really need so as to beguile you into putting them in power over you--whereupon they will proceed to ignore your wishes and act against your interests just as members of both parties have been doing all of your life.

Most importantly, you're in denial if you don't recognize that government lawlessness tolerated in any area and to any extent gets steadily worse and more extensive, and the only solution to that lawlessness is for YOU to stand up and do something about it. If you DO deny your personal, individual responsibility to act, and your personal responsibility for the consequences of your inaction, then you're just a sheep-boy (or -girl), and you might as well stop the jibber-jabbin'. No one's going to pay attention to you anyway-- nor should they. As Sam Adams, the architect of the last American revolution, put it:

> *If ye love... the tranquility of servitude greater than the animating contest for freedom, go home from us in peace. We seek not your counsel, nor your arms. Crouch down and lick the hand that feeds you. May your chains set lightly upon you; and may posterity forget that ye were our countrymen.*

The Truth About The "Exclusive Legislation" Clause In The U.S. Constitution

I can't think of how many times I have seen the assertion that Congress is free of all Constitutional restraints-- particularly tax-related restraints-- in the "federal zone" (DC and the "territories and possessions"). This notion is particularly widespread within the "tax honesty" movement, where it serves to prop up a variety of erroneous theories about the nature of the "income" tax.

It is, of course, complete nonsense.

Unfortunately, like most errors regarding important subjects, this inaccurate assertion is not a mere academic issue, but is actively harmful nonsense. The idea of rule-free taxing power within the federal zone serves to cause those exposed to it to incorrectly imagine that the tax is structured to capitalize on this "fact" and proceed down a path of ever-more elaborate misunderstanding with this error as the starting point. Every step down such a path is a step further away from the actual truth about the tax, and one step closer to becoming yet another loud voice spouting nonsense into the ears of the next traveler still uncommitted to the path down which he will choose to venture.

This myth about extra-Constitutional authority arises from misunderstanding the "exclusive legislation" provision in Article 1, section 8, Clause 17 of the United States Constitution. That provision gives Congress the power:

> *"To exercise exclusive Legislation in all Cases whatsoever, over such District (not exceeding ten Miles square) as may, by Cession of particular States, and the Acceptance of Congress, become the Seat of the Government of the United States, and to exercise like Authority over all Places purchased by the Consent of the Legislature of the State in which the Same shall be, for the Erection of Forts, Magazines, Arsenals, dock-Yards, and other needful Buildings;"*

To begin with, let's first recognize that the provision granting exclusive legislative authority over the area set aside as the seat of government (the District of Columbia) and such other areas as the several states may cede to federal control grants EXCLUSIVE legislative authority, not UNLIMITED or UNRESTRAINED legislative authority. Just on its face, there is nothing whatever in this provision supporting the myth about extra-Constitutional authority.

Further, the proposition is self-contradictory. A charter such as the Constitution can't grant authority to act outside the scope of the authority it has itself been ceded.

In fact the U.S. Constitution IS the constitution of the federal zone in precisely the same fashion that the Constitution of Michigan is the constitution of Michigan state territorial jurisdiction. The "exclusive" provision simply establishes that within the federal zone, no other jurisdiction obtains. Put another way, when exercised anywhere outside of the federal zone, such general federal jurisdiction as is authorized by the Constitution is, at best, concurrent with the territorial jurisdiction of one of the several states. Within the zone, only federal jurisdiction applies. However, while exclusive of any competition, even that exclusive jurisdiction is entirely bounded by the U.S. Constitution:

> *"And as the guaranty of a trial by jury, in the third article, implied a trial in that mode, and according to the settled rules of common law, the enumeration, in the sixth amendment, of the rights of the accused in criminal prosecutions, is to be taken as a declaration of what those rules were, and is to be referred to the anxiety of the people of the states to have in the supreme law of the land, and so far as the agencies of the general government were concerned, a full and distinct recognition of those rules, as involving the fundamental rights of life, liberty, and property.* ***This recognition was demanded and secured for the benefit of all the people of the United States, as well those permanently or temporarily residing in the District of Columbia as those residing or being in the several states. There is nothing in the history of the constitution, or of the original amendments, to justify the assertion that the people of this District may be lawfully deprived of the benefit of any of the constitutional guaranties of life, liberty, and property;..."***
>
> United States Supreme Court, Callan v. Wilson, 127 U.S. 540 (1888) (Emphasis added)

> *"The congress of the United States, being empowered by the constitution 'to exercise exclusive legislation in all cases whatsoever' over the seat of the national government, has the entire control over the District of Columbia for every purpose of government,-national or local. It may exercise within the District all legislative powers that the legislature of a state might exercise within the state, and may vest and distribute the judicial authority in and among courts and magistrates, and regulate judicial proceedings before them, as it may think fit,* ***so long as it does not contravene any provision of the constitution of the United States.*** *Kendall v. U. S. (1838) 12 Pet. 524, 619; Mattingly v.*

> *District of Columbia (1878) 97 U.S. 687, 690; Gibbons v. District of Columbia (1886) 116 U.S. 404, 407, 6 S. Sup. Ct. 427."*
> United States Supreme Court, Capital Traction Co. v. Hof, 174 U.S. 1 (1899) (Emphasis added)

(See your CtC Companion CD for both of these rulings in their entirety)

Another ruling is particularly worthy of review, since our focus here is the manner in which the myth of unrestrained authority in the federal zone distorts understanding of the nature and application of the taxing power:

> ***"Yet it is admitted, that the constitution not only allows, but enjoins the government to extend the ordinary revenue system to this district [of Columbia].***
>
> *If it be said, that the principle of uniformity, established in the constitution, secures the district from oppression in the imposition of indirect taxes, it is not less true, that the principle of apportionment, also established in the constitution, secures the district from any oppressive exercise of the power to lay and collect direct taxes.*
>
> ***After giving this subject its serious attention, the Court is unanimously of opinion, that Congress possesses, under the constitution, the power to lay and collect direct taxes within the District of Columbia, in proportion to the census directed to be taken by the constitution, and that there is no error in the judgment of the Circuit Court."***
> Loughborough v. Blake, 18 U. S. 317 (1820) (Emphasis added)

The reality about the nature and application of the federal taxing power is, of course, clearly, plainly (and exclusively) laid out in its entirety in 'Cracking the Code- The Fascinating Truth About Taxation In America'. Anyone actually wishing to learn the actual, liberating truth can easily do so with just a bit of light reading. (OK, maybe not exactly "light", but you get what you pay for...)

However, it is not enough that just the truly serious-minded and well-educated community of income-tax scholars know the truth, of course. As noted above, myths such as the "unrestrained power" nonsense are used to keep the existing regime of misapplication of the tax firmly fastened in place, and it is thus really important, and for the benefit of us all, that they not be allowed to persist even in the larger community.

Consequently, I am asking everyone who DOES understand the truth about this myth to become an adamant and forceful voice on behalf of that truth, wherever the issue arises.

Among other things, this will mean being sensitive to the appearance of this myth in larger bodies of work, even those to which it does not appear to be central or significant. The simple fact is, where a myth of this sort makes even a brief or apparently minor appearance, it serves as evidence of the overall work being rooted in misunderstanding (as well as a product of poor research), meaning that its broader analysis and conclusions are necessarily incorrect to one degree or another, as well.

I realize that this will be uncomfortable sometimes. Insisting on careful research and inflexible adherence to the facts is not always the path to popularity in some circles.

On the other hand, there is no other path to actually "getting it right" (and to becoming the persistent nightmare of the mendacious elements in the "tax agency/tax beneficiary" community that all of us ought to be). You will find that being right, and being a nightmare to the deserving and despicable crowd of systematic exploiters of ignorance, are a pretty satisfactory trade-off for enduring a little spite from those who wish to be spared the inconveniences of the actual facts.

The ultimate prize for sticking to the facts, of course, is finally winning this war on behalf of the rule of law, and that will be very satisfactory indeed...

So, I'm asking all of you to simply not permit the assertion of this myth, or any notion based (or dependent) upon this myth, to go uncorrected even one more time. Please.

Whenever you see it put forward, whether directly or indirectly, whether within the "tax honesty" community or the "mainstream", SHOUT IT DOWN (and teach the truth in its place). This myth is a confusing error at best, and more likely a deliberate lie intended to waste the energy of those who are willing and ready to act on behalf of the truth, but haven't yet gotten a clear sight of it.

What this myth is not is harmless. Never forget--confusion and lies are the tools of the enemies of the law, even when they are unwittingly deployed by others.

Please do your part.

The Effect Of A Social Security Number

One of the most persistent, and pernicious, bits of misdirection troubling the "tax honesty" community is the notion that having a Social Security number associated with oneself, or furnishing it to someone, makes one (or one's earnings) taxable. This is simply not so.

To begin with, furnishing a Social Security number to anyone doesn't constitute an exercise of privilege-- or an exercise of anything else other than one's authority to make prospective instructions concerning one's affairs. For instance, completing a W-4 instructing anyone how one wishes withholding to be conducted IF and WHEN one should actually come to be paid "wages" doesn't make one's pay into such "wages" anymore than completing an application for a fishing license makes everything one does at the lake "fishing". It is purely prospective.

Nor is a W-4 a contract or offer to contract of any kind-- no language to this effect of any kind appears on the form. Similarly, suffering the withholding of property in connection with "Social Security" "income" taxes is obviously neither the exercise of a privilege nor the acquisition of any other kind of benefit, nor does IT establish a contractual relationship between the person whose property is withheld and the federal government (except insofar as the government becomes obliged to return the withheld property if properly claimed).

First of all, one is not a "recipient of federal benefits" until one actually "receives the federal benefits". (And, of course, even if one were already "receiving the federal benefits", only those measurable benefit receipts would be taxable. The fact that certain of one's receipts are taxable does not make one's other receipts taxable.)

Second, contrary to the deep-seated misunderstanding of Social Security which is carefully nurtured by the beneficiaries of the overall "income" tax scheme, no one becomes "entitled" to Social Security by making 'contributions' (or any other way). Thus, even a (necessarily tortured) argument that vestiture in a future benefit constituted an "income"-taxable activity would not apply to Social Security, because no one is legally vested with a claim against the program.

The fact is, there is no legal relationship between the tax taken under the FICA and any benefits one might be given under the same act. When Social Security is called an "entitlement", the reference is to a merely political deal-- those in Congress recognize that it would be political suicide to stop giving money away to (especially) seniors under the mantle of the FICA, and so the recipients of those handouts are "entitled" to rely on them continuing into the foreseeable future. The FICA simply imposed another tax on "income", measured by remuneration paid to a particular group of federal workers (defined in section 3121).

(This class of remuneration was given the title of "wages", more particularly, FICA "wages", and is distinguished from the "wages" defined at 26 USC 3401. 3401 "wages" make up a broad and inclusive class (remuneration paid to all federal workers), within which is the subclass of FICA "wages". That is, all federal worker's pay qualifies as 3401 "wages", but only some also qualifies simultaneously as 3121 "wages", and is used to measure the additional "income" tax.)

All that should be needed to make this clear is to consider that, if that were the case, once someone had reached nominal "full vestiture" -- that is "40 quarters of contributions" (per the current arbitrary qualification)-- one would be finished making "contributions". If there actually was a contract involved, that would be the point at which the "contributor" would have satisfied his or her side of the bargain, with nothing more to do but wait until the payouts began. In case more is needed than that simple and straightforward logic, here is what the United States Supreme Court says on the subject in Helvering v. Davis 301 US 619 (1937):

> *"The proceeds of both [employee and employer FICA] taxes are to be paid into the Treasury like internal-revenue taxes generally, and are not earmarked in any way."*

...and in Flemming v. Nestor 363 US 603 (1960):

> *"The noncontractual interest of an employee covered by the Act cannot be soundly analogized to that of the holder of an annuity, whose right to benefits are based on his contractual premium payments."*

The court explains, also in Flemming v. Nestor, that:

> *"To engraft upon Social Security system a concept of 'accrued property rights' would deprive it of the flexibility and boldness in adjustment to ever-changing conditions which it demands..."*

It's that simple. There is no legal relationship of any kind between taxes withheld under the auspices of the FICA, and the receipt, or possible future receipt, of Social Security benefits-- and this is true even for those whose earnings really are "wages" as that term is defined in the law.

Congress could end Social Security payouts tomorrow, and no matter how many quarters of payments someone may have made, he or she would have no legal recourse by which to demand benefits. No one has an account at the Social Security Administration, in the sense of a reserved or claimable interest in any benefit. That the administration (or Congress) has elected to use "quarters of payments" as the nominal qualifier for receiving payments from the program is just the scheme de jure-- it could as easily be any thing else, and with just as much relationship to the benefit (from a legal standpoint) as the current scheme-- that is, none whatsoever. The designers of this tax simply settled on marketing it as though it were an insurance program, both to make it more immediately palatable, and to help create a constituency which would defend it in the future with the vigor attendant upon an imagined "ownership" interest. Without violating to the slightest degree its legal obligations under the Social Security Act or by virtue of the taxes it has collected under the name of "Social Security or Medicare contributions", Congress could announce tomorrow that benefits would henceforth be based on how many blue Volkswagens an applicant or current beneficiary had owned in the past (or owned now, for that matter).

Indeed, in 26 USC 86- *Social Security and tier 1 railroad retirement benefits* (a section within the "Items Specifically Included In Gross Income" part of Subtitle A), Congress must artificially designate Social Security benefits as to be *treated* as pension or annuity payments, for purposes of certain other sections of law, since such benefits don't actually qualify as pension or annuity payments inherently.

> *(f) Treatment as pension or annuity for certain purposes*
> *For purposes of—*
> *(1) section 22 (c)(3)(A) (relating to reduction for amounts received as pension or annuity),*
> *(2) section 32 (c)(2) (defining earned income),*
> *(3) section 219 (f)(1) (defining compensation), and*
> *(4) section 911 (b)(1) (defining foreign earned income),*
> *any social security benefit shall be treated as an amount received as a pension or annuity.*

(Social Security numbers are merely a creative element of this scheme, by the way-- being nothing more than a number under which qualifying "quarters" are recorded, but suggesting to the gullible the existence of a personally-owned numbered "account" financed by the FICA tax "contributions" extracted. However, as noted above, having such a number associated with oneself creates no ownership interest in any future benefits, nor does it have any legal affect on the character of one's earnings-- that is, it does not make earnings, which otherwise are not, into either 26 USC 3121 "wages" or 26 USC 3401 "wages".)

***

NOTE: Some are allowing themselves to be misled or distracted in regard to this subject by references to federal-retirement-benefit-vestiture within certain statutes, such as that at 5 USC 552a:

> *"(13) the term "Federal personnel" means officers and employees of the Government of the United States, members of the uniformed services (including members of the Reserve Components), individuals entitled to receive immediate or deferred retirement benefits under any retirement program of the Government of the United States (including survivor benefits)."*

(which is, by the way, just a "this section only" specification relating to federal authority to keep records...). Being shown the terms "entitlement" and "retirement benefits", they imagine that this language constitutes evidence that Social Security is an "entitlement" in a legal sense. However, the programs referred to are not Social Security and Medicare, but rather are the *"retirement program(s) of the Government of the United States"* (provisions of which can be seen elsewhere in the same title).

***

On another front, general misunderstanding of the true nature of Social Security, and of the context and meaning of language such as that in 5 USC 552a(13) is being abused with the promotion of the bizarre proposition that anyone having Social Security "income" taxes extracted from them are therefore "federal personnel", (and therefore are properly subject to the tax, in an interesting example of circular reasoning...), or are electing to be considered as such. That is, the misunderstanding of Social Security to be a legal entitlement is exploited to suggest that the reference in 5 USC 552a(13) to those *"entitled to receive immediate or deferred retirement benefits"* should be read as including people who have paid Social Security taxes (and are therefore imagined to be vested in benefits under the program). Then, goes the argument, since the subparagraph defines "federal personnel" as those *"entitled to receive either immediate or deferred retirement benefits"* (a class to which it is to be imagined those who have paid Social Security taxes belong), everyone who has paid Social Security taxes belongs, *Presto Change-O!*, to the class "federal personnel".

The "argument" concludes with the proposition that THIS is the clever mechanism by which Americans are made subject to the "income" tax (without any effort to address the fact that it is not merely "federal personnel" who are actually so subject, nor even are "federal personnel", except insofar as they engage in taxable activities). To describe the reasoning is to make clear its illegitimacy.

Much as was done by with the abuse of the language of the first half of Treasury Decision 2313 to push the "861 argument" (see 'A Cheap and Nasty Scam' elsewhere in this volume), this distraction relies on its audience not verifying its assertions, and thus not noticing that the immediately preceding subparagraph of the very same section of statute DOES reference mere welfare programs such as Social Security. That subparagraph specifically denominates programs of this sort as *"federal benefit programs"*, distinguishing them from *"retirement programs of the Government of the United States"* (and without any references therein to *"federal personnel"*):

> *"(12) the term "Federal benefit program" means any program administered or funded by the Federal Government, or by any agent or State on behalf of the Federal Government, providing cash or in-kind assistance in the form of payments, grants, loans, or loan guarantees to individuals;"*

Although it is not necessary to further illuminate this distinction, elsewhere in the same statute a competent researcher will find language clearly doing just that, such as the following subparagraph of 5 USC 552a(o)(1):

> *(D) procedures for providing individualized notice at the time of application, and notice periodically thereafter as directed by the Data Integrity Board of such agency (subject to guidance provided by the Director of the Office of Management and Budget pursuant to subsection (v)), to—*
> *(i) applicants for and recipients of financial assistance or payments under Federal benefit programs, and*
> *(ii) applicants for and holders of positions as Federal personnel,*

By the way, look at what the IRS has to say to those federally-connected entities making payments to persons <u>whom they have no reason to believe have ever been associated with a Social Security number</u>:

> <u>*Frequently Asked Questions about Backup Withholding*</u>
> *What is a Taxpayer Identification Number (TIN)?*
> *A TIN is one of the following four numbers.*
>
> 1. *A Social Security Number (SSN)*
> 2. *An Employer Identification Number (EIN)*
> 3. *An IRS individual taxpayer identification number (ITIN). Aliens who do not have an SSN, and are not eligible to get one should get an ITIN. Form W-7, Application for IRS Individual Taxpayer*

Identification Number, is used to apply for an ITIN.

4. *An Adoption Taxpayer Identification Number (ATIN). An ATIN is a temporary tax identification number issued for a child born in the U.S. An ATIN is used as an identifying number if the child is not eligible for an SSN.*

What should I do if a payee refuses or neglects to provide a TIN?

Begin backup withholding immediately on any reportable payments. Do the required annual solicitation (request) for the TIN. Backup Withhold until you receive a TIN.

Should I backup withhold on a payee who is a nonresident alien?

Yes. A nonresident alien is subject to backup withholding unless you have a signed Form W-8BEN, Certificate of Foreign Status of Beneficial Owner for United States Tax Withholding, or W-8, Certificate of Foreign Status, on file. Nonresident aliens are subject to backup withholding, and identified via Form W-8BEN.

Note the revealing qualifier in the language above: *"Begin backup withholding immediately* ***on any reportable payments****."* The issue is the nature of the activity in connection with which the payment is made (which is typically presumed to be a "taxable activity" when the payor is-- or is presumed to be-- a federal entity)-- NOT whether or not the payee has or has furnished a Social Security number.

Social Security Administration **Philadelphia Region**

"Committed to Quality and Creativity in Public Service"

Refer to:

401 E. Louther Street
Carlisle, PA 17013
(717) 243-0085 Ext.:
May 22, 1998

Mr. Mark R. James

Dear Mr. James:

I am responding to your recent inquiry concerning the requirements for a person to have and use a Social Security Number.

There is no law on the books which requires a person to have a Social Security Number. The Social Security Administration (SSA) issues numbers to persons who properly request them. SSN's are issued to report earnings and serve as taxpayer identification numbers. Once an SSN is issued SSA has no control over who might ask for the number.

The Internal Revenue Service (IRS) uses the SSN for tax collection purposes. Penalties and requirements are given in the Internal Revenue Code and IRS regulations. Employers can be penalized for non compliance of tax laws.

I have enclosed a copy of a few pages from SSA's Program Operations Manual which deal with the topic. Any questions you have about the use of the SSN should be directed to the IRS.

Sincerely,

Richard L. Hewitt
District Manager

*****

SOCIAL SECURITY

COPY

TEH2B
QR3572

January 27, 2009

The Honorable Gus Bilirakis
House of Representatives
Washington, D.C. 20515

Dear Mr. Bilirakis:

This letter is in response to your inquiry on behalf of Mr. C D , , who contacted you concerning the need for a Social Security number (SSN).

The Social Security Act does not require a person to have an SSN to live and work in the United States, nor does it require an SSN simply for the purpose of having one. However, if someone works without a number, we cannot properly credit the earnings for the work performed, and the worker may lose any potential entitlement to Social Security benefits.

Other laws require people to have and use SSNs for specific purposes. For example, the Internal Revenue Code (26 U.S.C. 6109 (a)) and applicable regulations (26 CFR 301.6109-l (d)) require a person to get and use a number on tax documents and to furnish it to any other person or institution (such as an employer or a bank) that is required to provide the Internal Revenue Service (IRS) information about payments to that person. There are penalties for failure to do so. The IRS also requires employers to report the number with employees' earnings. In addition, people filing tax returns for taxable years after December 31, 1994, generally must include the number of each dependent.

The Privacy Act regulates the use of SSNs by government agencies. They may require a number only if a law or regulation either orders or authorizes them to do so. Agencies are required to disclose the authorizing law or regulation. If the request has no legal basis, the person may refuse to provide the number and still receive the agency's services.

We hope that this information will help you respond to Mr. D . Please let us know if we can be of further assistance.

Sincerely,

Sheryll Ziporkin

Sheryll Ziporkin
Associate Commissioner
Office of Public Inquiries

Think about this as well: A Social Security number is assigned to most people as a minor, if not at birth, by action of another party (a parent, usually). There is no provision in law for expunging the number, its assignment, or the records associated with it by the government (in the sense of simply wiping them all out because the individual involved wishes them gone). Does anyone really imagine that a minor child can be thus made irrevocably subject to a tax-- or any other legal consequence or effect? This is absurd.

Further, let's not forget the decades of implementation and enforcement of the "income" tax before the institution of Social Security and its numbers in the late 1930s...

The simple and sordid reality is that to the extent that it is not just a tax-agency seeding of the "tax honesty" community with deliberate distractions and disinformation, notions about the "income"-tax-related significance of Social Security numbers are just erroneous "theories" in search of facts, rather than facts being considered in the formulation of legitimate theories.

*****

P. S. The fact that a payor may have an EIN ("Employer Identification Number")-- or that such a payor's payee may use such a number to help identify the payor-- is also immaterial to the issue of the "income" tax, as regards payments made to another. Although only actual "taxpayer" entities need such numbers, they are used for several purposes not necessarily involving "employment", "employees", or activity as an "employer". This is pointed out in the Internal Revenue Manual:

> *4.6.1.2.2 (06-20-2002)*
> *Employer Identification Number (EIN)*
>
> 1. *The EIN is a nine-digit number issued by IRS to identify the tax accounts of employers and certain others that have no employees. The digits are arranged as follows: 00-0000000. For more information, see Publication 1635, Understanding Your EIN.*
> 2. *An EIN is required if a taxpayer:*
>
>   *A. Pays wages to one or more employees, including household employees;*
>
>   *B. Is required to have an EIN to use on any return, statement, or other document, even*

> *if not an employer; e.g., withholding agent required to withhold taxes;*
>
> *C. Files a Schedule C, C-EZ, or F and has a Keogh plan or is required to file excise, employment, information, or alcohol, tobacco, and firearms returns. See the instructions to Form SS-4, Application for Employer Identification Number, for the complete list of taxpayers who must have an EIN.*

Needless to say, what a payor chooses to believe to be true about itself does not establish anything as true about anyone else, even someone who uses an applied-for and assigned "EIN" in identifying that payor. If your neighbor informed you that he was known to the town council as "The Queen of Sheba", and you, having occasion to do so used the title when communicating with the town council, your neighbor would not thereby become the Queen of Sheba. Nor would you become a Sheban (or whatever) simply using that title, or by virtue of doing business with your eccentric neighbor...

On Ignorance, The Income Tax, And The Federal Reserve

"There is nothing more frightening than active ignorance."
~ Johann von Goethe

While doing a radio show recently, I encountered a caller who nicely illustrated the widespread phenomenon known as GIGO-- Garbage In, Gospel Out. This fellow had called in to explain to me that the income tax was created in order to conceal the nefarious workings of the Federal Reserve. He was equipped with a number of attendant notions about the how the tax was applied, and so forth, all of which partook of its underlying, Federal Reserve-related purpose. The whole package of certain knowledge with which this caller was animated was based, or rested heavily, on the "fact"-- clearly never investigated or even questioned-- of the tax's birth in 1913, the same year the Federal Reserve Act was passed.

However, the tax actually began in 1862, of course-- 51 years before the Federal Reserve Act. As is noted in the preamble to the 1939 Internal Revenue Code:

> *The Revised Statutes of the United States and the Statutes at Large of the United States are the sources of*

> *the law codified. The Revised Statutes cover the period ended December 1, 1873. The Statutes at Large codified cover the period following December 1, 1873, and are published in the 35 volumes numbered 18 to 52, inclusive. The separate enactments carried into the internal revenue title, wholly or in part, from the Statutes at Large are 143 in number, exclusive of 93 statutes involving express amendment, reenactment, or repeal. The 277 Revised Statutes sections codified were derived from 21 basic statutes. The whole body of internal revenue law in effect on January 2, 1939, therefore, has its ultimate origin in 164 separate enactments of Congress.* ***The earliest of these was approved July 1, 1862****; the latest, June 16, 1938." (Emphasis added.)*

Even a brief glance at the derivation tables of either the 1939 IRC or the current 1954-1986 version will make clear that something on the order of 40% of the underlying body of "income" tax law pre-dates the federal reserve act. The imposition of the tax had nothing whatever to do with the Federal Reserve Act. Nor did the adoption of the 16th Amendment, which was submitted to the several states for ratification in July of 1909, well before the November, 1910 meeting at which the Federal Reserve was conceived.

Ironically, though, the very confusion from which my caller suffers about the "income" tax serves to conceal a probable nefarious reality about the Federal Reserve of a somewhat similar character to what he misunderstands about the tax. The fact is, while the tax was not adopted to conceal the ill effect of the Federal Reserve-- nor in any other way responsive to the as-yet unconceived central banking cartel-- the Federal Reserve System WAS almost certainly a response to the 16th Amendment, being a mechanism cleverly crafted to ameliorate the threat posed to the banking interests by the impending adoption of the amendment .

It must be remembered that the amendment's sole function is to bring the gains of national bankers (and others of the "Robber Baron" class) into the range of the tax by closing the Pollock Court loophole. As is pointed out in testimony by F. Morse Hubbard, legislative draftsman for the United States Treasury Department:

> *"[T]he amendment made it possible to bring investment income within the scope of the general income-tax law, but did not change the character of the tax. It is still fundamentally an excise or duty with respect to the privilege of carrying on any activity or owning any property which produces income."* House Congressional Record, March 27, 1943, page 2580;

and by the United States Supreme Court repeatedly over the decades:

> *"The Sixteenth Amendment, although referred to in argument, has no real bearing and may be put out of view. As pointed out in recent decisions, it does not extend the taxing power to new or excepted subjects..."* Peck v. Lowe, 247 U.S. 165 (1918)

and

> *"The legislative history merely shows... ...that the sole purpose of the Sixteenth Amendment was to remove the apportionment requirement for whichever incomes were otherwise taxable* [due the legal character of the activity by which the gains involved were generated]*."* South Carolina v. Baker, 485 U.S. 505 (1988)

Thus, the impending 16th Amendment promised to put a big hole in the otherwise unhindered and untaxed wallowing of that class in the very profitable intermingling of private interests and public power. It is highly likely that the Federal Reserve System (FRS) was dreamt-up by the banksters as a countermeasure by which the losses they were about to suffer from the "income" tax would be made up, at least in part, through the gains from exploiting the provisions of the FRS.

The supreme irony of the whole affair is that-- due in large part to confident ignorance about the "income" tax such as that demonstrated, and doubtless widely spread, by my caller-- it was only a matter of a few decades before we ended up with the vast bulk of the American people being fooled into unnecessarily paying the tax themselves. As a consequence, the financial burden on the much smaller group at whom the 16th Amendment was actually directed-- the banksters and their ilk-- is a great deal less than it otherwise would be. At the same time, we still have the legislative outrage originally intended to insulate its creators from that much higher burden which they had fully expected to be paying-- the Federal Reserve system-- steadily stealing wealth from all the rest of us for the benefit of those creators anyway!

What's more, the offsetting benefit offered by the Federal Reserve scam to the bankster class and its symbiotes is only maximized when the federal government is throwing money around in serious excess of current revenue streams (deficit spending). The acceptable justification for such excesses at the time the Federal Reserve Act received Woodrow Wilson's signature was war, and practically before that signature was dry there was a doozy of a war lined up (World War I, launched in 1914, entered by United States in 1917). The banksters and their ilk never looked back, and America has had endless war ever since (supplemented by the birth and various molts of the high-spending welfare state apparatus, as well). You can see how this has worked out (this graph only takes us to 1975; were it to go to present day, it would have to be MUCH taller...):

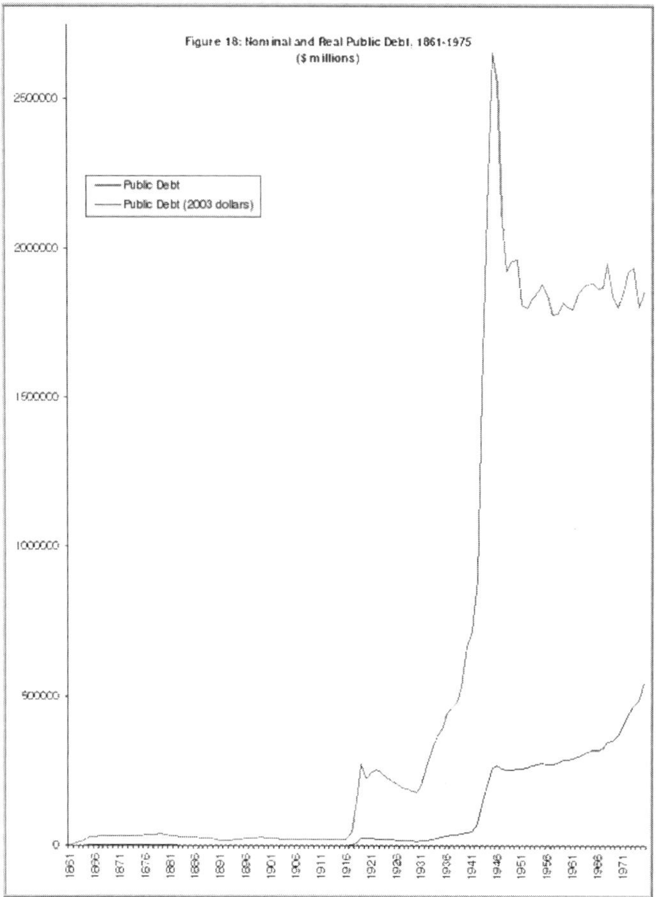

Source: EH.net: Nominal figures from "Principal of the Public Debt, Fiscal Years 1790-1975," *Annual Report of the Secretary of the Treasury on the State of the Finances, Statistical Appendix.* (Washington, DC: Government Printing Office, 1975), 62-63; real figures adjust for inflation and are provided by Robert Sahr, Oregon State University. http://oregonstate.edu/Dept/pol_sci/fac/sahr/sahrhome.htm.

***

There are two obviously important lessons to be learned here. One, of course, is that as we each step up to do our fair share on behalf of the rule of law by confining the "income" tax to its proper limits personally, we simultaneously help to restore a proper balance between the power and benefit of privileged moneyed interests and the rest of us in the aggregate.

The other is that scrupulous accuracy of information; and scrupulous and skeptical care in adopting the pronouncements and conclusions of those who claim knowledge; are of paramount importance for Americans trying to look after their own interests and properly supervise their agents. Bogus information must not only not be adopted, it must also not be left uncorrected, because the errors harbored by others can easily affect each of the rest of us.

There is a vast body of nonsense specifically about the 16th Amendment being used to protect the status-quo described above, of course. But every other error and misunderstanding about the "income" tax generally, and other matters of government, citizenship, law and so forth which clutter the landscape do so as well-- some directly and obviously, others by simply degrading the overall "signal-to-noise ratio", and making clarity of thought a struggle, if not an impossibility.

Fight them all.

A Little More On Social Security Numbers And The Income Tax

As has been noted, one of the most persistent, and most destructive, misunderstandings plaguing the "tax honesty" community is that having had a social security number (SSN) assigned to oneself, or furnishing such a number to others, causes a tax liability to arise (or causes that which otherwise is not taxable to become so).

SSNs can and do play a part, in some cases, in a fiction in which those whose activities are not subject to the tax are made to look, superficially, as though they are subject to the tax, for awhile. But such folks-- and/or their activities-- do not become subject by way of this pretense.

Rather, those invited (or effectively coerced) into the furnishing of social security numbers in connection with what are NOT actually activities subject to the tax are like people attending a party who, upon entering, are all asked to wear a tag with "Caterer" on it throughout the evening. At the end of the party, the announcement is made that whoever did the catering has to stay after and clean up.

The actual caterer of the party must stay and clean, of course. But those who DIDN'T actually cater the party, but are merely wearing tags saying "caterer" on them, just as obviously do not.

Someone may stand at the exit and point out each departing guest's tag to the doorman, who then commands them to stay and clean, but any guest who declares himself or herself to have NOT actually catered the party heads out the door without further ado (although the doorman might run after one or two unlucky guests for a bit, asking with an increasingly obnoxious whine, or threatening-sounding growl, "Did you really mean that you're not the caterer? Are you sure you don't want to change your mind? Caterers that don't own up get into trouble, you know!").

The doorman will also accost anyone trying to leave the party who ISN'T wearing a "caterer" tag, and demand that THEY stay and clean, as well, by the way. After all, a tag is just a tag. Just as wearing a "caterer" tag neither makes someone into a caterer in general, nor the caterer responsible for this party in particular, NOT wearing one doesn't make one NOT the caterer of the party. A tag is just a tag. <u>What actually happened is all that matters</u>.

But there is one caveat: Even those who DIDN'T cater the party CAN be made responsible for cleaning it up-- if they forget, or somehow don't understand, that they didn't really cater the party, and instead declare themselves to have done so. This might happen because the declarants had a few drinks, and everyone's been addressing them as "caterer" all evening; or maybe because they don't even know what "catering" means...

In any event, once anyone has made this declaration, the owner of the facility can sue them if they don't stay and clean. But this arising of liability has nothing whatever to do with the fact that the poor schmucks who didn't really do the catering but end up wiping down the tables anyway were wearing "caterer" tags. It is because they declared themselves to be among those liable for the clean-up when the question actually got asked of them at the end of the party. (Or, refused to say that they weren't when heading for the door and being confronted by that fellow making allegations.)

***

All of the above is exhaustively explained in '<u>Cracking the Code- The Fascinating Truth About Taxation In America</u>' (and supplemented in various places throughout losthorizons.com). Nonetheless, misunderstandings (and misdirections) concerning social security numbers persistently clutter up forums, newsgroups, chat rooms and everyone's email.

It's a shame that this goes on as a general matter, in that any and all misunderstandings interfere with the important work of helping each other gain an accurate understanding of the tax and the law, and that of spreading the word about these important matters to others outside the CtC-educated community. But the misunderstanding/mis-direction about SSNs is more pernicious than most.

This is so because for one thing, once assigned, SSNs are permanent. They don't belong to the person with whom they are concerned-- they are, after all, just Social Security Administration account numbers. That is, they are just the ID numbers under which records about a given individual are filed, and the individual has no more power to "rescind" or undo them than one would have in making one's library card number (and the records of library activity associated with it) go away.

Further, SSNs are demanded of people constantly, in connection with all manner of activities, and have been throughout the lives of most Americans. Thus, everyone has a sense of having intertwined their lives with these numbers.

Putting the three things together-- misunderstanding about the legal significance of the numbers, their ineradicable nature, and their ubiquity in the lives and affairs of those to whom they have been assigned-- creates a sense of hopelessness. After all, IF the numbers DID have the liability-generating effect that the myth-spinners suggest, most Americans would find themselves inescapably stuck in the "income tax" web.

Happily, the average American is NOT stuck in any such web. All that is required for liberty in this regard is an accurate understanding of the tax and the law, and enough courage and clear-headedness to declare the simple truth to the doorman when confronted.

There IS A Law By Which Any Person Can Become Liable For The "Income" Tax, And This Is How It Works

TO BEGIN WITH:

- There is a tax imposed on "income" in excess of the current exemption amount (as measured by the dollar value involved). What "income" is, and whether or not one actually received any, is irrelevant to this fact. There IS something called "income" which IS taxed. See the portions of The Revenue Act of 1938 pasted below, for instance. The rates, and various other aspects of the tax, have periodically been modified by individual enactments since this original enactment, the product of which are currently reflected in Sections 1, 61, 63, 6001, 6011(a), 6012(a) and 6065 of the IRC of 1986:

  AN ACT
  To provide revenue, equalize taxation, and for other purposes.
  Be it enacted by the Senate and House of Representatives of the United States of America in Congress assembled, That this Act, divided into titles

and sections according to the following Table or Contents, may be cited as the "Revenue Act of 1938":

SEC. 11. NORMAL TAX ON INDIVIDUALS.
There shall be levied, collected, and paid for each taxable year upon the net income of every individual a normal tax of 4 per centum of the amount of the net income in excess of the credits against net income provided in section 25.

SEC. 12. SURTAX ON INDIVIDUALS.
(a) DEFINITION OF "SURTAX NET INCOME".—As used in this section the term "surtax net income" means the amount of the net income in excess of the credits against net income provided in section 25 (b).
(b) RATES OF SURTAX.—There shall be levied, collected, and paid for each taxable year upon the surtax net income of every individual a surtax as follows: (a steeply graduated incremental tax rate table follows, up to a top marginal rate of 75%)

SEC. 21. NET INCOME.
"Net income" means the gross income computed under section 22, less the deductions allowed by section 23. For definition of "adjusted net income", see section 13 (a); for definition of "special class net income", see section 14 (a).

SEC. 22. GROSS INCOME.
(a) GENERAL DEFINITION.—"Gross income" includes gains, profits, and income derived from salaries, wages, or compensation for personal service, of whatever kind and in whatever form paid, or from professions, vocations, trades, businesses, commerce, or sales, or dealings in property, whether real or personal, growing out of the ownership or use of or interest in such property; also from interest, rent, dividends, securities, or the transaction of any business carried on for gain or profit, or gains or profits and income derived from any source whatever. In the case of Presidents of the United States and judges of courts of the United States taking office after June 6, 1932, the compensation received as

such shall be included in gross income; and all Acts taxing the compensation of such Presidents and judges are hereby amended accordingly.

SEC. 51. INDIVIDUAL RETURNS.
(a) REQUIREMENT.—The following individuals shall each make under oath a return stating specifically the items of his gross income and the deductions and credits allowed under this title and such other information for the purpose of carrying out the provisions of this title as the Commissioner with the approval of the Secretary may by regulations prescribe—
(1) Every individual who is single or who is married but not living with husband or wife, if—

> *(A) Having a net income for the taxable year of $1,000 or over; or*
> *(B) Having a gross income for the taxable year of $5,000 or over, regardless of the amount of the net income.*
> (Etc., etc., covering the usual categories familiar to all...)

SEC. 903. EFFECTIVE DATE OF ACT.
Except as otherwise provided, this Act shall take effect upon its enactment.
[Received by the President, May 16, 1938.]

[NOTE BY THE DEPARTMENT OF STATE.—The foregoing act having been presented to the President of the United States for his approval, and not having been returned by him to the House of Congress in which it originated within the time prescribed by the Constitution of the United States, has become a law without his approval.]

- There is also a law saying that anyone who has met the foregoing qualification (of the receipt of more than the current exemption amount of "income" dollars) must file an accurate and honest return-- with any appropriate accompanying forms or instruments-- reflecting this fact.

- Those who are actually capable of meeting the foregoing qualification (which is to say, those who ACTUALLY HAVE engaged in taxable activity resulting in the receipt of more than the current exemption amount of "income" dollars) HAVE VOLUNTARILY ELECTED TO MAKE THEMSELVES SUBJECT TO THIS REQUIREMENT AS PART OF THE PROCESS OF ENGAGING IN THAT ACTIVITY.
- The execution of an accurate and honest return includes appropriate self-assessment (thus possibly creating a liability) and remittance of the resulting amount of tax (if any).

It's that simple: There is no personal liability for John Doe specified in the law. BUT IF JOHN MEETS THE FOREGOING QUALIFICATIONS, HE IS OBLIGED TO DO SEVERAL THINGS, THE CONSEQUENCE OF WHICH IS THE <u>CREATION</u> OF A PERSONAL LIABILITY. That is the law that makes individual Americans liable for the tax, and how it works.

Now I know some are saying to themselves, *"AHA! I don't meet the foregoing qualifications! Therefore, there's no requirement for ME to file a return!"* Read on...

Here is the kicker:

- Sworn allegations on an "information return" (such as a W-2, 1099 or K-1) DECLARING that someone has received more than the exemption amount of "income" (and therefore meets the foregoing qualifications) WILL BE PRESUMED TRUE BY DEFAULT.
- Therefore, unless and until such allegations-- EVEN WHEN THEY ARE ERRONEOUS-- are formally and properly answered as provided for by law, they will be taken as imposing an obligation to file an honest and

accurate return, and they will support civil and criminal penalties (as well as the presumptive assessment of a tax based on the unanswered "information return" testimony) for a failure to do so.

And here is the somewhat ironic aspect to it all:

- The formal and proper means for answering (and, if appropriate, correcting) allegations that one meets the foregoing qualifications IS THE FILING OF AN HONEST AND ACCURATE RETURN.

The Revenue Act of 1862, Section 93:

> *"And be it further enacted,...that any party, in his or her own behalf,...shall be permitted to declare, under oath or affirmation, the form and manner of which shall be prescribed by the Commissioner of Internal Revenue,... ...the amount of his or her annual income,... liable to be assessed,... and the same so declared shall be received as the sum upon which duties are to be assessed and collected."*

Thus, even someone who DOESN'T actually "meet the foregoing qualifications", but who is declared to do so by someone else by way of an "information return", is <u>constructively</u> obliged to file a return.

(The return DOESN'T have to be a "Form 1040", by the way, although fears about hidden and harmful consequences of using such a form are unsupported by evidence... Any alternative DOES have to meet the "form and manner" specifications though, which means it must be legally identical to a 1040, while being a whole lot more trouble to produce.)

To those who might protest that it's just not right, and they shouldn't have to do ANYTHING when they didn't really have "income", I would say, *"I couldn't agree more. Nor could Congress, it would appear, since it has provided for civil action against those who produce bogus "information returns", codified at 26 USC § 7434..."*

Do You Know What You Aren't?

SUPPOSE YOU WENT OUT TO YOUR MAILBOX one afternoon and found a notice from Sears, Roebuck & Co. instructing "all employees" to report to the nearest company office for a staff meeting the next day.

Would you go?

If you DON'T work for Sears?

It'd be pretty stupid to go to the meeting if you don't work for Sears, wouldn't it?

So, when you're presented with a notice from the United States government instructing "all employees" to do this or that, why would you do whatever it says, if you DON'T work for the United States government?

***

HOW ABOUT YOU BUSINESS OWNERS? Suppose you found a notice from Sears in your mailbox one day declaring that "anyone to whom any employees report", and anyone who paid any contractors for services rendered or paid any dividends to stockholders, is to send information on all salaries and other payments made during the past year to the main office.

Would you send Sears such a list?

If your company is NOT a division of Sears?

It'd be pretty stupid to send in such a list if your company isn't a division of Sears, wouldn't it?

So, when you're presented with such a notice from United States government, why would you do what it says, if you're NOT a division of the United States government?

***

NOW, SUPPOSE YOU FOUND A NOTICE in your mailbox alerting you to the fact that someone has sent an affidavit to the Sears accounting department claiming that you were paid $50,000 by Sears last year-- and the Sears accounting department is going to debit your Sears charge account for what they figure your Christmas Club contribution, health insurance premium, retirement plan matching contribution, reserved parking space fee, and/or sundry other employee/contractor/investor-related expenses add up to.

Would you go to your local Sears store and pick up one of the "affidavit acknowledgment/correction/rebuttal forms" published by its accounting department, put $50,000 on the "amount paid to you by Sears" line on the form, spend 10.7 hours over a weekend figuring out how to take advantage of Sears company policy for reducing the related expenses for which Sears wants to charge you, and then sign the form and send it in-- feeling pretty good about how you reduced the hit that your Sears account is going to take?

Would you do all that?

If you HADN'T gotten paid by Sears?

It'd be pretty stupid to do all that if you hadn't actually been paid by Sears, wouldn't it?

SO, IF SOMEBODY SENDS YOU A COPY of an affidavit they've given to the IRS or a state tax agency on which they claim that you've been paid as a federally-connected person last year--such as a W-2, 1099 or K-1, which are only used to report such payments-- and it isn't actually true, why would you respond as though it is? Why wouldn't you use the IRS or state tax agency's "affidavit acknowledgment/correction/rebuttal forms" to correct, or rebut, the erroneous affidavit, both of which are among the primary functions of such forms?

It'd be pretty stupid to do anything else, wouldn't it?

***

It's All In Your Mind

LET'S PLAY A LITTLE MENTAL GAME. Imagine that you're someone who's been spared immersion in the State-dominated paradigm that controls the thinking of most 21st-century Americans. Perhaps you were educated by your loving parents rather than the government beneficiaries that operate public schools; maybe you were spared massive doses of television, as well. Perhaps you just naturally have what it takes to remain master of your own mind.

You learned to think logically and to avoid assumptions, and you learned that massive, power-obsessed institutions have no incentive to deal with you honorably. You learned, in fact, that massive institutions, whatever their pre-dispositions, are devoid of all integrity by virtue of their size and complexity, which permits and encourages each and every actor within them to presume that someone else has taken responsibility for the moral and legal propriety of the institution's practices.

In short, you are a clear-eyed, un-"conditioned", well-educated person.

NOW, THE TIME COMES when you choose to go into business, creating some product or delivering some service, and you set about organizing a little company for this purpose. Perhaps because it is more evocative of the independent and honorable contributions of those being described, it happens that when your structural purposes required any references to the staff you hire during this organizational process, you choose to call them "workers", rather than using the more demeaning term "employees" (which evokes an unpleasant sense that those so described are mere tools in your hands-- "human resources", as it were, "employed" in the same sense as you would "employ" any other resource to suit your purposes.

A "worker" <u>works</u>-- he brings his skills, his efforts, his brains, his integrity and his overall ability to produce wealth to the table and trades them for liquidity. An "employee", on the other hand, is just *deployed*-- he is simply a cog in someone else's machine.

IN ANY EVENT, it comes to pass that all your paperwork, and your practices in the workplace, exclusively refer to those you hire as "workers" (and refer to you in the same way, of course-- even if you were inclined to view your staff as mere tools and describe them accordingly, you could hardly view yourself as an "employee"!). Consequently, when the time comes that you first find an unsolicited notice from a government tax agency in your mailbox making reference to your "employees" you reflexively reject the application of the expression. Your first thought is, "I don't have any 'employees'!" and though you may immediately laugh at yourself for drawing what you imagine is a distinction without an intended difference, you are nonetheless prompted to a curiosity.

This curiosity is enhanced by your having noted that the use of the term "employee" in the correspondence you have received has an artificial flavor. There is no "conversational" character to its use. Rather than being one of several synonyms used interchangeably to describe those for whose labors your company is trading, "employee" is used invariably, and sometimes awkwardly. Indeed, its use has the feel of nothing so much as that of a legal term. The fact that the use of the term is alien to your own well-established habit makes this awkward artificiality much more pronounced to your eye than it would be to someone else's.

In turn, this perception of the deliberate and careful use of a legal term brings into sharp relief the fact that the correspondence in question has the character of a demand, as from a superior to a subordinate; or as though reflective of some obligation of contract. Those accustomed to thinking of their associates as "employees", being spared your visceral rejection of the correspondence's applicability, are that much less likely to be struck by its inaptness in this other respect, but you are now serendipitously alert to every nuance.

Thus, where others might forego the exercise due to not having had their hackles raised as yours have been (and due to a cognitively dissonant tendency to assume that when others act, it is only after having taken pains to ensure that they are doing so appropriately-- in other words, to assume that others HAVE engaged in the "due diligence" which the complacent object of their attentions is himself choosing NOT to exercise...), you are prompted to a painstaking "due diligence". Off you go to the library.

Part II

NOW, THE OBJECT OF YOUR INTEREST is the meaning of "employee" as used in the context of federal taxes, because that's what the notice you received was about. So you don't go to the local public library, where you might consult a dictionary-- instead you go to your nearest law library, where you can consult the statutes which explain and control the authority under which the notice was issued.

Once in the law library, you don't waste any time even looking in the legal dictionaries. The notice you're seeking to decipher doesn't allege a contractual, equity or tortuous issue. That is, nothing on the notice declares or even suggests that it was produced because of something you've done to someone else, or because of some duty to the sender which you accepted as part of an agreement or based on some equitable claim.

On the contrary, the notice just reeks with that inescapable, bizarre odor of something that would be sent from a superior to a subordinate-- as though it was sent by a company HQ to a branch office pursuant to some routine (and thus, written) internal policy. (Furthermore, the notice-- which is concerned with something called an "Employee Withholding Exemption Certificate"-- actually references a "Section 3402" of "26 USC", which you recognize as a federal statutory designation.)

So, "common-law" or other generic legal definitions such as will be found in a legal dictionary MIGHT eventually be found to be applicable, but where statutes are involved, it is to "statutory definitions" that one must look first. Only if any given term has no customized definition does one look outside the statutes for its meaning.

YOUR HUNT BEGINS in "Title 26" of the "United States Code"-- aka the "United States Internal Revenue Code". You're working with a digitized version of the "code", so you're spared flipping through thousands of pages in dozens of volumes to run down "section 3402"-- it appears on your screen in nano-seconds: *§ 3402. Income tax collected at source.*

You scan through the 6,584-word section and you find just one "definitions" portion-- a brief subparagraph offering definitions of "Supplemental unemployment compensation benefits", "Annuity" and "Sick pay", which explain the meaning of these terms as used in the preceding subparagraph providing for the treatment of certain payments as though they were payments of "wages", upon the request of the recipient. No definition of "employee" is provided, either in this subparagraph or anywhere else in "Section 3402"...

Concluding that you'll have to move to the law dictionaries next, you idly scroll back to the top of section 3402 before closing the window and notice that the section is actually a part of a "chapter" of Title 26. Having learned long ago the old folk-wisdom parsing of "assume" ("To assume is to make an ass out of u and me..."), and therefore unwilling to take for granted that the definition of a term used in a statutory section will necessarily be found in that same section (especially now that you know that the section is just part of a larger chapter), you click on the link to the chapter contents...

Bingo! Right at the top: "§ 3401. Definitions". You click on THAT link, and immediately find that not only are you now in the right place, but it's a richer informational mine-shaft than you would have had any reason to expect, because Lo and Behold! Not only is there a chapter-wide definition of "employee" provided, but even "wages"-- which you hadn't ever suspected of having a special meaning in any tax law-- is custom-defined here. And "employer", too! You resolve to return to those intriguing entries at some point in the future.

FOR NOW, OF COURSE, "EMPLOYEE" is your focus. This is what you read:

(c) Employee

> *For purposes of this chapter, the term "employee" includes an officer, employee, or elected official of the United States, a State, or any political subdivision thereof, or the District of Columbia, or any agency or instrumentality of any one or more of the foregoing. The term "employee" also includes an officer of a corporation.*

Upon seeing these words, you can't help but smile. Now the demeanor of the notice, as a command from a superior to a subordinate, makes sense. Obviously, the agency that sent it to you has mistaken your company for one of its own operations!

Even leaving aside the fact that this had all been a purely academic exercise in the first place (since you don't actually have any legal relationship with the tax agency or government involved), the class of "employees" with which the notice is concerned is revealed by this definition as being that of people working for (or at least, paid-for-services-rendered by), the government whose agency had sent it (or its subsidiaries). No other type of actor is listed. (As a sole proprietorship, the "corporate officer" reference wouldn't have anything to do with your company in any event, but even were your company incorporated, the context in which that reference appears, and the accompanying specifications, make clear that only officers of federal corporations like Fannie Mae or the RTC are meant even without looking more closely into that provision at the moment.)

The definition DOESN'T say: "In addition to others within the common meaning of "employee", or even just, "Employee" also includes...". Instead, the definition in the statute plainly and unambiguously identifies the objects of its attention, with no expansive modifiers at all.

As a businessman well-acquainted with reading, writing and occasionally litigating contracts and other legal instruments of the same "specifications/obligations" character as statutes, you are well aware that clarity is the very essence of such instruments. After all, they are created to express and respect jurisdictional limits, and vagueness or the appearance of overreach in such instruments risks rendering the entire affected clause-- and everything dependent on it-- inoperable and unenforceable.

Further, you know that when used in such "specifications/obligations" instruments, "includes" is a naturally restrictive term. In fact, you remember having looked into the very subject of federal legal doctrine regarding "includes and including" on a prior occasion, mostly due to having enjoyed the dry wit of Chief Justice John Marshall when expressing that fact in one of the earliest cases ever ruled on by the United States Supreme Court-- that of United States v. The Schooner Betsey and Charlotte in 1808. Disparaging (before flatly denying) the proposition that "including" was to be taken as being "expansive" in its effect, rather than restrictive, Marshall says,

> *"It [is argued that] the word "including" means "moreover", or "as well as"; but if this was the meaning of the legislature, it was a very embarrassing mode of expressing the idea.".*

You know that this (frankly self-evident) rule of construction is re-iterated by the Supreme Court elsewhere as well. Further, you recall the similarly self-evident rule-- that any term defined without modifying language specifying that its common meaning is retained loses every vestige of that common meaning-- has also been flatly observed by the Supreme Court in the face of periodic efforts to argue the contrary by "creative" litigants. In the case of Stenberg v. Carhart, for instance, in 2000, the court says,

> *"When a statute includes an explicit definition, we must follow that definition, even if it varies from that term's ordinary meaning."*

In the 1987 case of Meese v. Keene, the court is even more declaratory:

> *"It is axiomatic that the statutory definition of the term excludes unstated meanings of that term."*

This principle is so obvious that in 1945, the court makes its relevant observation almost conversationally:

> *"Of course, statutory definitions of terms used therein prevail over colloquial meanings."*

What's more (and what is, in fact, fully sufficient to make the whole point all by itself), context and jurisdiction rule everything in the construction and application of statutory language. You know that if, for instance, you were to declare a tax on the profits of all lemonade-stands operated on any driveway, the meaning of "driveway" in that context would obviously be confined to YOUR driveways, and wouldn't extend to those of anyone else, regardless of your failure to be more specific. As the United States Supreme Court has pointed out,

> *"Words having universal scope, such as 'every contract in restraint of trade,' 'every person who shall monopolize,' etc., will be taken, as a matter of course, to mean only everyone subject to such legislation, not all that the legislator subsequently may be able to catch."* American Banana Co. v. United Fruit Co., 213 U.S. 347 (1909)

While the U.S. Congress is perfectly free to issue dictats in regard to its own workforce (whether called "employees" or otherwise), it obviously hasn't got the same authority in regard to everyone else's...

Part III

However, alert now to the fact that the legislators of the "tax title" are not scrupulous about making sure that related specifications are in forthright proximity to each other, but must be hunted down, almost as though they were intended to be overlooked, you go to the further trouble of running a search on the whole, ugly mess, looking for any other "definitions" sections that might reveal that something else isn't quite what it superficially might be mistaken to be. After a moment or two a list appears, rocking you back in your seat. 741 "definitions" links! All in this one title!

Two hours later, you've narrowed things down to one single definition relevant to that of "employee" at 3401(c): A custom definition of "includes" and "including" in section 7701, a list of "title-wide" definitions applicable wherever an alternative, narrower-application definition for the same defined term isn't found. At first glance, this special definition of "includes" seems a tautology:

> *"The terms "includes" and "including" when used in a definition contained in this title shall not be deemed to exclude other things otherwise within the meaning of the term defined."*

But, being the well-educated fellow that you are, you recall another Supreme Court ruling (Helvering v Morgan's, Inc, 293 U.S. 121, 126 fn. 1 (1934)), in which the court observes:

> *"[T]he verb "includes" imports a general class, some of whose particular instances are those specified in the definition. This view finds support in § 2(b) of the Act, which reads: "The terms 'includes' and 'including,' when used in a definition contained in this title, shall not be deemed to exclude other things otherwise within the meaning of the term defined.""*

...and another (Federal Land Bank of St. Paul v. Bismarck Lumber Co. 314 U.S. 95, 62 S.Ct. 1 U.S. 1941), referencing and re-iterating the substance of the earlier observation:

> *"[I]ncluding... ...connotes simply an illustrative application of the general principle."*

...and then yet another (Massachusetts v. EPA, 549 U.S. 497 (2007)), doing the same yet again:

> *"The word "including" can indeed indicate that what follows will be an "illustrative" sampling of the general category that precedes the word. Federal Land Bank of St. Paul v. Bismarck Lumber Co., 314 U.S. 95, 100 (1941)."*

That is, when "includes" or "including" is deployed in a definition, the enumerated items that follow "illustrate"-- identify, and thus establish-- the characteristics of the class which the defined term creates and represents. In other words, the listed items establish the "general principle" of the custom-term's application (while at the same time, of course, any common meaning of the word being made into a statutorily-defined "term" has been entirely removed thereby...). The class can be considered expandable by other items not listed which share the characteristics of those which are-- that is, *"things otherwise within the meaning of the term defined"*, but not by anything else. As the Treasury Department has helpfully explained,

> *"Meaning of Terms: The terms "includes and including" do not exclude things not enumerated which are in the same general class"* 27 CFR 26.11 and 27 CFR 72.11, and previously also published in 26 CFR 170.59.

In sum, the provisions of 7701(c) make "includes" into a term of expansion, but only of LIMITED expansion-- not one which contradicts the Supreme Court's ruling in United States v. The Schooner Betsey and Charlotte in 1808. (Were definitions incorporating "includes" and "including" meant to be read as meaning "as well as", it would have been accomplished without the bother of making a special rule of construction for "includes" and "including" by the simple addition of an appropriate chapter or section preamble of, *"In addition to those within its common meaning-"* and an "also" to each use of either term where this meaning was intended; or the special rule of construction for the terms at 7701(c) would have been written to read something like:

> *Includes and including: The terms "includes" and "including" when used in a definition contained in this title shall be construed as adding members of the class that follows to those embraced by the common meaning of the preceding word or phrase*...)

Applying all this to the "employee" definition at 3401(c), you find that:

- "Employee" begins as an empty vessel, devoid of any pre-existing meaning by virtue of having been selected to receive a custom, statutory definition (a point rather heavily underscored in this particular case, where "federal employees" are enumerated in the statutory definition-- something obviously pointless if "employee" retained its common meaning...).
- The enumerated items in the definition after "...includes..." illustrate the class to which the newly-minted statutory term "employee" applies.
- All the enumerated items illustrating the class are government-connected entities even (you discover after a little further research) the "officers of corporations" reference, which concerns "a corporate agency or instrumentality" which is one "(a) a majority of the stock of which is owned by or on behalf of the United States, or (b) the power to appoint or select a majority of the board of directors of which is exercisable by or on behalf of the United States" per the Public Salary Tax Act of 1939.

You sit back in your chair, nodding to yourself. Just as you had concluded previously, the sender of the notice has indeed mistaken your company for one of its own operations, and your workers for its "employees".

Pulling the notice that had set you off on this exploration out of your briefcase, you read it through again, in light of your research. The thing purports to instruct you to require all "employees" to fill out a federal form before beginning work...

You can't help but smile ruefully and shake your head over having had to spend an afternoon looking this all up. Having now verified the nature of the mistake involved in the notice being sent to you in the first place, you're very conscious of what should have been your first thought on reading the thing when it arrived: *Who in his right mind would entertain for a moment the idea that some government has the lawful authority to require anyone that is not one of its own creatures, or under contract with it, to fill out a government form in connection with engaging in personal economic activity, such as trading personally-owned time, skills and effort for other goods?* The very idea is ludicrous.

Sighing over your lost time, but reflecting on the fact that you've at least had a nice reminder of the importance of remaining clear-eyed about core issues in a world in which others can't be relied upon to do the same, and in which silly mistakes like you being sent a notice by the federal government concerning its own "employees" can and will happen, you shut down the computer you've been using and get up to go. You drop the notice in the trash, and head back to work.

In The End, It's A Question Of Morality

The psychology of those in denial of the truth about the income tax laid out in cold, hard, unambiguous documentation on the previous pages has always fascinated me. These folks are presented with a simple choice between an obvious, patently ridiculous fiction and a plain, thoroughly-documented truth which has been being continuously acknowledged for years now even by the peddlers of the absurd fiction. Yet the deniers still manage to avoid choosing to embrace the truth.

On the one hand, these deniers are invited to imagine that their ancestors were drooling idiots, who inexplicably authorized their government agents to seize any portion of anybody's and everybody's earnings, at the whim of those agents, in perpetuity. According to this myth, the only "control" imposed on this utterly despotic power is that those who abuse it can be turned out of office afterwards (by what might then be an utterly ruined and subjugated population). Simply to describe this fantasy in plain words reveals it to be nonsense--indeed, even after what most of them would admit has been a life-time of conditioning to the acceptance of mammoth government, not one of the deniers themselves would be so daft as to grant such authority to the state.

The other choice simply requires facing the fact that the deniers themselves have been successfully snookered by a careful, disciplined, generations-long campaign to cultivate and exploit the myth just described, and to conceal most everything about the true nature and history of the "income" tax. This campaign is the project of a large, diverse community with a distinct self-interest in spreading and defending misunderstandings about the tax, which ranges from members of the political class to service-providers like "tax attorneys" and tax-preparers to beneficiaries of the largesse the misunderstandings have made available for distribution by the state over all these years. Even leaving aside simple common sense, ALL of the relevant evidence dismisses the first choice to the trash-can where it belongs and makes clear that the second is incontrovertibly true.

Let's be clear, these ARE the only two choices. There's no such thing as being "a little bit pregnant". When you sweep away all the cognitive clutter from decades of effort to create and exploit confusion about the tax by those who benefit thereby, what is left is straightforward. Choice One is that our ancestors authorized an effectively unlimited "economic activity" tax, entirely within the discretion of the federal government as to what it falls upon, how heavily and for how long-- a proposition so absurd and grossly incompatible with the United States Constitution that only the completely delusional could entertain it, even if the US Supreme Court had not flatly declared it to be untrue dozens of times both before and since the Sixteenth Amendment. Choice Two is that the tax is limited-- just as the Constitution plainly says it must be, and as the Supreme Court has repeatedly says it remains, even after the Sixteenth Amendment-- meaning nothing more remarkable than that it only applies to certain distinguished classes of gains and not to those which don't involve the use or exploitation of federal privileges or resources. Nonetheless, those who persist in denial refuse to get it right.

There was a time when I imagined that the problem was the strength of that lifelong conditioning to which the deniers have been subject. But the constantly-swelling ranks of Americans who DO shuck off the nonsense once presented with the truth proves that the conditioning is far from irreversible.

Then I began to suspect that embarrassment played a significant role in this persistent denial of the demonstrated truth. That it was just so mortifying for those in denial to admit having been so thoroughly taken in, and having needlessly handed over up to half of all their earnings over the years, that they simply couldn't bear to do so. Instead, the deniers would rather just go on paying massive tribute to their mental conquerors, in a particularly severe case of "cutting off your nose to spite your face". Nobody is THAT proud, though-- especially in light of the fact that nearly EVERYONE was taken in, and being just one of millions of victims carries no real stigma or shame...

So, I've come to realize that what is actually in play with those who persist in denial is a fundamental failure of moral courage. It's this simple: Acknowledging the truth about the tax inescapably imposes a moral duty upon a person to stand up and act in accordance with that truth, and some folks just don't want the burden of that kind of adult responsibility.

It is a "see no evil" dynamic-- manage to see none (or equip one's conscience with "plausible denial" of having seen any), and one is spared overt moral responsibility to denounce, and possibly confront, the evil-doer... Avoiding that obligation to denounce and confront is something for which many a moral coward is willing to go on paying even half the fruits of his or her blood, sweat and tears.

Such folks swaddle themselves in the comforting props of the "validating" fiction and the companionship of others similarly inclined. At the same time, they remain very conscious of the thoroughly-cultivated reputation of the IRS as an absolutely rabid junk-yard dog, utterly devoid of any respect for the law, and very unpleasant to confront and denounce, while never asking themselves why an agency of their own servant government would embrace and maintain such a reputation if all it did was administer a law the people themselves had properly authorized.

Now that IS shameful.

Happily, while the "see no evil" dynamic has little difficulty in finding a few warm places to live in any given group of people, those prone to persistent willful denial of reality are a small minority. That kind of deliberate sociopathy really doesn't come naturally to anyone, which is why we have a name for it, and a culturally-embedded scornful, contemptuous regard for those who embrace it.

Our natural predisposition is quite the contrary. To a man and woman, our admiration and emulation is reserved for those who eschew such hidey-holes, and face the facts, however inconvenient or demanding such moral honesty may be.

Thus, when all is said and done, however many deniers may clutter the landscape today, their ranks will steadily diminish. The ranks of those standing up with eyes open, proclaiming and acting on the truth, will continue to grow.

"I confidently trust that the American people will prove themselves...too wise not to detect the false pride or the dangerous ambitions or the selfish schemes which so often hide themselves under that deceptive cry of mock patriotism: 'Our country, right or wrong!' They will not fail to recognize that our dignity, our free institutions and the peace and welfare of this and coming generations of Americans will be secure only as we cling to the watchword of true patriotism: 'Our country--when right to be kept right; when wrong to be put right.'"

-Senator Carl Schurz, October 17, 1899